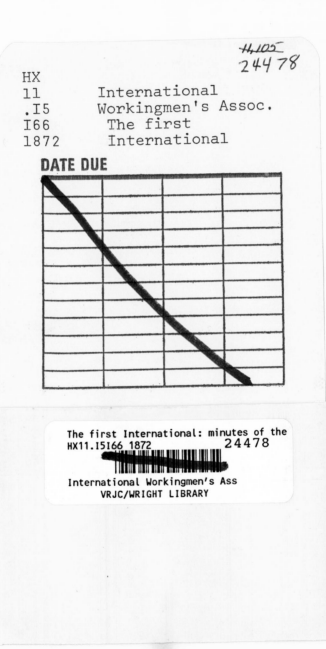

THE FIRST INTERNATIONAL

The

First International

MINUTES OF

THE HAGUE CONGRESS

OF 1872

WITH RELATED DOCUMENTS

Edited and Translated by HANS GERTH

The University of Wisconsin Press

Madison, 1958

Published by The University of Wisconsin Press,
430 Sterling Court, Madison 6, Wisconsin

Copyright © 1957, by the Regents
of the University of Wisconsin.
Copyright, Canada, 1957.
Distributed in Canada by Burns and MacEachern, Toronto

Printed in the United States of America
by Vail-Ballou Press, Inc., Binghamton, N.Y.

Library of Congress Catalog Card No. 57-11932

TO Dr. Hedwig Ide Gerth, nee Countess Reventlow, who was ousted by the Nazis from the University of Kiel which her ancestor Kay Reventlow had set on its modern course. She made her home in America and lived a life of work and care and love.

The Twenty-first of January, 1954
Requiescat in pace

PREFACE

The Minutes of the Hague Congress, never before published, were found among the papers of Hermann Schlüter, author of *Die Internationale in Amerika* (Chicago, 1918) and other works. Schlüter's library, including the Minutes, was presented to the Library of the University of Wisconsin by William E. Walling as part of the William E. Walling Collection.

William English Walling was a man of many fine causes. Vitally interested in social reform, he threw himself with energy into a host of activities. Among the many persons he came to know was John R. Commons, through whom he developed an interest in Wisconsin. In 1907 he had already made a gift of books to the Library, and he had further shown his interest in Wisconsin by urging Selig Perlman to complete his education at that institution. It was not an unnatural outcome that Mr. Walling in 1910 purchased the Schlüter collection for Wisconsin.

The International Workingmen's Association was founded in London in 1864 at a public meeting of British trade unionists, French labor delegates, and those, among them Karl Marx, who after 1848 sought refuge in Victorian England from political reaction and police persecution. Despite the conflicting objectives of others, Marx succeeded in making of the International an organ primarily devoted to Socialist propaganda. Because of his rivals, Marx in a few years recognized that he had to put an end to the meetings (called Congresses) of the International and move its General Council from England. This he accomplished at the Congress at The Hague in 1872. It is the Minutes of this Congress, recording the manner of Marx's victory, that make up the chief contents of this volume.

Because it was his intention to move the seat of the General Council of the Association, thus putting it at a distance from his rivals, Marx needed to deny seats at the Hague Congress to the delegates who were his enemies and to assure seats to those who were friendly. Those from Spain, Belgium, Holland, and England were in general dangerous to his plans. As the Minutes of the Congress show, Marx succeeded in holding the seats of his own delegates and in beating down a number of those that would have gone to the enemy. With this accomplished he was able to turn back the efforts of his rivals to limit the powers of the General Council and to succeed in his proposal to move the Council to New York. Finally, Bakunin and Guillaume, who in Bakunin's absence led the fight against Marx, were expelled from the Association.

Apparently the Minutes of the Hague Congress were written by a partisan of Marx. Engels must have been in error when he wrote to F. A. Sorge on September 21, 1872, that "due to the stupidity of the President no protocol was written as no secretaries were appointed." In the same letter Engels pressed Sorge for his "promised report of the credentials discussion," i.e., for these Minutes? Possibly Sorge wrote them and for one reason or another did not care to send them to London or to publish them in the United States. Sorge then was the General Secretary of the General Council of the International in New York, and he may have turned over these Minutes to his comrade Schlüter. Even if their publication may not reveal essential facts, unknown to the historians of the International, it may be agreeable to specialists to know that one more source confirms and/or supplements other reports such as those of Maltman Barry in the *Standard* or James Guillaume's memoirs.

Also first published here is the "Report to the North American

Preface

Federation of the International Workingmen's Association," written by Sorge. This document is useful chiefly for the light it throws on events as viewed by the Marxists, and it serves to illuminate the more formal record of the proceedings.

As Maltman Barry's *Report of the Fifth Annual General Congress, of the International Workingmen's Association, Held at The Hague, Holland, September 2–9, 1872* often adds color and human interest to the story and today is to be found in only a few libraries, we have included it here. Maltman Barry, a cobbler by trade, reported the Congress for the conservative *Standard*, which probably defrayed his expenses. His reports were reprinted from the *Standard* and in 1873 were issued in pamphlet form by F. Arnold in London. Our reprint is based on an original copy of the pamphlet in the Pierpont Morgan Library of New York.

ACKNOWLEDGMENTS

I should like to express thanks beyond words to my then co-worker and companion, Hedwig Ide Gerth. My thanks go to my then students, Norma Diamond and Daniel Kronenfeld, who have read and improved the manuscript in part. Mr. Louis Kaplan and Mr. Thompson Webb, Jr., of the Wisconsin Library and Press respectively have been patient and I owe them gratitude for this.

H. G.

INTRODUCTION

The Hague Congress of the International Workingmen's Association represents at once the zenith and nadir in the eight-year span of the turbulent career of the group. With the Hague Congress, which met in September, 1872, this deeply hated organization of revolutionary tradition and anticapitalist labor movements disintegrated. Two years after the Congress, Friedrich Engels, who had attended it, wrote from London to F. A. Sorge in New York, "The Hague Congress really was the end." [1] The subsequent withering away of the organization is of no interest. The seat of the International was removed to New York; Sorge was elected General Secretary; Johann Philipp Becker, the leading follower of Marx in Switzerland, worked hard at staging one more congress the next year—but it was all to no avail. At The Hague, however, things looked different. There appeared sixty-five delegates from twelve countries holding ninety-five mandates among them and representing the General Council in London, the leading executive body of the organization; federal councils which combined local sections; and finally also local groups.

Since the International was outlawed in France and Germany and restive labor suffered from severe repressive measures as well as administrative chicanery, the organization as a whole allowed for

[1] Letter of September 12 and 17, 1874, *The Selected Correspondence of Karl Marx and Frederick Engels, 1846–1895* (International Publishers, New York, 1942), p. 330.

diverse patterns of affiliation down to direct individual membership. In 1865 Marx wrote to his friend Dr. Ludwig Kugelmann: "As everybody who buys a card for one shilling can become a member of the Association; as the French have chosen this form of individual membership (ditto the Belgians) because they are forbidden by law to affiliate with us as an 'association'; and as things are similar in Germany, I have decided now to ask my friends here and those in Germany, to establish little societies of no matter how many members at a given place, each of whom takes out an English card of membership." [2] By the end of 1870 about 300 individual members were recorded, of whom over 170 were English.[3] Some smaller British trade unions were affiliated then, but the major trade union leaders such as George Odger, who had helped to found the Association and had served as president of the International's General Council, had lost interest in it since their immediate objectives had been won, namely, the franchise for the workingman and labor legislation. The ideological discussions of factitious Socialist and anarchist intellectuals had no interest for them.

And those who had not dropped out before the Franco-Prussian war and the Paris Commune were in a hurry to withdraw from the International after Marx's bombshell, *The Civil War in France.* This pamphlet in defense of the Paris Commune which depicted the Commune as a world historically significant event, the invention of a new model state of the revolutionary proletariat, did the rest. Marx drew the ire of a hostile European society upon himself and the International, for he published the pamphlet and several addresses in its name without being too scrupulous about prior consent and endorsement.[4] But though the International had no particular influence on the course of events in France and things would probably have taken the same course had it not existed at all, Marx succeeded with the help of the scapegoat-seeking press in snatching out of the reign of white terror, of the massacre of the Communards,

[2] Letter to Kugelmann of February 23, 1865, in Karl Marx, *Letters to Dr. Kugelmann* (Martin Lawrence, London, 1934), p. 27.

[3] Edward Hallett Carr, *Karl Marx: A Study in Fanaticism* (London, 1934, 1938), p. 194.

[4] "Some of the Englishmen whose names, as members of the General Council, were appended to it, afterwards declared that they had not seen its contents until it was published."—Carr, *Marx,* pp. 218, 223.

Introduction

a great political legend[5] which became especially important for modern Russian history. In Soviet historiography and history teaching to this day the Franco-Prussian war of 1870/71 matters only as the background to the rise of the Commune as a presumably new form of state, the dictatorship of the proletariat.

Marx was pleased with the reception of *The Civil War in France*. Three editions were sold in two months, "and I have the honour to be at the present moment the best calumniated and the most menaced man of London. This feels good indeed after twenty years of boring stagnation. Besides, scavengers of the press and men of all sorts crowd in on me to see the 'monstre' in person."[6] It was only after these events that Marx's name became known to a world-wide public as that of one of the modern revolutionary "isms."[7] In 1873 Engels wrote to Bebel, "The bourgeoisie, struck all of a heap, ascribed omnipotence to it [the International]."[8] Actually, however, things did not look good. The International was disintegrating. The fall of the Paris Commune and the regime of white terror put an end to the Jacobin democratic tradition of French labor. Paris ceased to be the center of European revolutionary democracy. After the labor movements revived, the European center shifted to Germany from the 1880's to the outbreak of World War I. The end of the First International marked the end of an era.

In 1864 Marx had written the Inaugural Address of the International and his draft had been accepted by French Proudhonists, social liberal trade unionists, and Marxists. It was a masterpiece of propagandist diplomacy. Everybody could find his aspirations satisfactorily embodied in the statement of policies and aims. Although pre-eminently the intellectual, Marx had to lean over backward to please all sides, and he was careful not to alienate any important body of opinion. He made compromises for the sake of unity. The following Congresses of the International at Geneva (1866), Lausanne (1867), Brussels (1868), and Basel (1869) served as a stage for airing well-nigh all the competing anticapitalist

[5] Heinrich Koechlin, *Die Pariser Commune im Bewusstsein ihrer Anhänger* (Basel, 1950).

[6] Marx, letter to Kugelmann, July 18 and 27, 1871.

[7] Arthur Rosenberg, *Democracy and Socialism* (New York, 1939), p. 204.

[8] *The Selected Correspondence of Karl Marx and Frederick Engels*, p. 325.

thought ways and policy proposals of nineteenth-century radicals. Johann Philipp Becker, a friend of Marx, wrote in the *Vorbote* in Geneva, "There were Fourierists, Cabetists, Considerantists, Proudhonists, Schultze-Delitssch followers, etc., thus communists, Phalanstère-men, Libre-Exchange-men, Mutualists and self-help men . . . . How the mossy heads of all schools of salvation were on the move with their tabernacles crowded with plans to benefit mankind; they entertained the proud expectation of loosening the entire old world from its moorings." [9] Becker might have added Bakunin and his followers.

Bakunin,[10] one of the "repentant noblemen" of Czarist Russia and a colorful romantic rebel, had built up a following in Italy, in Switzerland, and in Spain. Barricade fights, Czarist prison, exile in Siberia, escape and return to Western Europe from Siberia around the world through America, conspiratorial activity, intrigues, an incessant sequence of organizational schemes, mountainous correspondence, dramatic conversions of searching souls to his cause— these imparted to his life the phantasmagoric quality of a lived dream vision. He sought to conquer the International. He established an organization, the Alliance of Socialist Democracy, in Switzerland and applied for corporate affiliation with the General Council in London. The request was at first turned down. The General Council made affiliation conditional upon the dissolution of the Alliance, the transformation of its local branches into sections, and the substitution of Marx's formula "abolition of classes" for the programmatic Alliance formula "levelling of classes." Bakunin accepted the conditions. In the summer of 1869 he and his followers were received into the International.

Bakunin held forth at the Basel Congress of 1869, and although his ratiocinations about God, the state, and society could not compare with Marx's system-building, his personal magnetism, persuasive diction, and capacity to win intensely devoted followers made him the Menace. Marx and Engels set out to destroy him, using the Hague Congress for this purpose. It was the one Congress of the International which Marx and Engels attended. Bakunin could not

[9] This is cited by Dr. R. Meyer from the *Vorbote* in his *Der Emancipationskampf des vierten Standes* (Berlin, 1882), Vol. II, p. 432.

[10] Edward Hallett Carr, *Michael Bakunin* (London, 1937).

Introduction

come there, for he could not travel through France or Germany, where he was "wanted." He had to rely on James Guillaume, the editor of the *Bulletin Jurassien* and leader of the Jurassian Federation, the anarchist organization of Genevan building workers and watchmakers in the sweatshops of the Jura mountain valleys. Both the Anarchists and the Marxists prepared for the contest beforehand. Organizational and publicity skirmishes had been going on for quite some time. Cafiero,[11] a twenty-five-year-old convert to Bakunin's cause, had organized the Italian anarchist-minded sections into a federal council, and at the founding Congress at Rimini "before the workers of the whole world" he had declared that the new federation was breaking off all ties with the London General Council because the latter wished to impose the doctrine of the authoritarian German Communists upon the International. Hence the absence of any Italian delegates at The Hague.

In Spain Marx and Engels had Lafargue, Marx's son-in-law, and Mesa, a native Spanish anti-Bakuninist, on their side. Nevertheless, the Marxists here, too, lost out to the Anarchists. And since Marx possessed a profound insight into the peculiarities of the social conditions of the Iberian peninsula,[12] Bakunin's success must have been due to conspiratorial activities, not to "objective factors." Marx and Engels were firmly convinced that Bakunin was dishonest, that he maintained a secret society within the International. The Anarchists have always denied this. Given the small number of leading persons involved, personal attachment and devotion to their leader would seem to suffice for explaining the cohesiveness of Bakunin's lieutenants in control of various sections and federations in Switzerland, Italy, and Spain.

Engels, in a letter to Bebel, referred once to "old Hegel" as having said, "A party proves itself a victorious party by the fact that it *splits* and can stand the split." [13] This must have been the hope of Marx and Engels when they prepared for the purge of the International at The Hague. The choice of place was favorable to their followers; for the rest, they did what they could to "pack" the

[11] Gustav Mayer, *Friedrich Engels* (The Hague, 1934), Vol. II, pp. 238 f.
[12] G. Brenan shares this evaluation in his *The Spanish Labyrinth* (Cambridge, 1943).
[13] *The Selected Correspondence of Karl Marx and Frederick Engels*, p. 327.

Congress. Engels paid the fare for the five members of the General Council he brought over.[14] Marx in a much quoted letter of June 21, 1872, implored Sorge in New York:

At this congress the life or death of the International is at stake. You yourself and at least one or two others must come. As regards sections who send no direct delegates, they can send mandates.

The German mandates for me, Fr. Engels, Lochner, Karl Pfändner, Lessner.

The French for G. Ranvier, August Seraillier, Le Moussu, Ed. Vaillant, F. Cournet, Ant. Arnoud.

The Irish for MacDonnell, who turns out all right or if you prefer for one of the aforementioned Germans or French.[15]

A similar request was addressed to Kugelmann in July: "Germany must . . . have as many delegates as possible." [16]

When they arrived at The Hague, Marx and Engels could see at a glance that they had an assured majority, that victory was to be theirs. For the first time a sizable number of German delegates had appeared at a congress of the International. Moreover, Sorge had come from New York and had secured mandates from American sections for those who needed them.

The Anarchists had shown that they intended to fight the General Council to the finish, and Cafiero, who was at The Hague without attending the Congress, had broken away from the International. Marx and Engels therefore followed the policy of *à la guerre comme à la guerre*. Marx had secured "ammunition"—from Russia. Bakunin had contracted with a Russian publisher to translate Marx's *Capital* and had received an advance of three hundred rubles. Bakunin failed to meet his contractual obligation, and the publisher had to make an alternate arrangement and write off the three hundred rubles as a loss. A Russian friend of Bakunin's, the terrorist Nechaev, who believed in the "covenant of the gangsters" as a bond of political cohesion and who had an infamous murder to his credit, upon his return to Russia sought to help Bakunin by writing a threatening

[14] Gustav Mayer, *Engels*, p. 247.
[15] *Briefe und Auszüge aus Briefen von Joh. Phil. Becker, Jos. Dietzgen, Friedrich Engels, Karl Marx u.A. an F. A. Sorge und Andere* (Stuttgart, 1906), p. 59. Henceforth cited as *Sorge Correspondence*.
[16] Carr, *Marx*, p. 246.

letter to the publisher's agent, warning him to leave Bakunin in peace and to forget about the contract. Marx probably heard of this Nechaev letter from a member of the Russian colony in Switzerland. Marx at the last moment wrote to the Russian economist Danielson informing him of the affair and concluded his letter as follows: "It would be of the highest utility for me, if *this letter was sent me* immediately. As this is a mere *commercial* affair and as in the use to be made of the letter no names will be used, I hope you will procure me that letter. But no time is to be lost. If it is sent, it ought to be sent at once as I shall leave London for the Haag Congress at the end of this month." [17]

It worked. The publisher's agent himself sent Nechaev's letter. It was used against Bakunin in the quasi-judicial procedure of his expulsion. Marx, who had an abysmal scorn for the *Lumpenproletariat* and who hated Bakunin among other things for relying on such elements as political force, felt he had proof of Bakunin's association with criminals. Even Franz Mehring commented, "That Bakunin in questions of property was to be robbed of his honest name was inexcusable, and unfortunately Marx was to be blamed for this." [18] But, says E. H. Carr in his unsympathetic biography of Marx, "he was right in supposing that Bakunin, if he had had his way, would have wrecked the International, not merely in its existing form, but in any other form which could have been given to it." [19]

[17] Carr, *Marx*, p. 247.

[18] Franz Mehring, *Karl Marx, Geschichte seines Lebens* (Soziologische Verlagsanstalt, Leipzig, 1933), p. 539.

[19] Carr, *Marx*, p. 256.

CONTENTS

Contents

Protokoll des 5ten

allgemeinen Kongresses der

Internationalen-Arbeiter-Association

im Haag,

September 1872

Protokoll des 5ten allgemeinen Kongresses

der Internationalen Arbeiter-Association

im Haag, September 1872.

Diesem Kongress fiel nach dreijähriger Unterbrechung die Aufgabe zu, die Etwas gelockerte Organisation wieder zu befestigen & sie gegen äussere & innere Angriffe zu stärken. Während der drei Jahre seit dem letzten Kongress hatten sich natürlich viele Ansichten verschiedener Art kundgegeben & Versuche der manichfachsten Art waren gemacht worden, um die Association zu schwächen, zu theilen, zu zerstören oder ihren Zwecken zu entfremden.

Grosse geschichtliche Ereignisse hatten statt gefunden & waren nicht ohne Einfluss auf das innere Leben der Association geblieben. Diese Puncte müssen stets in Betracht gezogen werden bei Beurtheilung der Arbeiten dieses, des fünften Kongresses, worüber jetzt Bericht gegeben wird.

2

Es waren 65 Delegirte anwesend, davon 18 Franzosen,
15 Deutsche, 7 Belgier, 5 Engländer, 5 Spanier, 4 Holländer,
4 Schweizer, 2 Oestreicher, 1 Däne, 1 Ungar, 1 Australier,
1 Irländer & 1 Pole. Sie hatten 95 Mandate — davon
hatten gesandt Belgien 17, Deutschland 15, Frankreich 14, die Schweiz 11, Amerika 7, der Generalrath 6,
Spanien 5, England 5, Holland 4, Dänemark 2,
Irland 2, Ungarn 2, Portugal 1, Polen 1, Oestreich 1,
Australien 1. Unter den Delegirten waren 5
Schneider, 4 Drucker, 4 Lehrer, 4 Schriftsteller, 3
Schuhmacher, 3 Aerzte, 2 Zeichner, 2 Tischler,
2 Lohgerber, 2 Maschinisten, 1 Chemiker, 1 Bürst-
enmacher, 1 Handlungsbeflissener, 1 Instrumenten-
macher, 1 Weber, 1 Juwelier, 1 Lithograph, 1
Goldgräber, 1 Blumenmacher, 1 Porzellanmaler,
1 Graveur, 2 Ingenieure, 1 Leistenmacher & von
ungefähr 20 war das Gewerbe nicht angegeben.

Die Verhandlungen wurden vorwiegend
in französischer Sprache geführt, aber Uebersetzungen stets gegeben in 2 — 3 — ja - 4 Sprachen.
Dass die französische Nationalität vor-
herrschend war, gab dem Congress den Character

3

grosser, ja manchmal unangenehmer Lebhaftigkeit.

Sonntag, 1 Septbr, Abends 7 Uhr, fand die erste Sitzung, die sogenannte Vorversammlung, statt. Die Delegirten mussten sich durch gaffende Menschenmassen in den Saal drängen, der weder gut gelegen, noch sonst bequem war. Ein Komité des holländischen Föderal-Raths war anwesend, eröffnete die Versammlung. Nicht-Mitglieder mussten den Saal verlassen & Gerhard vom holländischen F. R. begrüsste die Delegirten, rief ihnen ein herzliches Willkommen zu & wies daraufhin, dass wir die Gastfreundschaft Hollands nicht aus Gnade, sondern auf Grund der Landesgesetze genössen, sowie dass eine behördliche Abweichung von diesen Landesgesetzen bei allen Parteien die heftigste Opposition hervorrufen würde. — Er fragt an, was nun zu beginnen sei? Eccarius sagt, dass nach Vorgang früherer Congresse diese Vorversammlung nur geselliger Natur sei, dass morgen das Vollmachtsprüfungskomité zu ernennen sei & dann die Arbeit beginne. Longuet verlangt Festsetzung der Tagesordnung

für morgen, Engels — dass die Delegirten ihre
Namen einreichen. Fränkel fordert sofortige Einsetzung des Mandat-Komité's & dass die Delegirten
nicht genöthigt seien, den Ort ihrer Sectionen
anzugeben, da daraus Gefahr für die Mitglieder
entspringe, welche aus Ländern kämen, wo die
I. A. A. verboten sei, & wir von Spionen umringt
seien. Sorge beansprucht für solche Delegirte das
Recht, einen andern Namen zu führen. Beides
wird als sich von selbst verstehend betrachtet. —
Ranvier beantragt Eröffnung der Sitzung morgen,
Montag, 9 Uhr Morgens unter Vorsitz des holländischen
Föderal-Raths, um sofort ein Mandatprüfungs=
Komité niederzusetzen etc.

Marx fügt hinzu, ~~dass~~ die Sitzung geschlossen
sein müsse ~~ausser~~ für die Mitglieder der Haager
Section. Hales fordert, dass alle Mitglieder der
I. A. A. zugelassen werden & Marx nimmt diesen
Zusatz an, vorausgesetzt, dass die Mitgliedschaft
nachzuweisen ist. — Diese Anträge von Ranvier,
Marx & Hales wurden einstimmig angenommen,
worauf sich die Versammlung vertagt bis

Montag Morgens 9 Uhr. — Die Delegirten zerstreuten
sich nach ihren Wohnungen, die sie anstarrte wie
Wunderthiere (Ungeheuer. ——

    Montag, 2 September, Morgens 9½ Uhr wird
die erste Sitzung des Kongresses eröffnet. — Engels
verlangt, dass kein Berichterstatter über die ge=
schlossenen Sitzungen berichten dürf. (Bezieht
sich auf Delegirte, welche zugleich als Berichterstatter
für Zeitungen handeln) Dupont fordert, dass alle
Nicht-Delegirte den Saal verlassen, & wenn sie Mitglieder der I. A. A. sind, auf die Gallerie gehen.
Guillaume beantragt, einstweilen officielle Ueber=
setzer zu ernennen. Dupont, Fränkel & Eccarius
werden zu Uebersetzern ernannt. — Longuet ist
gegen Zulassung irgend welcher Berichterstatter
für Zeitungen. Ranvier verlangt Beschluss=
nahme darüber & findet längere Verhandlung
statt über die Berichterstatter etc. Es wird be=
schlossen, dass alle welche nicht Delegirte sind,
den Saal zu verlassen haben — gegen 2 Stimmen. —
    Engels bringt hierauf den Antrag ein, ein
Komite zur Prüfung der Vollmachten, aus

7 Personen bestehend, zu erwählen. Soura beantragt
dagegen, ein Mitglied aus jeder Föderation dazu zu
nehmen. Vaillant, dass es nur aus (5) fünf Personen
bestehe; & die Mandate aus Ländern, wo die I. A. A.
verboten sei, zu vernichten habe. Soura verlangt das
Recht, seinen Antrag zu erläutern & zu vertheidigen, was ihm zugestanden wird. Er sagt, man
solle nicht den Verdacht aufkommen lassen, es
sässen nur Anhänger des General-Raths im Komite
& darum solle man aus jeder Föderation 1 Mitglied in das Komite wählen. Es wird hierauf
der Antrag Engel's (Komite von 7 zur Prüfung der Vollmachten) angenommen einstimmig. Soura
nimmt seinen Antrag wiederum auf & verlangt
Abstimmung darüber. (Nicht beachtet vom Präsidenten)
Dem Komite wird die Befugniss ertheilt, sich
mit den Delegirten aus Ländern, wo I. A. A.
verboten & verfolgt ist, zu verständigen. Guillaume
verlangt gleich Soura 1 Mitglied von jeder Föderation, Seraillier dagegen sagt; „wir haben mehr
als 7 Föderationen, in manchen Ländern mehrere,
in andern Ländern keine" u. s. w. man könne
darum nicht nach Föderationen wählen.

Longuet ist nach Serailliers Ausführungen
gegen Soura's Antrag, wünscht aber, dass nicht
blos Anhänger des G. R. in das Komité kommen,
obwohl er selbst Vertheidiger desselben sei
Guillaume sagt, die I. A. A. bestehe aus Föderationen,
darum müssen die Föderationen im Komité
vertreten sein. Bedauert, dass Longuet den G. R.
vertreten wolle, — er (G.) vertrete die Internationale
Dupont erklärt, dass wir die Vertreter der Arbeiter-
Bewegung, nicht eines Landes seien. Schluss
der Debatte wird beantragt & angenommen. —
Seraillier; Antrag, die Komitemitglieder unter-
schiedlos aus der Versammlung zu wählen, wurde
hierauf zum Beschluss erhoben mit 48 gegen
9 Stimmen & 4 Enthaltungen. Morago gibt die
Erklärung ab, dass er & seine Mitdelegirten von
Spanien, die bestimmte Weisung hätten, sich
der Abstimmung zu enthalten, bis die Abstimmung nach Kopfzahl der vertretenen Mitglieder
Stattfinde. Lafargue erklärt, dass er obwohl auch
Delegirter für Spanien, diese Weisung nicht erhalten habe. Es wird jetzt Pause von 10 Minuten
gemacht, um die Stimmzettel vorzubereiten.

Nachdem die Sitzung wieder eröffnet, wird auf Antrag Doainard, beschlossen, relative Mehrheit bei dieser Wahl für genügend zu erachten & die Zählung der Stimmzettel begonnen, deren 58 abgegeben wurden, während 3 (Spanier) sich der Abstimmung enthielten. Erwählt wurden Marx mit 41, Ranvier mit 44, Roch mit 41, Mc Donnell mit 39, Dereure mit 36, Gerhard mit 50 & Fränkel mit 22 Stimmen. Auf Antrag Sorge's wird das Komite beauftragt, sich zurückzuziehen & sofort seine Arbeit zu beginnen, während der Kongress sich bis 7 Uhr Abends vertagt, um dann den Komitebericht entgegenzunehmen. — Dereure verlangt, dass alle Anträge schriftlich eingereicht werden & dass die Delegierten dem Mandatskomité ihren Namen, Beschäftigung & Wohnort einreichen. Die Sitzung schloss um 3 Uhr. —

Die Abendsitzung begann erst um 8½ Uhr, da das Mandatkomité nicht früher erschien.

7

Als Vorsitzender fungirt seit diesem Morgen van den

Abeel, Delegirter von Gent (Belgien.) — das Mandats-

Prüfungskomité berichtet als in Ordnung mit

dem G. R. & berechtigt zu Sitz, Stimme.

Swarn für eine französische Section

Lucain   „   „   „   „

Longuet   „   „   „   „

Joannard   „   „   „   „

Ranvier   „   „   „   „

Vaillant   „   „   „   5

                 Section zu La cheaux de fonds

Fränkel für eine französische Section

Walther   „   „   „   „

Vichard   „   „   „   „

Vilmot   „   „   „   „

Cyrille   „   „   „   „

Dereure   „   die amerikanische Föderation

Sorge   „   „   „   „

Marx   „   „ Section I New York

        5   „   die Section Leipzig

        8   „   den General Rath.

Guillaume   „   die jurassische Föderation

Schwitzguebel „   „   „   „

H. Scheu   „   eine Wiener Section

   „   „   „   „ Esslinger „

   „   „   „ Königsberger Section

G. Ludwig für eine Mainzer Section
Sorera   „   die Sectionen 29 & 42 in Amerika
O. Farkas   „   zwei ungarische Sectionen
Hein   „   eine böhmische Section
Mc Donnell „   „ irländische   „
B. Becker   „   „ Braunschweiger Section
  „   „   „ Chemnitzer Section
Le Mouson   „   „ franz. Section in London
Dr. Sexton   „   den General Rath
B. Splingard „   Sectionen zu Charleroi
  „   „   „   „ Couxelles
  „   „   „   „ Deponts
Pihl   „   Dänemark
Gerhard   „   den holländischen F. R.
Roch   „   „ brittschen F. R.
  „   & Stratford Section.
G. Schuhmacher für Section zu Solingen
Eberhard für belgischen F. R.
  „   „ Schuhmacher, Anstreicher ek
Lafargue für Madrider Föderation
  „   „ andere spanische Föderation
  „   „ Lissabon (Portugal) „
Dr. Kugelmann für Section zu Celle
Dietzgen   „   „ „ Dresden
A. Hepner   „   „ No 8 New-York
Cournet   „   Dänischen F. R.
  „   „ G. R.
Dupont   „   G. R.

11

Arnond   für die Section zu Parouge,

Wroblewski   "   Polnische Section London & G.R.

van der Hout   für Section zu Amsterdam

Harcourt   "   "   " Victoria (Australien)

Barry   "   "   N.3 Chicago

Serraillier   "   den G.R.

Halles   "   die Section zu Hackneyroad

Brismée   "   "   "   " Brüssel.

F Engels   "   "   "   " Breslau

"   "   "   " N.6 " New.York.

Milke   "   "   " zu Berlin

"   "   "   " Crimmitschau

" Mottershead   ,   ,   " Bethnal Green (London)

Lessner   "   deutsche Section zu London

Cuno   "   Section zu Düsseldorf

"   "   " " Stuttgart

Eccarius   "   die Leistenmacher (London)

Coenen   "   " zu Antwerpen

J. Ph. Becker   "   " Section zu Basel, Genf, Luzern & s.w. & romanischen Föderat Rath

van den Abeel   " Section zu Gent

Friedländer   "   "   " Zürich

Herman   "   "   " Lüttich

Das Komite berichtet ferner, dass Hues als Delegirter für das Vesdre Thal (Verviers) erschienen, aber nicht im Besitz einer richtigen Vollmacht sei; dassgegen

V. Dave, Delegirter der Haager Section, Anklagen vor-
liegen, welche erst entschieden werden müssen, dass
Alerini nicht zuzulassen sei als Delegirter einer Section
zu Marseille; ebensowenig Jonkowski als Delegirter
der Section de la propagande et action revolutionaire
zu Genf; die Zulassung von Morago, Marcelau, Targa
Pelicer & Alerini als Delegirten der Spanischen Föderation
zu verschieben, bis dieselben sich mit dem G. R. in
Ordnung gesetzt; das Mandat von Section 2 zu New York
zu annulliren, weil diese Section vom amerikanischen
F. R. ausgeschlossen & nicht mit dem G. R. in Ordnung
sei; & ebenso das Mandat von W. West zurückzuweisen,
weil derselbe der Sect. 12, dem Philadelphier Congress &
dem Princestreet Föderal-Rath angehöre & angehört
habe.

Unterdessen kam noch ein Mandat für J. Ph. Becker
an, sowie mehrere für Herman aus Belgien. —
Splingard zieht die von ihm über V. Dave gemachten
Ausserungen zurück & Fluse gibt demselben ein gutes
Leumundszeugniss. Ranvier beantragt Abstimmung
über die nicht Beanstandeten. Schwitzguebel verlangt nochmalige Verlesung & Zulassung Aller
derjenigen, gegen welche kein Einwand erhoben wird,
die Letzeren aber zurückzustellen. Eccarius & Sorge

13

sind dagegen. Das Comité nimmt Dave & Flues als
vollberechtigt an nach den verschiedenen Erklärungen
Seitens belgischer Delegirten. Engels erklärt sich für
den Antrag Schwitzguebels, ebenso Saura, welcher sofortige Entscheidung verlangt. Ranvier fordert die
Abstimmung als Vertrauensvotum für das Mandat=
Comité, & schnelle Handlung, da wir sonst nicht vor
Mittwoch mit den Mandaten fertig werden & keine Zeit
zu anderen Arbeiten behalten. Lafargue für Schwitzguebels
Antrag & sofortige Abstimmung. Alerini verlangt,
dass die sämmtlichen Mandate einem Komité-Mitgliede
übergeben werden, damit Jeder sie aber besichtigen könne.
Barry fragt, warum man denn das Comité ernannt
habe? Marx sagt, das Comité habe nur zwei Sachen zu
untersuchen gehabt; 1, ob das Mandat richtig ausgestellt
sei & 2., ob die Aussteller in Ordnung mit dem G.R.,
also zur Ausstellung berechtigt seien. Schwitzguebels
Antrag, unterstützt von Saura, Lafargue & Anderen,
alle Beanstandeten zurückzustellen & die Uebrigen
nach nochmaliger Verlesung im Ganzen (en bloc) anzunehmen, wird genehmigt, gegen Alerini & Sorge.
Die Verlesung geht wieder vor sich, & Targe Pelicer
verlangt nach Lesung der ersten Namen von französ.
Sectionen zu wissen, ob dieselben bezahlt haben, worauf

14

Ranvier sagt, dass das Komite gerade dies zu er-
kunden gehabt habe. Pelica, wollte blos wissen, ob
das Komite alle gleich behandelt habe. — Bei der nun
vor sich gehenden Verlesung wird das Mandat Vaillants
beanstandet durch Schwitzguebel, Dereure's & Sorge's durch
Saura, Saura's durch Sorge, Lafargue's durch Alerini,
Barry's durch Hales, Dasjenige der Delegirten des General-
Raths durch Guillaume. Alle Uebrigen, 51 an der Zahl,
werden auf einmal zugelassen, die Delegirten des General-
Raths eingeschlossen, obwohl Brismée verlangt, daß die
Frage über diese Letzeren Später zu behandeln sei. —
Lafargue fordert die Beanstandeten auf, sich in den
Hintergrund des Saales zurückzuziehen. —
Der Vorsitzende meint, dass man jetzt das Bureau
wählen solle, wogegen Sorge & Dereure sich erklären.
Hales protestirt gegen Sorge's Recht zu sprechen ebenso
Hues. Die Sitzung wird geschlossen um 9½ Uhr. —
Dienstag Morgens 9½ Uhr (3 Sept.) wird die Sitzung
wieder eröffnet & bedauert der Vorsitzende, daß so
viele Mitglieder säumig sind. Es wird beschlossen,
4 Sekretäre zu erwählen: Le Moussu für die französische,
Hepner für die deutsche, Roche für die englische & van der
Hout für die holländische Sprache. — Engels stellt den
Antrag, 2 Redner für & 2 Redner gegen jeden Fall mit

13

15 Minuten Redezeit anzuhören & dann abzustimmen.
Das Mandatkomité bringt ferner Mandate ein aus
Belgien für Flues aus Frankreich für Servillier, vom
romanischen F. R. zu Genf für Dural, welch angenommen
werden. Ranvier will den Fall Vaillant's aufrufen,
wogegen Schwitzguebel protestirt. — Saura spricht gegen
die fünf Minuten & verlangt 10 Minuten, um alle Protestationen, (er hat deren 4) vorlegen zu können; er hält
diesen Antrag für eine Taktik (Mittelchen) seiner Gegner,
um ihn mundtodt zu machen. Dereure erklärt dies
für eine Beleidigung, da die 5 Minuten für uns eben-
sowohl gelten, als für euch. Dural kann Saura nicht
verstehen. Eberhardt sieht doch ein Kunstgriff darin,
so prophezeit", dass es schlecht ausfallen werde. Saura
& Lafargue stellen das Amendement, 10 Minuten den
ersten beiden Rednern zu geben. Guillaume, Schwitzguebel & Saura machen das Amendement, die Redezeit
auf 10 Minuten festzusetzen & die Anzahl der Redner
nicht zu beschränken. Das Amendement von Saura
& Lafargue wird mit 24 gegen 24 verworfen. Auch
das Amendement von Guillaume, Schwitzguebel & Saura
wird abgelehnt & hierauf der ursprüngliche Antrag

(Engels) angenommen gegen 6 Stimmen mit grosser Mehrheit. — Zu dem Mandate Vaillant, von La Chaux de fonds gibt Schwitzguebel blos die Erklärung ab, dass dies keine französische Section sei, sondern einfach zur romanischen Föderation gehöre. Vaillant hat Auftrag, die romanische Föderation zu vertheidigen gegen die jurassische Föderation, in welcher von einigen Führern Prinzipien aufgestellt werden, welche nur dazu dienen, die I. A. A. zu zerreissen. Guillaume spricht gegen das Mandat Vaillant's, dessen Name von anderer Hand später eingefügt worden ist. Diese Section von La Chaux-de-fonds ist verbündet mit den Revolutionairen & alten Royalisten des Kantons Neuchâtel. Sie halten es mit den Royalisten, wie die Genfer mit den Radikalen, — Beide halten & stimmen mit den Bourgeois. Elsenrel durch royalistische Beihülfe erwählt, Grasselin durch radikale — Vaillant wird vom Congress fast einstimmig anerkannt. — Serraillier verlangt, daß man über den einzelnen Fall, nicht über allgemeine Prinzipien spreche. Bei dem Mandate Dereure's sagt Saura, dass er viele Proteste habe, aber keine Zeit, sie vorzulesen, legt sie daher auf dem Bureau nieder. Section 2 halte dafür, dass der amerikanische Kongress schlechte Eingebungen gehabt

habe, indem er zur Wahl von Delegirten schritt gegen die
Vorschrift der Statuten. Es sei dies eine Wahl im zweiten Grade,
ausserdem hätten Sorge & Dereure vom amerikanischen
Kongress die Vollmacht bekommen, 5 Mitglieder des General-
Raths auszuwählen, um ihnen Mandate zu ertheilen.
Ferner konnte der amerikanische Kongress nicht 2
Delegirte erwählen, da er nicht 1000 Mitglieder vertrat,
es müsse also Einer von Beiden ausgeschlossen werden.
Aber Welcher? Section 42 protestirt gegen die Erwählung
durch den amerik. Kongress als eigenmächtige (autoritaire)
Handlung, sie will ihre eigene Souveränität nicht
aufgeben & protestirt auch gegen die Steuer von
55 Cts. zu deren Ausschreibung der Nordamerik.
F. R. kein Recht gehabt habe, da die Statuten nur
15 Cts erlauben. — Der Vorsitzende fragt an, ob er
alle ihm vorgelegten Schriftstücke verlesen soll, was von
dem Kongress verneint wird. Dereure bedauert, dass
sie nicht gelesen werden, sowie dass wir durch Serailliers
Antrag in der Diskussion beschränkt seien, da es sich
hier wesentlich um Prinzipienfragen handle. Wenn
man indirecte Wahl nicht gelten lassen wolle, müssten
sich die Meisten der anwesenden Delegirten zurückziehen.

Der amerik. Kongress war ausdrücklich berufen, um
Delegirte zu erwählen, folglich müssen sich die Sectionen
fügen, welche daran Theil genommen haben. Prismée
sagt, dieser letzere Grund sei für ihn entscheidend.
Dereure's Mandat wird vom Kongress anerkannt mit
allen gegen Saura's Stimme. Sorge's Mandat wird
angefochten wiederum von Saura wegen Mangel an
Mitgliederzahl (es seien nicht 1000). Sorge meint daß
richtige Auslegung der Statuten uns das Recht auf
mehr Mitglieder gäbe. Er fragt, welche Erwählung
directer sei, als die durch einen zu diesem Zweck berufenen
Kongress? Welches Mandat gültiger, als das von
einem allgemeinen Kongress ausgestellte. Die Behauptung Saura's, dass Dereure & Sorge noch 5 Mitglieder des
G. R. auszuwählen, ist falsch, der Beschluss des amerik.
Kongresses lautet: „daß der Kongress zwei Abgeordnete
wähle & auf allgemeine Kosten schicke, & dass die
einzelnen Sectionen aufgefordert werden, Mandate
an bewährte Parteigenossen zu schicken." Gönnt
Section 42 ihre Souveränität, aber bestreitet ihr das
Recht, sich gegen Beschlüsse aufzulehnen, welche
unter ihrer Mitwirkung gefasst sind. Glaubt gerne,
dass dieselbe Section gegen die 55 Cts protestirt, weil

7

sie nicht zahlen will. Es wäre etwas Anderes, wenn sie nicht zahlen könnte. Sie sollte offen handeln, nicht hinter dem Rücken. — Sorge's Mandat wird vom Kongress anerkannt einstimmig, Saura's ausgenommen. Saura's Mandat von Section 29 & 42 wird angefochten von Sorge, welcher sagt, dass Section 29 nirgends hin gehöre, also auch nicht bezahlt haben könne; dass Section 42 seit dem amerik. Kongress nicht zu finden gewesen sei (introuvable), nicht ihre Beiträge zu den allgemeinen Kongresskosten bezahlt & dieses Mandat nur heimlicher, hinterlistiger Weise ausgestellt habe, um Saura den Eintritt zu ermöglichen, da sie selbst gefürchtet, dass es mit dem Mandat von Sect. 2 schlecht stehe. Das ganze sei nur ein schlau angelegtes Manöver. — Saura sagt, es gebe eben Sectionen in den Ver. Staaten, welche sich den bestehenden Zwistigkeiten halber nirgends angeschlossen, sondern unabhängig geblieben seien, wie z. B. Sect 29. Es sei Verläumdung, zu behaupten, dass Sect. 42 wegen den 55 Cts. oponire; Sie oponiren, weil der amerik. Kongress die allgemeinen Statuten ändern wolle. Uebrigens sind Sect. 29 & 42 in Ordnung mit dem

G. R., da sie bezahlt haben. — Le Moussu sagt, es sei den Sectionen 29 & 42 wohl bekannt gewesen, dass der F. R. im 10 Ward-Hôtel allein vom G. R. aner- kannt war; hätten also durch den F. R. bezahlen müssen. Uebrigens habe ihm Laura selbst ge- sagt, dass er in London schnell zum Schatzmeister Jung gelaufen sei, um solchen Einwänden zuvor zukommen, was beweise sie selbst ihre schwache Stellung erkannt & mit List versucht haben, herein zukommen. — Fränkel wird es bedauern, wenn später solche Fälle wie derjenige Laura's, vorkommen sollten, kann aber jetzt nicht anders handeln, als Laura anerkennen, weil die Statuten leider noch das Bestehen von Sectionen ausserhalb der nationalen Centralisationen gestatten. (Le Moussu's Mittheilung von Laura's eigner Aussage war weder von Fränkel, noch von Eccarius übersetzt worden.) Laura erklärt, dass Le Moussu einen traurigen Gebrauch von seinem Vertrauen gemacht hat, dass er sich wohl hüten wird, ihm wieder Mittheilungen zu machen. Le Moussu sagt, dass allgemeine Interessen ihm vor den persönlichen stehen. Marx setzt aus

21

einander, dass Sectionen entweder den nationalen Föderationen angehören oder vom G. R. direct anerkant sein müssen. Sect. 29 ist keins von Beiden. Unabhängige Sectionen sind in gewissen Fällen ganz nützlich, müssen dann aber vom G. R. anerkannt sein ç direct mit demselben in Verbindung stehen. Er ist entschieden gegen Anerkennung Sauva's. Dereure beantragt Zulassung Sauva's als Delegirter der Sect. 42, wenn die Sectionen 2, 29 ç 42 sich verpflichten wollen, die Handlungen ç Beschlüsse des amerikan. allgemeinen Kongresses anzuerkennen ç dem gemäß zu verfahren. Marx stimmt zu. Sauva nimmt diesen Kompromiss nicht an, denn Sect. 29 warte nur auf das Resultat des Haager Kongresses als Richtschnur ihres ferneren Verhaltens. Dereure zieht seinen Antrag zurück. Auf die Frage, ob diese Sectionen in Ordnung seien, erklärt Engels, dass keine von Beiden mit dem G. R. in Ordnung sei. Unter ziemlicher Verwirrung wird die Abstimmung vorgenommen ç Sauva als Delegat von Sect. 29 ç 42 zugelassen mit 30 gegen 20 Stimmen. ——

22

Cuno beantragt Tadel des Vorsitzenden, weil er zuviel Redner habe sprechen lassen; worauf derselbe erwiedert, daß es sich um 2 Mandate gehandelt habe. Lafargue's Mandat von der Madrider & einer anderen Spanischen Föderation, wird angefochten von Alerini, welcher sagt, dass die Redacteure der „Emancipacion" nur Sectionen gebildet haben, welche der Spanische F. R. nicht anerkannt habe, worauf sich jene an den G. R. gewandt, der sie zugelassen habe mit der Erklärung, „dass es absurd sei, einen FR zu fragen, welcher in seiner Mehrheit zusammengesetzt sei aus Mitgliedern einer geheimen, der I.A.A. feindlichen Gesellschaft" Der Spanische F. R. protestirt gegen die neue Madrider Föderation, weil der G. R. sie statutenwidrig aufgenommen habe. Die andere Spanische Föderation, deren Mandat Lafargue habe, befände sich in gleicher Lage mit der ganzen Spanischen Landesföderation, welche noch nicht ihre Beiträge bezahlt haben. — Guillaume verbessert einen deutschen Uebersetzungsfehler. — Lafargue liest einen Artikel aus der „Emancipacion" vor (anerkannt von Morago), welcher den Grund zur Ausstossung der Redacteure

23

der 'Emancipación' gegeben, die von nur 15 Mitgliedern
(unter 130) beschlossen worden sei, ohne den Angeklagten
nur die geringste Notiz oder Gelegenheit zur Vertheidigung
zu geben. Der spanische F. R. hat diese ungesetzliche
Ausstossung genehmigt, & darum mussten wir uns
an den G. R. wenden. Morago ist schon 2 mal Ver-
räther an der Sache geworden, als er nach Lissabon
floh & als er nach Sagasta's Dekret der I. A. A. den
Rücken wandte. — Jene 15 Mann stellen sich immer
autonom, sind aber ausserordentlich autoritär, wenn
es in ihren Kram passt. Die Motion zu ihrer Handlungs-
weise seien verdeckt; es sei geschehen, weil er in der Liberté
die 'Alliance' angegriffen habe. Morago sagt, dass der
G. R. unter Verletzung aller Regeln & Gesetze, nach
bloss eingebildeten Gründen entschieden habe. Der
Spanische F. R. habe doch mit den inneren Angelegenheiten der Sectionen nichts zu thun. Die
Ausstossung sei regelmässig erfolgt, da die Sections-
Statuten regelmässige Sectionsversammlungen
vorschreiben, deren Beschlüssen sich die Mitglieder
zu fügen haben, wenn sie nicht anwesend sind,
ob sie nun von 5 oder 15 oder 50 gefasst seien.

24

Die spanische Föderation sei die streitbarste aller
internationalen Föderationen. Aller Zwist in Spanien
sei nur entstanden nach Ankunft & Einmischung
dieses einen Individuums. — Sie stellten sich nur
auf den Standpunkt der Statuten, welche zu verletzen
der G. R. kein Recht hat. Wir wollen keine Persönlichkeiten
hereinbringen, aber auf dem nächsten spanischen Congress
entscheiden, ob die Ausstossung gerechtfertigt & in
Ordnung war. Engels sagt, wir müssen entscheiden,
ob die I. A. A. noch fernerhin nach demokratischen
Grundsätzen verwaltet werden soll, oder regiert von
einer Clique, geheim organisirt, in Verletzung der Statuten
der I. A. A. Hier sind 6 Personen anwesend, welche
dieser geheimen Gesellschaft angehören, die 4 Spanier
& Schwitzguebel & Guillaume. — Guillaume unterbricht:
„das ist falsch". Engels fährt fort. Ich habe die Beweise
hier (zieht sie aus der Tasche). Guillaume wird genöthigt,
seinen Ausdruck zurückzuziehen. Engels sagt ferner,
dass die Ausstossung der Madrider ungesetzlich
gewesen sei, da man die statutengemässe Ernennung
einer Ehrenjury nicht vorgenommen habe. Die neue
Section habe nur das ihr zustehende Recht ausgeübt,
als sie sich von dem spanischen F. R. losgesagt &

direct dem G. R. angeschlossen habe. Wohl hat der G. R. die
Statuten überschritten, aber mit vollem Bewusstsein &
mit der Absicht, dadurch die J. A. A. in Spanien
zu retten. — Die Alliance handelt in Spanien mit
dem Gelde der J. A. A. & der spanische F. R. zählt unter
seinen 8 Mitgliedern 5 Brüder der „Alliance". Der G. R.
war sich seiner Verantwortlichkeit wohl bewusst, musste
aber handeln. — (Marcelau sagt, Yes, o Yes! als Engels
erklärt, dass die gegenwärtigen spanischen Delegirten der
Alliance angehören.) Tounnard verlangt Fortsetzung der
Diskussion, um den Spaniern volle Redefreiheit zu gewähren
& dem Vorwurf zu begegnen, dass ihnen das Wort abgeschnitten
sei. Fränkel ist dagegen, weil derselbe Fall später wieder
vorkommt. Verlängerung der Diskussion wird verworfen
& Lafargue als Delegirter der Madrider Föderation zugelassen
mit 40 Stimmen gegen Keine. — Marx beantragt Aus=
stossung der Alliance aus der J. A. A. & verlangt Einsetzung
eines Ausschusses, um Dokumente & die ganze Angelegen=
heit zu untersuchen. Die Sitzung wird auf 2 Stunden
ausgesetzt. —

Wiedereröffnung um 4 Uhr. Beim Namensaufruf fehlen
22 und Cuno tadelt den Vorsitzenden, dass er nicht pünktlich
begonnen habe. Dural beantragt, noch 15 Minuten zu
warten. Vorsitzender spricht längere Zeit & ruft dadurch

26.

Proteste hervor. Er verliest die Namenslisten zum zweiten
Male. Marx gibt Nachricht von einem aus P. Mauricio, nahe
Genua, angelangtem Schreiben einer Section mit Glück=
wünschen. Mc. Donnell wird zum englischen Sekretär
an Stelle des abwesenden Roche ernannt. Lafargue's An=
trag, jede Sitzung mit Namensaufruf zu beginnen, die Fehlenden
einzutragen & die betr. Föderationen zu benachrichtigen, wird
angenommen. — Barry's Mandat beanstandet von
Hales. Da Hales nicht mehr anwesend, war Saura p. gefällig,
an Stelle & im Auftrag Hale's das Mandat anzufechten,
aber ohne einen einzigen Grund anzugeben. — Sorge fragt
nach Gründen, ob irgend Jemand das Recht der Section
bestreite, das Mandat auszustellen? Da absolut
keine Antwort erfolgt & gar kein Grund des Angriffs
angegeben wird, so hat er auch Nichts zu vertheidigen,
macht aber diese Leute verantwortlich für den Zeit=
verlust, den sie dem Kongress verursachen; die Arbeiter=
Klasse wird sie zur Rechenschaft ziehen für diese Ver=
geudung von Zeit, welche der Besprechung von Arbeiter=
Fragen & Arbeiterintressen gewidmet sein sollte.
Wendet sich besonders gegen Saura. — Mottershead
fragt, warum Barry gerade von einer ausländischen
deutschen Section gewählt sei, während er zu Hause

27

in England nicht zu den Führern gehöre, & nichts gelte? —
Marx sagt, es gehe Sie nichts an, wen die Section wähle.
Uebrigens gereiche es Barry zur Ehre, nicht zu den sogenannten Führern der engl. Arbeiter zu gehören, denn
diese seien Alle mehr oder weniger der Bourgoisie & der
Regierung verkauft. Barry sei nur desshalb angegriffen
worden, weil er sich nicht zum Werkzeug Hale's habe
machen lassen wollen. — Barry's Mandat wird
anerkannt gegen Laura's & Motterhead's Stimmen. —
Das Mandats-Komité berichtet Ankunft & Anerkennung weiterer Mandate für Duval aus der Schweiz,
für Mc. Donnel aus Dublin, für A. Hepner aus Regensburg. Alerini's Mandat von einer Section zu Marseille
wird vom Mandat-Komité selbst beanstandet. Ranvier
verlangt, daß Seraillier Auskunft gebe. Seraillier erklärt,
dass er niemals Nachricht von Marseilles, also auch
keine Beiträge erhalten habe. Kann demgemäss nicht
zugelassen werden. Doch sei ihm mitgetheilt worden,
dass sich kürzlich verschiedene Orts-Sectionen gebildet,
um Delegirte auf den Congress zu senden. — Alerini
ist schmerzlich bewegt, so Etwas zu hören in dem
Augenblick, wo die Marseiller erklären, dass sie zur

28

revolutionären Arbeiter-Klasse der Welt gehören. Er entsagt
jetzt diesem Mandat. Er findet, dass hier jetzt Manöver
statt finden, um die Association in gewissem Sinne zu reinigen
& den Händen einiger Weniger zu überliefern. Letztes Jahr
wollte der G. R. den Marseillern Geld zur Beschickung der
Londoner Konferenz übersenden, unterließ es aber, als die
Marseiller nicht in das Horn des G. R. blasen wollten.
Serailler stellt den Antrag, dass so gemachten Ankläger
sofort erwidert werden dürfe. Angenommen. Serailler
erklärt hierauf als Sekretär für Frankreich, dass er während
der ganzen bezeichneten Periode weder einen Brief nach Marseille
geschrieben, noch von dort empfangen habe, also Alerini's Anklage
zu Bodenfalle. — Duval erzählt, dass zwei Leute von
Marseilles nach Genf geschrieben, um sich mit der
romanischen Föderation in Verbindung zu setzen. Ein
Mitglied des romanischen F. R. sei kürzlich nach
Marseille gegangen & dort haben ihm die Marseiller
selbst erklärt, dass es unmöglich, dort eine Section
zu bilden. — Cyrille vermuthet, dass doch Sectionen
bestehen können, ohne mit dem G. R. in Verbindung
zu stehen. Alerini will wieder sprechen. Sorge fragt,
ob Diskussion der Zwischenfragen erlaubt sei. Alerini
sagt, Combe's Mandat von Marseilles sei schon aus-

29

gestellt gewesen & Bastelica habe im Namen des G. R. dorthin korrespondirt. Seraillier verlangt, es möge zu Protokoll genommen werden: dass Bastelica den Marsaillern Geld versprochen habe, sowie dass Bastelica niemals das Recht gehabt habe, auch nur einen einzigen Brief im Namen des G. R. zu schreiben. Fränkel verlangt Abstimmung, ob die Section in Marsailles bestehe oder nicht. Abstimmung wird angeordnet. Seraillier enthält sich der Abstimmung, um nicht zu erklären, dass Alerini ein falsches Mandat abgegeben habe, der vielleicht selbst getäuscht worden ist. Alerini protestirt dagegen. Das Mandat Alerini's von Marsailles wird verworfen mit 38 Stimmen gegen 14 Enthaltungen. — Das Mandat Jonkowski's von der Section de propagande d'action révolutionaire et socialiste zu Genf wird von dem Mandatkomité beanstandet, dessen Vorsitzender Ranvier, erklärt, dass es Föderationen in der Schweiz gäb, die von Jonkowsky vertretene Section aber weder vom romanischen F. R. noch vom G. R. anerkannt sei. Die Section appellirt daher an den Kongress, verlangt die Gründe der Abweisung vom G. R. zu wissen. Dural erzählt, wie die französischen Flüchtlinge bei ihrer Ankunft in Genf versuchten, sich der Égalité

30

zu bemächtigen. Viele derselben traten ein in die Alliance.
Diese wurde allerdings am 6 August aufgelöst, unmittelbar
vor der Konferenz, aber stand sofort wieder auf unter dem
Namen Section de propagende revolut. etc., die sich keinem
anderen Körper anschloss. Brismée sprach sich aus gegen
das Auftreten der Franzosen als Sectionen in Genf, Brüssel
& a. O. Sie sollten sich nur als Gruppe zusammen finden,
um ihre Beiträge zu zahlen. Gingen wahrscheinlich
nicht in die Sectionen, weil man in den belgischen
Sectionen Stellung & Moralität der Aufzunehmenden
untersucht, um keine Schelme aufzunehmen. —
Marx sagt, die Alliance sei aufgenommen worden, weil
man zu Anfang ihren geheimen Character nicht kannte.
Wir wussten wohl, dass sie sich wieder gebildet hatte, doch
konnte die Conferenz gegenüber der amtlichen Auf-
lösungs-Erklärung vom 6 August 1871 Nichts anderes
thun, als die bekannten Beschlüsse fassen. Ich
spreche nicht gegen geheime Gesellschaften als solche —
denn ich habe selbst dergleichen angehört — sondern
gegen geheime Gesellschaften, welche der I. A. A. feindlich
& schädlich sind. — Der romanische F. R. protestirte
heftig gegen Zulassung der fraglichen Section, darum
wies sie der G. R. zurück in Befolgung der Statuten

31.

In Brüssel stand es anders. Die dortige französische
Section schrieb dem G. R., dass Mitglieder des belgischen
F. R. ihnen selbst gesagt, dass Zulassung zu der belgischen
Föderation sie der belgischen Polizei überliefern würde.
Der G. R. konnte daher nicht umhin, die Brüsseler
französische Section unabhängig anzuerkennen z
aufzunehmen, z mit der zweiten dortigen französischen
Section ebenso zu verfahren. Guillaume fordert das
Wort nach Jonkowski. Engels gegen Verletzung der
angenommenen Geschäftsordnung. Guillaume's Ford-
erung wird abgewiesen. Jonkowski sagt, dass seine
Section sich nicht an den romanischen F. R. gewendet
habe. Es gibt in Genf eine Centralsection, welche die
Propaganda im Kanton zum Zweck hat. Die franzos.
Flüchtlinge wussten zuerst nicht, wohin sich wenden.
Einige gingen in die Centralsection. Da sie aber nicht
im Kanton Genf, sondern in Frankreich Propaganda
machen wollten, so bildeten sie diese Section,
welche durchaus nichts gemein hat mit der Alliance,
der fast kein einziges Mitglied früher angehört hat
er selbst war wohl Mitglied, aber nur als Section
der I. A. A., ohne sie als geheime Gesellschaft zu
kennen. Die Mitglieder seiner Section verwahren

32.

sich stets gegen Beschäftigung mit den Angelegenheiten
der Alliance's verlangen jetzt Zulassung als Section
der I.A.A. Ranvier beantragt, die Erledigung
dieser Angelegenheit zu verschieben bis zur Verhandlung
über den Marx'schen Antrag gegen die Alliance. Angenommen. Mandat von Moraga, Farga Pelicer, Marselau
& Alerini vom Ausschuss beanstandet, weil sie ihre
Pflichten dem G. R. gegenüber nicht erfüllt haben.
Ranvier verlangt, dass man die Entscheidung darüber
verschiebe bis zur Entscheidung über die Alliance.
Farga Pelicer sagt, dass ihre Sectionen mit der Zahlung
etwas im Rückstande sind, weil sie theilweise zu arm
sind, was wir alle begreifen sollten. Sie bitten daher
um Stundung der letzten 3 Monate, weil sie es
selbst noch nicht erhalten haben. Wundert sich über
Ranviers Antrag auf Zurückstellung bis zur
Entscheidung der „Alliance" Frage, da sie doch nur
wegen Nichtzahlung beanstandet seien. Die
Spanischen Sectionen seien sehr thätig im Kampfe
mit dem Kapital, das sie vielleicht bald zu vernichten
gedenken. — Engels findet es sehr sonderbar, daß
die Spanier das Geld in der Tasche behalten, anstatt
es mit ihren Mandaten niederzulegen, wie das immer

33

auf Konferenzen & Kongressen geschieht & geschehen
soll. Die Span. Delegirten wundern sich, dass man
die Alliance hereinziehn, & haben doch heute selbst ihre
Mitgliedschaft in derselben zugegeben. (Marselau & die
Anderen sagen, dass sie nicht mehr darin sind, aber
dazu gehört haben). Engels glaubt, sie seien noch
immer darin, nur unter anderem Namen. Wenn sie
sich auf das Blühen der I. A. A. in Spanien berufen
sollte man bedenken, dass der frühere F. R. (die in Madrid
ausgestossenen) dieses Wachsthum herbeigeführt habe. —
Marselau meint, Engels sei nicht genau. Sie wollen das
Geld nicht in der Tasche behalten, sondern erst ihr
spanisches Geld umwechseln, was ihnen bis gestern
Abend noch nicht gelungen sei: Sie hätten sich
allerdings Etwas zurückgehalten als diese unerwartete
Opposition gegen ihre Mandate aufgetreten sei.
Er ist Mitglied der „Alliance" gewesen, die Alliance
hat die I. A. A. in Spanien eingeführt & empor-
gebracht. Die Alliance sind ergebene Parteifreunde
ächte Soldaten der Revolution. Ich bin zufrieden,
wenn man uns hinauswirft. Diese Frage ist
vorher entschieden. Ich spreche die Wahrheit & fürchte
nicht den Tod dafür. Unsere Zerwürfnisse datiren

34

nur von der Ankunft eines Individuums. Wir Mitglieder der Alliance haben Mehr für die Sache gelitten, als alle Mitglieder des G. R. etc. die uns exkommuniciren wollen. Sagt es doch frei heraus, dass wir hinaus geworfen werden sollen & wir werden gehen & Euch das Geld lassen, welches Euch gehört. Die Alliance wurde auf dem Congress zu Saragossa aufgelöst, nachdem sie ihr Werk der Propaganda vollführt hatte & nicht mehr nöthig war. Vorher war sie nöthig weil wir in Spanien kein Versammlungsrecht hatten. —

Ranvier wies darauf hin, wie die Frage der Alliance überall hereintritt, also erst entschieden werden muss ehe wir den Fall der Spanier aburtheilen können. Er habe den Spaniern gestern Abend ehrlich gesagt, sie möchten zahlen, um dieses Hinderniss hinweg zu räumen. Wir müssen die Alliance-Frage vornehmen.

Coenen spricht für die Zulassung der Spanischen Delegirten, wann sie vom G. R. anerkannt sind & bezahlt haben, Was ihm erledigt erscheint. Sein Mandat gebiete ihm, die Sitzung zu verlassen, wenn die Spanier nicht zugelassen werden. Ranvier verwahrt sich gegen die Drohung von Splingard, Guillaume & A. den Saal zu verlassen, — was nur beweise, dass ihre Mandanten die Angelegenheit schon im Voraus

35.

abgeurtheilt hätten. Er wünscht, dass alle Polizeiorganten
der Welt so ihren Abschied nähmen. — Marago erklärt,
dass sie Delegirte der spanischen Föderation, nicht
der Alliance seien, also auch damit Nichts zu thun haben.
Man würde die ganze spanische Föderation durch solche
Verletzung der Gerechtigkeit zerstören. Handelt es sich
jetzt um die Alliance, um die Autorität, um die geheimen
Gesellschaften? Die Alliance hat die J. A. A. gegründet,
gehoben & verbreitet. Alle unsere Wähler wussten, dass
wir zur Alliance gehört (denn es war der Polizei mitgetheilt)
Ihr habt nur zu untersuchen, ob unsere Mandate
in Ordnung sind, weiter Nichts. Wir sind die Vertreter der spanischen Föderation, & hier ist die Absicht
vorhanden, uns draussen zu halten. Ihr habt nur
zu sehen, ob Siegel, Beiträge etc in Ordnung sind.
Lafargue vertheidigt sich gegen die Vermuthung,
dass er mit der spanischen Polizei in Verbindung stehe,
weil er die Alliance angegriffen habe. Sie sollten
darin keine Gefahr finden, da sie keine Politik
treiben, also keiner Regierung gefährlich sein können.
Marselau sagt, Lafargue habe das Blatt zur
Denunziation gegründet & die eben gehörten
Sophismen habe er erst jetzt erfunden.

36.

Wenn Lafargue von Verräthern spreche, könne er
(Marcelau) nicht gemeint sein. Lafargue giebt das
zu, aber Andere". Splingard meint wir hätten
nur mit den Mandaten zu thun, nicht mit
der Alliance, weist auf die zahlreiche Mitglied=
schaft in Spanien hin. Unterbrechungen treten
ein. Ranvier ist gegen Abstimmung, bevor
die Spanier ihre Beiträge gezahlt & die Frage der
Alliance gelöst sei. Fargo Pelicer überliefert jetzt
dem Vorsitzenden die Beiträge der Spanier mit
Ausnahme des letzten Quartal's. Ranvier ist
für Gestattung dieser Ausnahme & beantragt jetzt
ihre Zulassung ohne damit die Frage der Alliance
zu entscheiden. Die spanischen Delegirten
werden hierauf zugelassen; nur Vaillant enthält
sich der Abstimmung, weil die spanischen Delegirten
zwar der Alliance nicht mehr angehörten, aber
nicht erklärt haben, ob sie Artikel IX der
Konferenzbeschlüsse anerkennen & halten
wollen. —

Das Mandat der Section 2 (New York) wird
vom Ausschuss nicht erklärt, weil diese Section
nirgend wo Anschluss habe, nirgendhin gehöre.

37

Saura ist in Verlegenheit wegen der heute morgen gefassten Beschlüsse. Section 2 hat ihre Beiträge gezahlt, ist also in Ordnung mit dem G.R., zählt 169 Mitglieder — 235 darin gewesen —, hat Sectionen in St. Louis, Baltimore, Springfield, Chicago & a. O. gegründet. Gegentheilige Entscheidung würde ernste Folgen für die amerikanische Föderation haben. Schloss sich nach dem Staatsstreich (Eccarius applaudirt) dem Prince-Street Council an & organisirte die Trauerprozession, gegen welche Sect. 1 protestirt hat. Wandte sich zuletzt gegen den Prince street-Council, weil dieser dem G.R. nicht gehorchen wollte & mit der Apollo Hall Geschichte in Verbindung stand. Eccarius übersetzt & fügt seine eignen Bemerkungen hinzu, was von Sorge gerügt wird. Dereure fragt, ob eine Section sich den unter ihrer eignen Mitwirkung gefassten Beschlüsse eines Kongresses entziehen kann. Sorge weist die Beschuldigung gegen Section 1 zurück unter Anführung des Thatbestand's. Marx sagt, diese Section 2 bestehe gar nicht für uns, da sie sich nicht als unabhängige Section mit dem G.R. in Verbindung gesetzt habe. Herman sagt, der

38

belgische Kongress habe auch Mehrheitsbeschlüsse
gefasst, könne deßhalb die Minderheit nicht ausschließen. Es dürfe in der J. A. A. keine Mehrheit geben,
also auch in Amerika nicht. Dereure erklärt, dass
sich die Delegirten der amerikanischen Föderation
zurückziehen werden, wenn Section 2 zugelassen
wird. Brismee erzählt, wie man in Belgien mit solchen
wiederspänstigen Sectionen verfährt, indem man
sie nicht blos suspendirt, sondern vollständig
streicht. Sorge erklärt, dass er die von Dereure
gestellte Kabinetsfrage erst bei Section 12 gestellt
haben würde, wo man zeigen werde, welch' un-
geheures Unrecht der Arbeiterklasse & Arbeiter-
Bewegung in Amerika durch diese Elemente
zugefügt werde. Fränkel ist entschieden gegen
Zulassung von Section 2 unter Hinweis auf
Vorgänge in der Kommune, wo auch von einzelnen
Sectionen in Maueranschlägen etc. gegen den
F. R. intriguirt worden sei. Spricht für die
Centralisation gegen die sogenannte Autonomie,
gegen die Eitelkeit. Man dürfe Auflehnung gegen
jeden Beschluss nicht mehr dulden & Disciplin

muss aufrecht erhalten werden. Eccarius sagt,
Section 2 sei die zweitälteste in den Ver. Staaten,
Section 1 habe sich durchaus nicht freundlich gegen
die Procession benommen, wie er aus den durch
seine Hände gegangenen Briefen wisse. Barry
verwahrt sich gegen Verletzung der angenommenen
Regeln. Ranvier spricht gegen Zulassung von
Section 2, welche sich von allen Andern, von ihrer
eignen Familie losgesagt habe, nun auf einmal
den Kongress beschicken wolle, & zu diesem Zweck
am 26 August die Beiträge an den Schatzmeister
zahle, als eigentlich kaum noch die G. R. bestand.
Das sei nur leerer Vorwand & hinterrücks gehandelt.
Wenn wir solches Verfahren fernerhin zugeben, hat
die I. A. A. kein Recht mehr zu bestehen. Man
mache dann lieber Freimaurerei daraus & der
Secten so viel man wolle. Joannard verlangt Lesung
eines von Saura eingereichten Schriftstück's & besteht
in der heftigsten Weise darauf. Engels verliest es,
den Brief Bolte's vom 4 August an Section 2.
Ranvier tritt nochmals im Namen des Mandats-
Ausschusses entschieden auf gegen Zulassung
von Section 2. Das Mandat derselben wird
nichtig erklärt mit 39 Nein gegen 9 Ja & 11

Enthaltungen. — Marx theilt mit, dass West die Frage wegen Section 12 (New-York) auf Morgen verschoben wünsche; dass der Ausschuss damit einverstanden sei. Er erinnert an die Frage der Alliance; erklärt, dass er nur die Ausschliessung der Alliance, nicht der Spanischen Delegirten, beantragt habe. Sitzung schliesst 10 Uhr Abends.

Mittwoch, 4 Sept., Morgens 9½ Uhr, wird die Sitzung eröffnet; fehlen ziemlich viel Mitglieder. Vilmot fordert Verbot des Rauchens im Saale. Guillaume dafür, wenn es auch nur Einen belästige. Barry; Sexton dagegen. Das Rauchen wird verboten mit 15 gegen 13 Stimmen. Lafargue beantragt Tadel gegen Hales wegen Verlassen des Kongresses, zieht den Antrag nach Erklärungen Seitens englischer Delegirter zurück. Ein Mandat von San Francisco für Vaillant wird Jerner angemeldet & genehmigt; der Kongress schreitet zur Diskussion des Mandats von Section 12 (New-York) für W. West. Saura beantragt, dass für diesen Fall die 5 Minuten-Regel aufgehoben werde, was mit 31 gegen 8 Stimmen angenommen wird. Seraillier erhebt sich gegen Jonkowski's Recht zu Stimmen, Guillaume spricht dafür. Der Kongress entscheidet mit 26 gegen 10 Stimmen; 6 Enthaltungen, dass Jonkowski kein Recht zu Stimmen

41

habe. Morago verlangt Abänderung des Abstimm-
ungsmodus — nach Mitgliederzahl — da sie, die Spanier,
Auftrag haben, nicht zu stimmen, bis das erledigt ist.
Es findet Zwiegespräch zwischen dem Vorsitzenden &
Joannard, Ranvier statt & treffen zwei neue Mandate
für Marx ein. — Marx beantragt im Namen des
Mandatausschusses Nichtigkeitserklärung des Mandats
von W. West, weil er 1, Mitglied einer suspendirten
Section sei; 2, Mitglied des Philadelphier Kongresses &
3, Mitglied des Prince street Council gewesen sei.
Mandat West's ist unterzeichnet von Vict Woodhull,
welche auf die Präsidentschaft schon seit Jahren speculirt,
Präsidentin der Spiritisten ist, free love predigt, Bank-
Geschäft hat etc. Section 12 gegründet von V. Woodhull,
bestand Anfangs fast aus lauter Bourgeois, agitirte
besonders für das Frauenstimmrecht & erließ den
famosen Appeal an die englisch sprechenden Bürger
der Ver. Staaten, worin die J.A.A. mit allerlei Zeug
belastet wurde, & auf Grund dessen sich verschiedene
Sectionen im Lande gründeten. Unter anderem war
darin die Rede von persönlicher Freiheit, socialer
Freiheit (freie Liebe), Kleiderordnung, Frauenstimmrecht,
Universalsprache u. s. w. Sie erklärten am 28 October,

42

dass die Emancipation der Arbeiterklasse durch sie selbst nur bedeute, dass die Emancipation der Arbeiterklasse nicht gegen den Willen der Arbeiter selbst vollzogen werden könne. Sie stellen die Frauenfrage der Arbeiterfrage voraus; verwahren sich gegen die Annahme, dass die I.A.A. eine Arbeiterorganisation sei. Section I protestirte gegen dies Vorgehen der Section 12; verlangte, dass die Section aus wenigstens 2/3 Lohnarbeiter bestünden, weil in den Ver. Staaten jede Arbeiter-Bewegung durch die Bourgeoisie verpfuscht & ausgebeutet wird. Section 12 verwahrte sich gegen die Forderung der 2/3 Lohnarbeiter, höhnisch fragend, ob es ein Verbrechen, kein Lohnsclave sondern frei zu sein. — Beide Parteien riefen die Entscheidung des G.R. an, welche sie am 5 & 12 März gab, & Section 12 suspendirte. Darum kann West nicht zugelassen werden. Trotz ihres Anrufs der Entscheidung des G.R. verweigerte Section 12 & ihre Anhänger die Anerkennung dieser Entscheidung. West war auch Mitglied des Kongresses zu Philadelphia & des Prince Street Council, welche Anerkennung des G.R. verweigerten & in Verbindung mit der jurassischen Föderation standen, welche ihnen laut Zeitungsberichten anriethen, keine Beiträge

43

zu zahlen, um so den G. R. auf's Trockne zu setzen.
West spricht ungefähr 1½ Stunden lang, sagt, das
Urtheil sei schon vorausgefällt; doch komme er
4000 Meilen weit, um seine Pflichten seinen Wählern
gegenüber zu erfüllen. Will sich nur an die 3 Puncte
des Berichts halten, nicht an unbewiesene Anschuldig-
ungen; ist Mitglied der Section 12 & stolz darauf, denn
Section 12 hat englische Sectionen gegründet; verlangt Gericht hier gegen die falschen Anklagen &
Verläumdungen, welche von der anderen Seite durch
Briefe gegen Section 12 gemacht worden sind. Die
Suspension war ungesetzlich, denn sie war Anklage,
Urtheil & Strafe auf ein Mal ohne Anhörung des
Angeklagten. Section 12 ist unschuldig wie ein
neugebornes Kind, unschuldig, bis sie schuldig befunden wird. Darum verweigerte mein Freund
Eccarius Absendung des Urtheils. Wisset, dass in
der ersten Erwägung der Suspension kein Wort wahr
ist, denn Section 12 hat nie einen solchen Beschluss
gefasst, sondern ihn blos besprochen & amendirt.
Section 12 wollte sogar den G. R. als Richter anerkennen, wenn sie billiges Gehör & Tribunal fände.

44.

Zweite Erwägung ebenfalls falsch, denn wir haben Nichts gethan noch gesagt, was nicht in den Statuten, Kongressbeschlüssen u. s. w. selbst enthalten & begründet ist. Die Arbeiterfrage ist auch eine Frauenfrage, & die Frauenemancipation muss der Arbeiteremancipation vorausgehen, Woodhull & Andere sind Spiritisten & free lovers! Könnt ihr das verbieten? Könnt ihr Liebe gebieten, wo keine vorhanden ist? (allgemeines Gelächter.) Geht Euch gar Nichts an. Wir haben uns streng an die Statuten gehalten. Zuerst sind wir Menschen, ehe wir Arbeiter oder Bourgeois sind. Die Entwicklung & Lösung der socialen Frage geht auf folgende Weise vor sich: Erst ist der Mensch Waare, dann wird er Lohnarbeiter, dann wird er Bourgeois — Mittel-Classman etc., & dann tritt durch die höhere Intelligenz des zum Bourgeois avancirten Menschen in die allgemeine Kooperation ein, d. h. die Substitution der Gesellschaft für die individuelle Arbeit. Die Bourgeois haben & gewinnen die nöthige Erfahrung & Intelligenz, welche wir in der Bewegung brauchen. Ich bin allerdings Mitglied des Philadelphier Kongresses gewesen, doch hat dieser Kongress Nichts gegen den G. R. gethan, übrigens habt ihr gestern

45

hier das Mandat einer Section anerkannt (29), welche
dort vertreten war. — Bin wohl Mitglied des Prince-
Street Councils gewesen, aber auf Verlangen desselben
zurückgezogen worden. Wir haben das heilige Recht
der Empörung gegen jeden Despotismus. Der G. R. hat
zweimal seine Pflichten verletzt. Die Amerikaner konnten
die 2/3 Regel nicht annehmen. Der G. R. könnte ja
alles mögliche thun, wenn wir nicht das Recht der
Empörung hätten. Wir wollen nicht, dass andre Leute
Hirn für uns denke, daß der G. R. uns in Amerika Etwas
vorschreibe. Wir sind für die Kommune, das allgemeine
(Frauen-) Stimmrecht, die directe Gesetzgebung. Wir
finden, dass unsere Republik misslungen ist, wollen
eine andere gründen. Man sollte auch die Schweizer
ausschließen, welche das Referendum & andere
politische Rechte einführten. Section 12 hat sicherlich
das erste Jahr bezahlt, was Sorge bezeugen wird & er will
schwören, dass sie auch das 2te Jahr bezahlt haben.
Spricht von Sorge-Partei & West-Partei. Sorge verwahrt
sich gegen Verbindung seines Namens mit dem-
jenigen West's. Der Kongress ist ungeduldig wegen
der vielen von West verbrauchten Zeit. Brismée &

46

Ranvier sind besonders ungehalten über solche
Zeitverschwendung. — Sorge erwiedert West, sagt,
seine Aufgabe sei leicht, erzählt, wie Section 12 unter
falschen Angaben aufgenommen wurde (West erklärte
nämlich, "daß S. 12 in der Mehrheit aus Lohnarbeitern
gleich ihm bestände"), dass der andern Seite genügende
Nachricht von den Forderungen der Gegner der S. 12
gegeben sei, dass der G. R. die ⅔ Regel nur empfohlen,
nicht dekretirt habe; dass Frau Woodhull persönliche
Zwecke in der Association verfolgt, wie ihm West selbst
gesagt; dass man ihnen nie das Recht bestritten,
allerlei Ansichten über Frauenfrage, Religion ek
zu haben, aber wohl die Berechtigung, die I. A. A.
dafür verantwortlich zu machen; dass Section 12
& ihre Anhänger schamlos alle Streitigkeiten vor
dem gesammten Publikum bloss gelegt hätten;
dass sie nicht für dieses Jahr bezahlt hätten; dass sie
mit Vergnügen die Mittheilung von der jurassischen
Föderation & dem univers. Föd Rath in London empfangen hätten; dass sie hinterrücks intriguirt &
die Oberleitung der I. A. A. in Amerika vom G. R.
verlangt, & die gegentheiligen Beschlüsse des G. R.

47

unverschämte Weise als zu ihren Gunsten ausgegeben
hätten; dass sie sich gegen die französischen Kommunisten
& die deutschen Atheisten verwahrt; dass wir Disciplin
verlangen, Unterwerfung nicht unter Personen, aber
unter das Princip, unter die Organisation; dass
wir die Irländer brauchen in Amerika, sie aber
nicht gewinnen können, ehe wir jeglicher Verbindung mit Section 12 & den free lovers ledig sind —
Arbeiterklasse in Amerika besteht 1, aus Irländern,
2, aus Deutschen; 3, aus Negern & erst 4, aus Amerikanern
— Gebt uns freies Spiel, freies Feld, damit wir Etwas
Ordentliches aus der Internationale in Amerika
machen können! — Saura will nicht für S. 12
sprechen, bricht aber eine Lanze für die Leistungen &
guten Eigenschaften der Frau Woodhull & der Sect. 12,—
die 100 Dollars für die Trauerprocession, Frau
Woodhull sei grosse Rednerin, habe für die
Kommune gesprochen, Sectionen gebildet usw. Sect. 2
glaube, dass der G. R. zu hastig gehandelt habe in der
Suspension der Sect. 12, welche sicherlich ihre Beiträge
bezahlt habe. Die gegen die französischen Kommunisten
& die deutschen Atheisten geschleuderten Anklagen

48

seien nicht officiell. Guillaume behauptet, dass die jurassische Föderation niemals nach Amerika ge-schrieben, dass aber er (G.) bei den sich widersprechenden Nachrichten über den amerikanischen Zwist einen Privat-Brief an Verpillier in New-York geschrieben habe, um sich Auskunft über die Sachlage zu erbitten. Dieser habe ihm folgenden Privatbrief als Antwort geschickt, den er verliest, & die Anklagen gegen Sorge, die rechte Hand Marx's, & seine Kreaturen enthält & sagt, dass seine Section (18) sich nie jenen anschliessen könne, welche die Urheber der Spaltung seien, den Staats-streich gemacht hätten, von welchem Sorge nur seine Kreaturen unterrichtet habe u.s.w. Der Brief ist datirt vom 4. August. — Sorge verlangt Abschrift des Verpillier'schen Briefes, um den Verfasser in Amerika zu belangen; zeigt, wie die Gegner nur immer zu verläumden, weil sie glauben, dass doch etwas hängen bleibt; erläutert dies an dem Beispiel Elliot in seinem Brief an den Star v. 9 Dez. 1871, der nie ein Wort auf Sorge's Antwort erwiedert habe, worin ihm dieser vor jedem Komité, dass er (E.) gelogen, zu beweisen sich erboten. — Guillaume verspricht den Brief dem Bureau einzuhändigen.

49

Le Moussu protestirt gegen den Brief Langrands, der
im Bulletin der féd-jur. abgedruckt, voller Lügen & Beleidigungen sei. – Brismée stellt den Antrag, dass
die J. A. A. keine aus Bourgeois gebildete Section
anerkenne. West will über den Antrag sprechen, darüber
entsteht Unruhe, während welcher Cyrille den Saal
verlässt. Auf Seraillier's Antrag findet namentliche
Abstimmung statt. Für Brismée Antrag stimmen:
Arnoud, J. Ph. Becker, Brismée, Barry, Cournet, Cuno,
Coenen, Dupont, Dave, Dural, Dereure, Eberhard, Flues,
Forkas, Friedländer, Fränkel, Guillaume, Gerhard,
Herman, Hepner, Hein, Joannard, Marx, Kugelmann,
Lessner, Lucain, Lafargue, Le Moussu, Milke, Mottershead,
Pihl, Ranvier, Swarm, Saura, Sorge, Sohen, Seraillier,
Sexton, Schumacher, Splingard, Walther, Wroblewski,
van den Abeel, Vaillant, Vichard, Dietzgen Vilmot.
Der Abstimmung enthalten sich Ecarius, Harcourt,
Roche, Schwitzguebel, von den Hout, Forga Pelicer, Morago,
Alerini, Marcelau. 6 sind abwesend. – Bei der
nun folgenden Abstimmung über das Mandat West's
stimmen gegen dasselbe: Arnoud, J. Ph. Becker,
Brismée, Barry, Cournet, Cuno, Coenen, Dupont,
Dave, Dural, Dereure, Eberhard, Flues, Forkas,

50.

Friedländer, Fränkel, Gerhard, Herman, Hepner, Heim, Joannard, Marx, Kugelman, Lessner, Lucain, Lafargue, Le Moussu, Milke, Pihl, Ranvier, Roche, Swarm, Laura, Sorge, Scheu, Seraillier, Sexton, Schumacher, Splingard, Walther, Wroblewsky, van den Hout, van den Abeel, Vaillant, Vichard, Dietzgen, Dumont, Mc. Donnell & Vilmot. Der Abstimmung enthielten sich Eccarius, Guillaume, Harcourt, Mottershead, Schwitzguebel, Farga Pellicer, Morago, Alerini & Marcelau. — Das Mandat West's war also ungültig erklärt mit 49 Nein gegen kein Ja & 9 Enthaltungen. Die Spanier enthalten sich des Stimmens, bis die Art der Abstimmung geregelt ist, haben übrigens selbst schon ähnliche Beschlüsse gefasst. Harcourt hat die Frage nicht verstanden. Eccarius erklärt dass er Geschäftsbeziehungen mit den Secessionisten gehabt & noch habe, er ist selbst in dieser Sache Angeklagter & die Briefe an den G. R. seien Lügen. Sorge habe ihn in Deutschland der Intrigue angeklagt & doch sei Sorge selbst die ganze Ursache des Streites, was er beweisen wolle. Mottershead hat sich enthalten wegen des Barry'schen Mandats. Roche, weil mit dem ersten — Bristwice'schen Beschlü

51

die Hälfte des G. R. austreten müsste. Guillaume
weil man West nicht noch einmal habe sprechen lassen,
übrigens durch Eccarius Erklärung bestärkt. Schwitzguébel ist noch nicht genug aufgeklärt. — Es kommt
der Antrag ein, die Angelegenheit der Allianz einer
Kommission zu unterbreiten & in geschlossener Sitzung
zu verhandeln. Auf Serailliers Vorschlag wird beschlossen,
diese Anträge heute Abend zu verhandeln, Abendsitzung
um 7 Uhr & morgen öffentliche Sitzung zu halten.
Schluss der Sitzung gegen 4 Uhr Nachmittags.

Abendsitzung wird um 7½ Uhr eröffnet. 13 Mitglieder abwesend beim Namensaufruf. Sorge beantragt,
sofort zur Wahl des Bureau's zu schreiten. Dupont
verlangt Lesung der Protokolle. Der Vorsitzende
hält dies nicht für nöthig — & erklärt, dass West
kein Recht hat, anwesend zu sein. Sorge verlangt
die Dringlichkeit seines Antrags. Einstimmig angenommen. Das Mandatkomité berichtet Ein-
treffen eines Mandat's für die Delegirten der franz.
Föderation. Sorge besteht auf der Wahl. Herman
schlägt Brismée, Gerhard & Dupont vor. Heßner
nominirt Ranvier, Sorge & Gerhard. Gerhard lehnt ab

52

Vilmot verlangt besonderen Wahlgang für jeden der
drei Vorsitzenden, Fränkel einen Wahlgang für alle
Drei. Fränkels Antrag wird angenommen. In der
nun folgenden Wahl wird Ranvier zum Präsidenten,
Gerhard & Dupont zu Vicepräsidenten erwählt. Dupont
lehnt ab zu Gunsten Brismée's. Brismée nimmt
nicht an & Sorge wird durch Acclamation zum
Vicepräsidenten ernannt. Auf Kugelmann's Vorschlag
spricht der Präsident dem bisherigen Vorsitzenden
den Dank der Versammlung aus, & er (Ranvier) übernimmt den Vorsitz als eine Ehre, die man nicht
ihm, sondern der Section Ferré, der Stadt Paris,
der Kommune erweist. Zu Uebersetzern in die
verschiedenen Sprachen werden erwählt Cuno,
Fränkel, Eccarius, Vilmot, Dave, van den Abeel,
Marcelau & Alberini. Auf Antrag Sorge's werden
die bisherigen Sekretäre durch Acclamation bestätigt,
mit Ausnahme Roche's, an dessen Stelle Mac-Donnell
für die engl. Sprache tritt & Marcelau wird Sekretär
für die Spanische Sprache. Van den Abeel hat der Presse
mitgetheilt, dass morgen um 10 Uhr öffentliche Sitzung
sein wird & dass Plätze für die Berichterstatter reservirt

53

seien. Der Kongress genehmigt diese Mittheilungen.
Der holländische F. R. ladet den Kongress zu einer
Sitzung in Amsterdam ein am Schluss des Kongresses.
Wird für später zurückgelegt. Joannard verlangt
geschlossene Sitzung um 8 Uhr Morgens & Ausgabe von
Eintrittskarten, um Skandal zu vermeiden.
Van den Hout sagt, dass verschiedene Mittheilungen
von den Behörden eingelaufen seien. Gerhard ver-
langt dass man 1 Gulden Eintrittsgeld erhebe.
Friedländer protestirt dagegen. Eccarius meint,
man solle die ganze Angelegenheit den Haager Partei-
Genossen überlassen, was durch Uebergang zur
Tagesordnung geschieht — Es kommt ein der
Antrag von I. Ph. Becker & Genossen, sofort zur
Berathung zu schreiten über die Vollmachten des
G. R., Bestimmung seines Sitzes, Abhaltung
des nächsten Kongresses & Revision der Statuten —
Saura will erst den Bericht des G. R. hören, den-
selben interpelliren, hat dem G. R. viele Fragen zu
stellen. Auch müsse man den G. R. wählen. Lafargue
ist für den Antrag Becker's, denn die Berichte,
Interpellationen u. s. w. gehören in die geschlossene
Sitzung, & wir müssen den Deutschen, welche nach

54

Mainz zu gehen haben, die Gelegenheit dazu geben. Scheu, Unterzeichner des Antrags, sagt, ihr Verlangen sei ein durchaus loyales, denn der deutsche Arbeiterkongress sei richtig, die socialdemokratische Arbeiterpartei Deutschlands sei ein Zweig der I. A. A. Gebt uns Gelegenheit, unsere Mandate zu erfüllen! — Brismée für vorherige Berathung der Statuten, weil möglicher Weise kein G. R. übrig bleibt. Die Belgier wollen keine Vermehrung der Vollmachten des G. R., sondern eine Verminderung derselben; sonst würden sie sich wieder vereinigen; Massregeln treffen wie die Spanier, Italiener, Schweizer u. s. w. Erklärt ferner, dass der G. R. sich nicht in die Angelegenheiten der Belgier gemischt habe, dass die Belgier sich nicht über den G. R. zu beklagen haben, dass aber die amerikanischen, spanischen & andere Geschichten zeigen, daß der G. R. zu viel Macht hat, & dass ihm das Recht genommen werden muss sich in die inneren Angelegenheiten eines Landes zu mischen. J. Ph. Becker schließt sich Scheu an, meint aber dass man viel falsche Vorstellungen mache. Das Verlangen Saura's nach dem Bericht ist selbstverständlich, aber das nothwendigste Geschäft ist die Bestimmung der Stellung des G. R., & muss zuerst erledigt werden, ist auch früher schon zweimal so

55

gehalten worden. Wir hoffen auch, dass der Kongress durch diesen Antrag zur Eile getrieben werde. Die Gründe sind also ausgezeichnet, & ausserdem sind fast alle deutschen Delegirten Abgeordnete zum Mainzer Kongress, was wir sicherlich in Betracht zu ziehen haben. Morago protestirt, dass er nicht zum Worte gelangt. Guillaume verlangt das Wort für Morago. Hepner erläutert den Antrag, der verlangt, dass das Nöthigste zuerst gethan werde. Gerade die Gegner sollten erst recht dafür sein, damit sie ihre Klagen gegen den G. R. recht bald vorbringen könnten. Sie hätten das ganze Jahr gebrummt & jetzt wolle man hören, was sie eigentlich wollten. Es wird die Debatte geschlossen & der Antrag Becker & Genossen mit grosser Mehrheit (41 Stimmen) angenommen. — Es kommt der Antrag der spanischen Delegirten zur Verlesung & Berathung, welcher fordert dass die Abstimmungen im Congresse fernerhin nach Kopfzahl der Vertretenen vorgenommen werden sollte. Morago spricht dafür, es sei eine Aenderung der Abstimmung im demokratischen Sinn; sie seien beauftragt, nicht eher zu stimmen, als bis eine solche Reform beschlossen sei,

56.

so dass nicht der Abgeordnete von 100 Mitgliedern ebenso viel Macht besitze, wie derjenige, welcher 2000 vertritt. Engels dagegen, weil es Statutenaenderung ist, also jetzt nicht am Platze; übrigens als Pangermanist dafür, weil man es in Deutschland so macht; es nicht unsere Schuld, dass die spanischen Delegirten sich in so trauriger Lage befinden (nicht stimmen zu können) übrigens sei die Instruction nicht von der Föderation, sondern von dem spanischen F. R. gegeben worden. Herman sagt die Belgier stellten dasselbe Verlangen, wie die Spanier. Hepner macht darauf aufmerksam, dass der Kongress soeben beschlossen, gewisse Angelegenheiten vorerst zu berathen, also zur Tagesordnung übergehen müsse. Vilmot dagegen. Präsident theilt mit, dass wir der vorgerückten Stunde halber (11½ Uhr) den Saal verlassen müssen. Die Dringlichkeit des Antrags der Spanischen Delegirten wird abgelehnt mit 7 Stimmen gegen eine grosse Mehrheit. Guillaume erklärt, dass die Jurassier nicht mehr stimmen werden. Der Präsident erklärt, dass die Statuten nicht das Werk des G. R., sondern der I. A. A. sind, also diese Angriffe nicht dem G. R., sondern der Internationalen gelten. Geschlossene Sitzung wird

57

anberaumt auf Morgen früh 8 Uhr. Schluss der Sitzung
nach Mitternacht. —

Donnerstag, 5 Sept, Morgens 8 Uhr kann die Sitzung
nicht eröffnet werden, weil keine Delegirtenliste
vorhanden ist. Nach geraumer Zeit wird zur Arbeit
geschritten; der Präsident theilt die Tagesordnung
der öffentlichen Sitzung & eingelaufene Korrespondenzen
mit. Guillaume verlangt Einsetzung eines Komités,
um das Orginal des Langrand'schen Briefes mit dem
Abdruck im bulletin de la féd. jur. zu vergleichen.
Marx erklärt, dass der Brief Langrand's voller Lügen
& Beleidigungen ist. Le Moussu ist gegen Einsetzung
des Komité's, weil die Jurassiers sich durch Veröffentlichung zu Helfershelfern jener Gemeinheiten &
Lügen gemacht haben. Marx, Joannard & Lafargue
werden als solches Komité ernannt. Es läuft eine
telegraph. Depesche von Genf ein gegen die Aechtheit
des Mandats der Section de propagande et d'action
revolutionaire, wollen Brief nachsenden. Jonkowski
sagt, die Unterzeichner der Depesche seien nicht
Mitglieder seiner Section. Engels protestirt gegen
die Anwesenheit West's im Sitzungssaal & erzählt
West's Aeusserung, dass er (W.) auf jeden Fall Zutritt
zum Kongress haben werde, "wenn nicht durch die

58

Thür, dann durch das Fenster; wenn nicht durch
das Fenster, dann durch den Rauchfang." West muss
sich zurück ziehen. Der vielfach gezeichnete Antrag
auf Einsetzung eines Untersuchungs Ausschusses
über die "Alliance" kommt zur Berathung.
Sorge schlägt vor, dass zu diesem Zweck ein Komite
von fünf Mitgliedern erwählt & Pause von 5 Minuten
gemacht werde. — Marx theilt mit, dass der Bericht
des G. R. nur für die Oeffentlichkeit bestimmt sei,
da der G. R. über verschiedene nationale Organisationen nicht berichten darf, & mehrere Föderationen,
z. B. die jurassische, ihre Pflichten bezüglich der
Berichte nicht erfüllt haben, so dass der G. R. nicht
einmal in den Stand gesetzt war, genauen Bericht
zu geben. Er erwähnt, dass die nordamerikanische
Föderation die einzige sei, welche alle Pflichten
betreffs der Berichte, Beiträge u. s. w. genau
erfüllt habe. Er fügt den Wunsch hinzu, dass man
Verfügung über die öffentlichen & geschlossenen Sitzungen treffe. — Betreff des Sorge'schen Antrag's
bemerkt Guillaume, dass die Minderheit bis jetzt
kein einziges Mitglied eines Komite's durchgesetzt

59

habe, & verlangt, dass man den Mitgliedern der
Alliance gestatte, <u>ein</u> Mitglied des Untersuchungs-
Komite's zu bezeichnen. Dies wird gestattet; nach
Berathung mit den Spaniern theilt Guillaume mit,
dass R. Splingard von ihnen dazu erkoren sei.
Marx macht darauf aufmerksam, dass man,
um zeitraubende Uebersetzungen zu sparen,
nur französisch redende Mitglieder in das Komite
wählen solle. — Bei der nun erfolgenden Abstimmung werden als Untersuchungsausschuss für die
Angelegenheit der „Alliance" erwählt: Cuno,
Splingard, Walther, Lucain & Vichard. —
Alerini & Guillaume stellen den Antrag, ein Komite
von fünf unbetheiligten Mitgliedern zu ernennen,
um die Anklagen gegen den G. R. & dessen „unter-
irdische Wühlerei" (Leipziger Hochverrathsprocess) zu
untersuchen. Sorge erklärt sich dafür, wenn auch
Eccarius darin zur Untersuchung gezogen werden
kann. Moussu wünscht, dass dies Komite nicht
gewählt, sondern von den <u>Anklägern selbst</u> ernannt werde. Auf Antrag Guillaume's wird
diese Untersuchung dem Ausschuss über die Alliance
mit überwiesen — (14 gegen 4 Stimmen) & es wird

jetzt Pause gemacht, um die öffentliche Sitzung 60

einzurichten. —

Kurz nach 10 Uhr wird die öffentliche Sitzung

eröffnet. Zahlreiches Publikum füllt die demselben

reservirten Räume, viele Berichterstatter In-&

Ausländischer-Zeitungen besetzen die Gallerie & der

Namensaufruf der Delegirten ergibt nur 3 Abwesende.

Der Präsident hält eine Anrede an die Versammelten,

worin er zuvörderst die bekannten Gründe an-

gibt, warum der allgemeine Kongress in den vor-

hergehenden zwei Jahren nicht habe abgehalten

werden können & dann übergeht zur Stellung der

I. A. A. zu der Kommune. Er vertheidigt die

Kommune gegen die gewöhnlichen Angriffe, weist

nach, dass die der Kommune gemachten Vorwürfe

& Beschuldigungen vor die Thür der Versailler

gehören & ertheilt den Ländern ein Lob, welche den

flüchtigen Kommunarden ein Asyl gewährt &

das niederträchtige Auslieferungsbegehren des

infamen J. Favre gebührend zurückgewiesen

hätten. Auch Holland gibt er ein Lob & schliesst

mit einem Hoch auf die I. A. A. Es wird die

61

Einladung des holländischen F. R. zu einer ge-
selligen Zusammenkunft in Amsterdam verlesen
& auf Antrag Lafargue's zur Verhandlung in
geschlossener Sitzung zurückgelegt. — Sexton raliest
jetzt den Bericht des General-Raths in englischer,
Longuet in französischer & Marx in deutscher Sprach,
worauf ihn van der Abeele in 's holländische übersetzt. Der Bericht schildert besonders die Verfolgungen,
denen die J. A. A. überall ausgesetzt ist, in Oeste=
reich, Frankreich, Spanien, Deutschland, Dänemark
u. s. w, wie das Bestehen der J. A. A. als uner-
träglich mit den jetzigen modernen Einrichtungen
der Gesellschaft in allen Ländern angesehen, desshalb
als Hochverrath betrachtet wird; wie diese neue
Rechtsanschauung sich von Wien fast über den
ganzen Kontinent verbreitet hat, wie die J. A. A,
die Vertreterin der Arbeit, um so mehr erstarkt
sei & neuerdings besonders Boden gefasst habe
in Irland, Dänemark, Holland, Portugal, Aus-
stralien, Neuseeland & Buenos-Ayres. Welch grossen
Fortschritt die proletarische Bewegung gemacht,
sehe man besonders daran, dass es Jahre lang

gewährt habe, bis die Arbeiter der verschiedenen
Länder den Junikampf (1848) verstanden hätten;
dass sie aber jetzt in allen Ländern der Kommune
sofort zugejauchzt hätten. —

Der Bericht des G. R. wird einstimmig angenommen, immer mit der stereotypen Enthaltung der Spanier.

Es wird ein Antrag eingebracht & einstimmig
angenommen: Den Verfolgten der Arbeiterpartei
in allen Ländern unsere Sympathie auszu-
drücken & unseren brüderlichen Gruss allen
leidenden Freunden darzubringen, in Frankreich,
Deutschland, Dänemark u. s. w.

Auf Brismée's Vorschlag wird beschlossen, die
geschlossenen Sitzungen während des Tages, die
öffentlichen Sitzungen des Abends abzuhalten.

Sorge beantragt jetzt eine Pause von 15 Minuten,
Joannard von mindestens 1 Stunde. Brismée
spricht für Sorge's Antrag. Das Amendement
Joannard wird angenommen. Cuno macht
eine persönliche Erklärung gegen den früheren
Preussischen Konsul Schramm zu Mailand & droht

63

ihm, ihm einen feigen Dieb nennen zu wollen, sofern
er nicht nach der Sitzung Rede stehen werde. Der Genfer
Föderationskongress schickt einen telegraphischen
Glückwunsch; d'Osten einen Gruss an seine Genossen
von der Kommune. Die Liste wird verlesen & die
Sitzung geschlossen um 3 Uhr.

Um 4 1/4 Uhr wird die öffentliche Sitzung
wieder eröffnet durch Namensaufruf. Dietzgen
zeigt schriftlich seine Abreise an. Sohn ist auch
abgereist. Präsident Rauvier verliest theilweise
eine Denkschrift der Section Ferré von Paris, welche
sich in scharfen Ausdrücken gegen Bonaparte,
Bakunin, Malon, Gaspar Richard, Blanc &
A. ergeht, sowie gegen die Föderation, welche solche
Elemente enthält; hegt etc. Vilmot verwahrt
sich gegen Betrachtnahme des Briefes, & Guillaume
gegen die Verbindung solch ehrenwerther Namen
wie Bakunin & Malon mit den Namen solcher
Elenden wie Richard, Blanc etc. — Longuet
spricht gegen Vilmot's Bedenken & der Kongress
geht hierauf zur Tagesordnung über. —

64

Es läuft ein Antrag ein von Arnaud, Cournet, Dereure, Le Moussu, Ranvier & Vaillant, der sich gegen die Enthaltung von der Politik ausspricht, verlangt, dass die streitbare Organisation der revolutionairen Kräfte des Proletariats & des politischen Kampfs auf die Tagesordnung des nächsten Kongresses gestellt, der G. R. angewiesen werde dem nächsten Kongresse darüber eine umfassende Vorlage zu machen. — Auf Antrag Dupont's wird beschlossen, ein Komité niederzusetzen, welches alle Eingaben an den Kongress zu prüfen & darüber zu berichten hat. In dieses Komité werden gewählt Dupont, Hepner, Fränkel, Dereure, Lafargue, Brismée. — Zur Tagesordnung, Berathung über den General Rath & seine Vollmachten, ergreift Herman das Wort & schildert die Ansicht der Mehrheit der Belgier, welche wohl einen G. R. beibehalten, aber aller Macht entkleiden wollen. Lafargue verlangt den Ausführungen Herman's gegenüber zuerst Abstimmung über die Frage, ob der G. R. fortbestehen solle oder nicht.

65

Dave tritt gegen Lafargue für Herman auf. Longuet
verlangt zuerst Generaldebatte, 2 für, 2 gegen die
Vorlage, dann Specialdiskussion. Dupont fordert
einfache Tagesordnung, welche genehmigt wird,
worauf Lafargue für das Institut des G. R. spricht,
dessen Nothwendigkeit aus den ökonomischen Gesell=
schaftsbedingungen nachzuweisen versucht & mit
der Erklärung der Portugiesen schließt: „Wenn
wir keinen G. R. hätten, müssten wir schnell
einen erfinden"! Guillaume ergreift das Wort
& sagt, dass zwei grosse Ideen in der Bewegung
nebenhergehen, die der Centralisation in der
Hand weniger Männer & die der freien Föderation
derjenigen, welche die Gleichheit der ökonomischen
Zustände jedes Landes zur Einheit der Idee der
Interessen in allen Ländern vereinigt. Die
Bewegung kann nicht die Auffassung eines
einzelnen Gehirn's sein. Man braucht zur
Leitung der Bewegung keinen G. R. mit Autorität.
Wir wollen keine Autorität & wir in der jurass.
Föderation besitzen keine. Wir stützen uns

66.

auf Erfahrungen. Brauchen wir im ökonomischen Kampfe (grieve) den G. R. hat er schon jemals eine grieve organisirt oder gemacht? Brauchen wir zum politischen Kampf einen G. R. Der G. R. hat noch niemals Barrikaden gebaut & wird sie nie bauen. Was hat er hier & dort genützt? Wenn man fragt: Braucht die I. A. A. keinen Kopf? antworten wir "Nein". Sorge antwortet Guillaume: Wir haben auch Erfahrungen & möchten gern sehen, was die Jurassier mit diesen Ideen geleistet. Was haben sie denn aufzuweisen? Guillaume sagt, sie hätten keine Autorität in der Jura-Föderation. Wäre dem nur so, dass sie keine Autorität gehabt hätten, den lügnerischen, infamen Brief Langrand's zu veröffentlichen. Wenn der G. R. bei den Ausständen Nichts genützt habe, so verweise er ihm auf den Fall der Pariser Bronzearbeiter, der englischen Maschinisten, der New-Yorker Näh-maschinenarbeiter, die schnell erkannt hätten welchen Nutzen ein solches internationales Band gewähre. Wenn der General Rath auch kein General wäre, so sollte er doch ein Generalstab

67

sein, der die cadres formire & organisire. Wenn
Guillaume die I. A. A. ohne Kopf haben wolle,
so erniedrige er uns zu den thierischen Organismen
der niedersten Art. Wir wollten nicht blos einen
Kopf, sondern einen Kopf voll Gehirn, & wenn unsre
Feinde mit Kanonen schössen, wollten wir
nicht mit Erbsen antworten. Morago sagt,
seine Sympathien waren für Abschaffung des
G. R. & nur für Beibehaltung eines Mittelpunktes
der Correspondenz & Statistik. Die Spanische
Föderation sei durchaus autonom & verlange
die wahre, freie, autonome I. A. A. Der
G. R. dürfe durchaus keine Macht haben
weder über Sectionen, noch über Föderationen.
Auf die Zahl der G. Rathsmitglieder kommt es
uns weniger an. Wenn der Kongress dem G. R.
noch mehr Macht geben will, so wird die Span.
Föderation sich Nichts auferlegen, aufhalten
lassen, da sie frei & autonom ist, & durchaus
nicht beherrscht sein will. Diejenigen, welche
die Macht des G. R. so vermehren wollen, mögen
auch die Folgen davon tragen. — Seraillier &
& Dupont schlagen vor, die öffentliche Sitzung

68.

auf Morgen Abend 6 Uhr zu vertagen, was genehmigt
wird. Schluss 11 Uhr.

Freitag, 6 Sept., Morgens 9 Uhr, wird die Sitz=
ung durch Namensaufruf eröffnet, der 71 Anwesende
ergibt. Walther erbittet für die Untersuchungs=
kommission die Erlaubniss, sich zurückzuziehen
zu dürfen, um an ihre Arbeit zu gehn. Genehmigt.
Sorge, Becker & Genossen bringen einen Dring=
lichkeitsantrag ein, dass man sofort zur Berathung der Statuten über die Vollmachten des
G.R. schreite, je 1 Redner für & gegen Fünf Minuten
sprechen lasse & dann zur Abstimmung schreite.
Dove verlangt die Lesung der Protokolle, Dupont
eine geschlossene Sitzung zu diesem Zwecke.
Van den Abeel spricht gegen den Dringlichkeitsan-
trag, Vaillant dafür, indem er ausführt, dass
wir hieher gekommen sind, die Organisation
zu verbessern, also zum Werke schreiten müssen.
Der Sorge'sche Antrag wird angenommen mit
34 gegen 4 Stimmen. Zur Diskussion gelangt
jetzt die Dringlichkeit des folgenden Antrags,
von denselben Mitgliedern eingebracht:

69

Allgemeine Regeln. General-Rath.

Art. 2 Der G. R. ist verpflichtet die Kongressbeschlüsse
auszuführen & darüber zu wachen, dass in jedem
Lande die Grundsätze, Statuten & allgemeine
Regeln der I. A. A. genau beobachtet werden.

Art. 6 Der G. R. hat gleicher Weise das Recht,
Zweiggesellschaften, Sectionen, Föderal-
Räthe oder Komites & Föderationen der
I. A. A. zu suspendiren bis zum nächsten
Kongress.

Gegenüber zu einer Föderation gehörigen
Sectionen soll er jedoch dieses Recht nicht
ausüben bevor er den betr. F. R. um Rath
gefragt hat.

Im Falle der Auflösung eines Föderal-
Raths oder Komite's soll der G. R. sofort die
Wahl eines neuen Föderal-Raths oder Komites
durch die Sectionen der betr. Föderation binnen
30 Tagen ausschreiben.

Im Falle der Suspension einer ganzen
Föderation soll der G. R. unmittelbar allen
anderen Föderationen davon Nachricht geben.

Wenn die Mehrheit der Föderationen es
verlangt, soll der G. R. eine ausserordentliche

70

Konferenz, bestehend aus einem Delegirten
jeder Nationalität, berufen, welche einen Monat
nachher zusammen treten & den Fall ent-
giltig entscheiden wird.

Hierbei bleibt es wohlverstanden, dass diejenigen Länder, in welchem die I. A. A verboten
ist, dieselben Rechte ausüben werden wie die
regelmässigen Föderationen.

Da Ph. Becker für sofortige Inbetrachtnahme
sagt, dass wir eigentlich nicht mehr nöthig
haben sollten, darüber zu sprechen, da wir
dasselbe schon früher beschlossen haben; müssten
Gewissensbisse darüber empfinden, dass wir
heute, am 5ten Tage noch Nichts beschlossen
& ausgeführt haben; selbst die sogenannte
Opposition könne den Vorwurf nicht auf
sich nehmen, dass die Opposition uns Opposition
mache. Das vorliegende sei die Hauptsache;
wenn die erledigt würden wir mit dem Anderen
bald fertig werden; wir alle fühlen das Be-
dürfniss, bald heim zu gehn, & unser Geldbeutel
mahnt uns sicherlich daran. — Vaillant
spricht auch dafür; wir müssen arbeiten, nicht
Reden halten; diese Hauptfrage müssen wir

71

erst abmachen, dann können wir die Fragen der
Politik & der Erhöhung der Beiträge aufnehmen.
Brismée sagt, es sei ganz unnütz, über die
Vollmachten des G. R. in Berathung zu treten;
wir (Belgier) wollen keine Macht des G. R.; dies
ist eine Prinzipienfrage, über die wir in Belgien
alle einig sind; die Delegierten des Vestu Thales
verlangen sogar vollständige Abschaffung des
des G. R.; wir fordern, dass der G. R. nur der
Kommis der I. A. A. sei & nie sich in die inneren
Angelegenheiten eines Landes mischen dürfe. –
Longuet meint, das Volk könne doch nicht
überall sein, es müsse doch Beauftragte haben,
welche gewisse Arbeiten thun, die nicht jeder
verrichten kann; Flues, der die vollständige Abschaffung des G. R. verlange, sei logischer als Brismée;
denn zu den Arbeiten, welche Brismée dem G. R. überlassen will, brauche man eben keinen G. R., da
sie ganz gut ohne ihn besorgt werden könnten. –
Guillaume sagt: Wir haben unsere Ansichten schon
ausgesprochen & werden solche Anträge nicht dis-
kutieren; ich beantrage daher sofortige Abstimmung.

72

möge die Majorität den Muth haben, vollständig
hervorzutreten; glaubt übrigens, dass Viele der Delegirten
Niemand vertreten. — Seraillier erklärt, er sei nicht
gebunden hier, wie Guillaume & Genossen, welche sich
vorausverständigt haben, da sie mandat impératif
angenommen, sich zurückzuziehen oder in gewissem
Sinne zu stimmen. Wirft daher Guillaume's Worte
auf diesen selbst zurück, erklärt & will beweisen, dass
er Frankreich vertritt, welches jetzt in 30 Departements
besser organisirt sei, als unter dem Kaiserreich &
die Konferenzbeschlüsse über Politik & die Handlungen
des G. R. vollständig anerkenne. Schluss der Diskussion
wird angenommen mit allen gegen 5 Stimmen.
Saura glaubt, dass je 1 Redner für & gegen nicht alle
Meinungen vertrete. — Der oben angeführte Artikel 2
kommt zur Berathung. Morago führt aus, dass
der G. R. die Kongressbeschlüsse, Statuten u. s. w.
nach seiner Weise auslegen könne, & man dann
kein Mittel gegen den G. R. habe; welche Garantie
sei gegen etwaige Ausschreitungen des G. R. geboten?
Wir halten den Beschluss für gefährlich & sind gegen
jede Machtbefugniss des G. R., da wir von Niemand
regiert werden wollen. — Lafargue erklärt daß das,
was Morago gegen die Vollmachten des G. R. vorbringt

1

73

sich auch gegen einzelne Sectionen sagen lässt,
die in Ländern, wo die I.A.A. verboten ist, manchmal aus Spionen & Polizeiagenten sich bilden;
wenn Morago so viel gegen etwaigen Despotismus
des G.R. sich auslässt, muss ich ihm sagen, dass
sein Auftreten dahier das allertyrannischte ist, indem er & seine Genossen verlangen, dass man ihnen
nachgebe unter der Drohung, sich andern Falls
zurückzuziehen. — Der Artikel 2 wird verlesen &
angenommen mit 40 Ja gegen 5 Nein & 11 Enthalt=
ungen. — Dumont verlangt Tadel gegen die Abwesenden. Van den Hout spricht sich aus gegen die
mandats impératifs & wünscht, dass die Majorität
der Minorität mehr Konzessionen mache. —
Zur Berathung gelangt der oben angeführte Artikel
6. — Saura sagt, dass hier irrthümlich (deh. Sorge)
die Behaupthung aufgestellt worden sei, als ob
die Franzosen in den Ver. Staaten für eine Macht-
erweiterung des G.R. seien; sie seien nur für Beibe=
haltung des G.R.; sein Mandat sei; dass der
G.R. das Recht der Suspension von Sectionen &
Föderationen nur in vom Kongress bestimmten
Fällen habe, sonst nicht. — Herman versucht

74

Beispiele anzuführen, worin das Recht der Suspension unangenehme Folgen habe. — Marx sagt: Wir verlangen diese Befugnisse nicht für uns, sondern für den künftigen G.R.; wir wollen den G.R. lieber abschaffen, als nach dem Wunsche Brismée's eine Briefbox daraus machen; in solchem Falle würden auch Journalisten, d.h. meistens Nicht-Arbeiter die Leitung der Association in die Hände bekommen. — Wundert sich, wie die jurassische Föderation (die Abstractionisten) die Section 12 unterstützen konnte, welche aus der Association ein Mittel & Werkzeug zur Unterstützung einer Bourgeoispolitik machen wollte; wenn man ungläubig über Polizeisectionen lächelt, so möge man wissen, dass solche in Frankreich, Oesterreich & a. O. gebildet worden seien. der G.R. sei von Oesterreich aus angegangen, keine Section anzuerkennen, die nicht durch Delegirte des G.R. oder der dortigen Organisation gegründet sei; Vésinier & Genossen, kürzlich aus der französischen Flüchtlingschaft ausgestoßne, seien natürlich für die Jurassische-Föderation. — Der belgische F.R. sei beim G.R. so arg angegriffen worden, wie irgend einer wegen Ausschreitungen, Nepotismus etc. & zwar von

75

belgischen Arbeitern, worüber die Briefe vorlagen,
Bursche wie Vesinier, Landeck & Kons. bilden meinet-
wegen zuerst einen Föderal-Rath, dann hinterher
eine Föderation; Bismarck'sche Agenten mögen
dasselbe thun; der G. R. muss daher das Recht haben,
einen F. R., eine Föderation aufzulösen oder zu
suspendiren; dann kommt die Berufung an die
Sectionen, die manchmal recht angemessen
sein mag, um zu entscheiden durch des Volkes Stime,
ob ein F. R. noch der Ausdruck des Volkswillens sei;
in Oesterreich bildeten Schreier, Ultraradikale &
provocateurs Sectionen, um die I. A. A. zu kompro-
mittiren; in Frankreich bildete ein Polizeikomondant
eine Section; trotzdem ist die Association am Besten
da, wo sie verboten ist, denn Verfolgungen bringen
dieses Resultat immer hervor; der G. R. könnte
schon jetzt eine ganze Föderation suspendiren, indem er eine Section nach der anderen suspendirte;
im Falle der Suspension eines F. R. oder einer
Föderation setzt sich der G. R. unmittelbar hinterher einer Zurechtweisung, einem Tadel aus, &
wird daher das Recht einer solchen Suspension nur
in den allernöthigsten Fällen ausüben; ob wir

76

aber dem G. R. das Recht eines Negerfürsten oder russischen Czars zugestehn & zuschreiben, seine Macht ist doch null, sobald er aufhört, der Ausdruck der Mehrheit der I. A. A. zu sein; der G. R. hat keine Armee, kein Büdget, sondern nur eine moralische Macht & wird stets ohnmächtig sein, wenn er nicht die Zustimmung der ganzen Association hat. Lafargue sagt, man habe dem G. R. vorgeworfen, daß er den Kongress nach dem Haag berufen, um sich dort eine Mehrheit zu sichern; man sehe sich einmal, wie die Holländer immer mit den Belgiern gegen den G. R. stimmen, um zu begreifen, wie wohl der G. R. sich vorbereitet habe. — Dave fragt an, warum der Kongress nach dem Haag berufen worden sei? Marx sagt, das es auf den Vorschlag der Belgier geschehen sei (Bismée bejaht dies.) Guillaume gibt die Erklärung ab, dass die jurassische F. R. das Redactionskomité des bulletin sei & als solches der Föderation verantwortlich. — Bei der nun folgenden Abstimmung wird der Artikel 6, wie oben, angenommen mit 36 Ja gegen 6 Nein & 15 Enthaltungen. —

Vaillant, Arnoud & Cournet beantragen, jetzt den Artikel über politische Handlung der Arbeiter-

Klasse, über Erhöhung der Beiträge in Berathung zu ziehen. — Die englischen Delegirten legen gemeinsam Protest ein wegen Missachtung ihres Rechts zu sprechen, & machen den französischen Delegirten Vorwürfe, dass sie das Diskussionsrecht monopolisiren, & mittelst ihrer Lebhaftigkeit & Heftigkeit zu ihrem Ziel gelangen. — Der Vorsitzende Ranvier sagt, es sei eigne Schuld der Engländer, welche sich immer zu spät zum Worte melden, & verspricht, von jetzt an die englische Uebersetzung immer zuerst geben zu lassen, womit sich die englischen Abgeordneten befriedigt erklären. — Longuet schlägt vor, den Artikel über die politische Handlung der Arbeiterklasse auf die Tagesordnung der öffentlichen Sitzung zu stellen. Generalkonsul Schramm erscheint & verursacht grosse Unruhe mit seinen Protestationen, bis Cuno sich mit ihm zurückzieht. — Schwitzguébel verlangt Berathung des spanischen Antrags auf Aenderung des Abstimmungsmodus. — Engels, Marx & andere Mitglieder des bisherigen G. R. schlagen vor, dass der Sitz des G. R. für das Jahr 1872–1873 nach New-York verlegt werde, & der G. R. aus folgenden Mitgliedern des dortigen F. R. bestehe: Karanagh, St. Clair, Oetti, Levicle, Lawel, Bertrand,

78

Bolte & Carl, mit dem Recht sich bis zur Zahl von 15 zu ergänzen. — Jvannard ist gegen London als künftiger Sitz des G. R., aber Engels Antrag habe nicht den Vorrang; er sei nicht mit sich einig, wohin der G. R. zu verlegen sei. — Ranvier schlägt vor als Tagesordnung für die öffentliche Abendsitzung: Beendigung des gestern Begonnenen, Abstimmungsmodus; drittens die politische Handlung der Arbeiterklasse. Dies wird genehmigt & Engels nimmt das Wort für den Antrag, den G. R. nach New-York zu verlegen. Der G. R. sei bisher immer in London gewesen, weil er dort allein international, dort allein Papiere & Dokumente in vollständiger Sicherheit sein konnten. In New York sind unsere Papiere aber mindestens eben so sicher, als in London, & an keinem anderen Orte in Europa sind sie so sicher, nicht einmal in Genf oder Brüssel, wie man an gewissen Vorkommnissen gesehen hat. Die Parteizwistigkeiten seien in London so arg geworden, dass der Sitz verlegt werden müsste. Ausserdem sind die Anschuldigungen & Anklagen gegen den G. R. so heftig & unausgesetzt geworden, dass die Meisten seiner bisherigen Mitglieder dessen müde

79

geworden & entschlossen sind, keine Stelle mehr
darin anzunehmen. Er könne dies z. B. bestimmt
erklären für K. Marx & sich selbst. Auch sei die bisherige G. R. durchaus nicht immer einmüthig gewesen,
was alle Mitglieder bezeugen könnten. Der G. R. sei jetzt
8 Jahre lang an einem Orte gewesen & es sei ganz
gut, ihn zu verlegen, um einer gewissen Verknöch-
erung vorzubeugen. Marx habe aus ähnlichen
Gründen schon im Jahre 1870 beantragt, den G. R.
nach Brüssel zu verlegen, aber alle Föderationen
hätten sich damals für sein Verbleiben in London
erklärt. – Wohin nun sollte man den G. R. verlegen?
Nach Brüssel? Die Belgier selbst erklären, dass das
nicht gehe, weil keine Sicherheit dort für sie herrsche
Nach Genf? Die Genfer verwahren sich entschieden
dagegen, theilweise aus demselben Grunde, wie
die Brüsseler & weisen auf die Angelegenheit Outine's
hin. So bleibt denn kein anderer Ort als
New-York. Dort sind unsere Papiere sicher, dort
haben wir eine treue, starke Organisation, dort
ist unsere Partei recht international, wie an keinem
anderen Orte der Welt. Man sehe sich z. B. den V. Yorker
F. R. an, der aus Irländern, Franzosen, Deutschen

80.

Italienern & Schweden bestehe, & bald auch ein-
geborene Amerikaner zu sich zählen werde.
Der Einwand, dass New York zu fern liege, ist
nicht stichhaltig; denn das wird ein gewisser Vortheil
für die europäischen Föderationen sein, welche eifer-
süchtig gegen Einmischungen des G. R. in ihre
innern Angelegenheiten sind, da eben diese räumliche
Entfernung solche Einmischungen erschweren & es
verhindern wird, dass einzelne Föderationen einen
zu grossen Einfluss im G. R. erlangen; & übrigens
hat ja der G. R. das Recht, vielleicht sogar die Pflicht,
für gewisse Fälle & Länder Vollmachten in Europa
auszustellen, wie es der G. R. ja bisher immer
gethan. — Vaillant tritt gegen die Verlegung
nach New-York auf, gibt zu, dass nächst London
New-York der beste Platz für den G. R. sein würde,
doch seien in Amerika selbst jetzt zu grosse Streitigkeiten & ein Theil der Organisationen sogar in
Bourgeoispolitik verwickelt, New York sei zu fern
vom Schauplatz der Handlung, zu fern von denjenigen
Ländern, wo die I. A. A. verboten & desshalb am
Besten ist (Oesterreich, Ungarn, Frankreich, Deutschland).
Wenn er es auch sehr bedaure & es grosse Schade sei,

81

dass so viele bewahrte Männer austreten & nicht
mehr im G. R. dienen wollten, so gäbe es doch so
viele gute Internationale in London, dass man
leicht einen ordentlichen General-Rath in London
wählen könne. — Laura erklärt sich für eine
Veränderung des Sitzes & des Personals des G. R.,
ist aber noch nicht mit sich einig darüber, ob
New-York der beste Platz sei; jedoch für New-York,
wenn er zwischen London & New-York zu wählen
habe, ist gegen die Zuziehung von Mitgliedern
(Ergänzung); der Kongress sollte selbst den G. R.
vollständig wählen, aber ihn nicht in die
Hände von einer Gruppe von Leuten geben, welche
mit ausgezeichneten Absichten (sagt dies wiederholt)
viel Uebles angerichtet haben; der nordamerikanische
F. R. könne sich mit den besten Absichten
nicht den Persönlichkeiten entschlagen & vertrete den Autoritarismus mindestens ebenso stark,
ja stärker als der bisherige G. R. — Schluss der
Debatte wird angenommen. Serraillier verlangt
Abtheilung des Engels-Marx'schen Antrag in
3 Theile: 1, Soll der G. R. verlegt werden?
2, Wohin? 3, Wahl der Mitglieder desselben.

82

Vilmot will nur 2 Abtheilungen. Seraillier's
Vorschlag wird angenommen. — Die erste Frage:
Soll der Sitz des General-Raths verlegt werden? wird
bejaht mit 26 Ja gegen 23 Nein. Marcelau be=
schwert sich darüber, dass man lache, wenn er
& seine Genossen sich des Stimmens enthalten; sie
hätten bestimmten Auftrag dazu. Ranvier, daß
er nichts gegen die Delegirten habe, aber gegen das
sonderbare Mandat, welches sie in so eigenthümliche
Lage bringe. Alerini erklärt, dass sie dieses
Mandat frei angenommen haben & vollständig
billigen. — Farge Pelicci & Alerini bringen einen
Antrag ein, den G. R. nach Brüssel zu verlegen
& aus 2 Personen für jede Föderation, von diesen
selbst gewählt & nur diesen verantwortlich, be=
stehen zu lassen. — Die Abstimmung über die
Frage: Wohin soll der G. R. verlegt werden? ergibt
31 Stimmen für New-York, 14 für London, 1 für
Barcelona, 11 Enthaltungen. —
Cuno bringt eine Erklärung vom früheren General-
Konsul Schramm ein, in welcher der Letzere sich entschuldigt
& Cuno's Auslassung nicht übel nehmen will weil er nicht
die von C. gemeinte Person sei.

83

Engels verlangt Einsetzung einer Komission zur
Untersuchung der Kassenangelegenheiten des
General Raths, aus je einem Mitglied jeder Föderation
zu bestehen. Dies wird auf die öffentliche Sitzung
verschoben & die Sitzung vertagt bis Abends 6 Uhr.
Abends 6 Uhr öffentliche Sitzung. Der Namensaufruf ergibt 2 Abwesende. Vaillant verlangt, daß
die Diskussion über den G. R. als geschlossen
erklärt werde, da sie nach den in der administrat.
Sitzung gefassten Beschlüssen völlig unnütz sei.
Kepner fragt, ob dann dem gestern gesagten
keine Entgegnung folgen könne? Er & Heim verlangen zu diesem Zwecke das Wort. van den Hout
hält eine Ansprache an das versammelte Publikum, worin er mit vielem Feuer die Verdächtigungen
& Lügen des Haager Dagblad zurückweist. — Der
Vorsitzende verliest hierauf die in der Morgensitzung
gefassten Beschlüsse über den General-Rath, seine
Befugnisse & seinen Sitz. — Cuno verliest die
Entschuldigungs Briefe vom Generalkonsul Schramm
& zieht seine gestern gemachte Erklärung gegen
denselben öffentlich zurück. — Guillaume verlangt,
dass die Art & Weise der Abstimmung berathen
werde. Joannard beantragt, dass dies in

84

geschlossener Sitzung geschehe, was die Versammlung genehmigt & zu der Berathung der neuen Statutenparagraphen über die politische Handlung der Arbeiterklasse übergeht: Paragraph, einzuschalten zwischen §§7 & 8 der allgemeinen Statuten:

„ In seinem Kampfe gegen die verbündete Macht
„ der besitzenden Klassen kann das Proletariat als
„ Klasse nur auftreten & handeln, indem es sich
„ selbst als besondere politische Partei in Gegensatz
„ zu allen alten von den besitzenden Klassen ge=
„ bildeten politischen Parteien constituirt.
„ Diese Stellung des Proletariat's als politische Partei
„ ist unerlässlich, um den Triumpf der socialen
„ Revolution & ihres obersten Zieles, der Aufhebung
„ der Klassen, zu sichern.
„ Die in den ökonomischen Kämpfen schon er=
„ langte Vereinigung der Arbeiterkräfte muss in
„ den Händen dieser Klasse auch als Hebel in
„ ihrem Kampfe gegen die politische Macht ihrer
„ Ausbeuter dienen.
„ Da die Grundherren & Kapitalisten, sich ihrer polit=
„ ischen Privilegien stets bedienen, um ihre
„ ökonomischen Monopole zu vertheidigen & zu
„ verewigen, & die Arbeit zu unterjochen, – so wird

85

" die Eroberung der politischen Macht die grosse Pflicht
" & Aufgabe des Proletariats. "

Vaillant ergreift das Wort für Aufnahme dieser
Beschlüsse in die Statuten. Man braucht Gewalt
gegen uns, & Gewalt kann nur durch Gewalt re-
trieben werden; der ökonomische Kampf muss Eins
werden mit dem politischem Kampf & in der
Revolution durch die proletarische Dictatur
die Abschaffung der Klassen durchsetzen. Wir
haben gegen uns die Abstentionisten in zwei
Abtheilungen; 1, Abstentionisten aus Unwissenheit
& 2, Abstentionisten aus Politik, die von der Politik
leben, Geschrei machen & toben, & heute in Versailles
sitzen; ein Versailles gibt es aber überall, nicht
blos in Frankreich. Wir müssen eine eigne Partei
bilden gegen alle Parteien der herrschenden besitzenden Klassen, ohne jeglichen Zusammenhang mit
den bürglichen Klassen; schon in der Inaugural-
Adresse wurde die politische Handlung der
Arbeiterklasse empfohlen & der G. R. ist seiner
desfallsigen Pflicht nie untreu geworden; die
Londoner Konferenz begriff die Richtigkeit auch sehr
wohl, übernahm die Verantwortlichkeit für die

86.

Kommune; die Proletarier schlossen sich überall
derselben an. Hepner hat geglaubt, dass alle
Internationalen diese Frage verständen, man
hat gestern Abend von zwei grossen Ideen gesprochen,
der Centralisation & der Föderation, die letztere
sich ausdrückend in der Abstention. Die Enthaltung von politischer Thätigkeit führe in's
Polizeibureau; diese Erfahrung sei in Deutschland
gemacht worden. Diese bakunistische Partei in
Deutschland sei der allgemeine Deutsche Arbeiterverein
unter H. von Schweitzer gewesen, & H. v. Schweitzer
sei notorischer Polizeiagent gewesen. Diese Leute
waren bei Ausbruch des Krieges sehr patriotisch;
während wir uns neutral verhielten & nicht allein
„Nieder mit Napoleon." sondern auch: „Nieder mit Bismark!
riefen, schimpften uns unsere Schweitzer'schen Gegner
Vaterlands-Verräther & warfen uns die Fenster ein,
dahin führe die politische Enthaltung; erst nach
der Anexion von Elsass & Lothringen fingen sie an,
den Fehler ihres Chauvinismus zu begreifen; wohin
führt politische Enthaltung? Dass wir mit den
Händen in der Tasche ruhig zusehen, wenn in
Frankreich eine Revolution gemacht wird, eine
politische Handlung vorgeht; die internationale

Bewegung kennt keine politische Enthaltung. —
Man hat von Aufocterierung gewisser Doctrinen
gesprochen. Uns ist keine aufcelegt worden.
Nennt doch Eine! Wenn ihr keine Antwort
ertheilt, seid ihr nur Störenfriede. Der G. R. hat
nur von Zeit zu Zeit Manifeste erlassen & wer von
uns hat nicht mit Freuden diese Manifeste be-
grüsst? Nachdem wir die Adresse über den
„Bürgerkrieg in Frankreich" in mehr als 4000
Exemplaren im „Volksstaat" verbreitet, haben wir
noch Separatausgaben von mehr als 8000 Stück
veranstaltet. Die deutschen Arbeiter nehmen
solche Manifeste gewiegter bewährter Männer &
Parteigenossen freudig auf, man spricht gegen
Autorität, auch wir sind gegen Uebergriffe jeder
Art; aber eine gewisse Autorität, ein gewisses Ansehen
wird immer nöthig sein, um der Partei Zusammenhang zu geben; logischer Weise müssten diese sogenannten Anti-Autoritäre dann auch die Föderal-
Räthe, Komite's, Föderationen, ja Sectionen selbst
abschaffen, weil überall mehr oder weniger Autorität geübt wird, & die absolute Anarchie her-
stellen, d. h. aus der streitbaren Internationalen
(Internationale Militans) eine Spiessbürgerliche

88

Partei in Schlapock & Pantoffeln machen; wie
kann man nach der Kommune noch gegen
Autorität auftreten? Wir deutschen Arbeiter
wenigstens glauben, dass die Kommune grossentheils
durch Mangel an Autorität & Autoritätsübung gestürzt
worden ist. Uebrigens, welche seltsame Logik der Anti-
autoritäre! Guillaume beschuldigt den G. R., im
ökonomischen & politischem Kampf nichts gethan, keine
Autorität geübt zu haben & verlangt in demselben
Athem die Abschaffung des General Raths wegen Aus-
übung zu grosser Autorität. Der Unsinn der
Antiautoritäre zeigt sich darin glänzend ferner,
dass man dem G. R. vorwirft, er habe keine
Revolution gemacht. Sind diese Leutchen so
unwissenschaftlich, zu glauben, dass man Revolution machen könne; wissen sie noch nicht,
dass Revolutionen nur auf natürlichem Wege
entstehen, Stadien der geschichtlichen Entwicklung
sind? Haben diese Leute noch nicht einmal
die Barrikadologie überwunden? —
Während der Uebersetzungen wird das Publikum
ungeduldig & laut. Guillaume verlangt
Räumung des Saales (sehr autoritär wird ihm
zugerufen). Sorge beantragt Unterbrechung
der Sitzung bis der Saal frei sei. Es entsteht

89

wieder Etwas Ruhe & Guillaume antwortet: Es
besteht ein Missverständniss zwischen uns, müss ich
in meinem & meiner Kollegen Namen hier erklären;
hat sich schon in Basel gezeigt. Wir stehen auf dem
Standpunkt, den Hins in Brüssel einnahm, als er erklärte,
wir wollen uns nicht in die heutigen Regierungen, in
den Parlementarismus mischen; wir wollen alle Regier=
ungen stürzen (applaudi.) Leider haben wir uns Abstent=
ionisten nennen lassen, ein von Proudhon sehr
schlecht gewählter Ausdruck. Wir sind Anhänger einer
gewissen Politik, der Socialen Revolution, der Zer=
störung der Bourgeoispolitik, des Staates; Hepner
sprach von der Anhänglichkeit der deutschen Arbeiter
an den G. R. & seine Manifeste; dies ist sehr natürlich,
denn darin waren vertreten die Ansichten der
besonderen deutschen Socialisten-Partei, aber nicht
anderer Länder. — Auf den Vorwurf, dass die Kommune
zu wenig autoritär gewesen, mögen die Kommunarden
antworten; in Frankreich sei die Abstention von
Proudhon & Longuet gepredigt worden (zwischenruf:
Gaspar Richard & Blanc.), gegen den Vorwurf Hepner,
dass die Abstentionisten in Deutschland Chauvinisten
seien, erwiederte, dass bei ihnen in der Schweiz die
politisch Thätigen & Grossrathswähler mit der

90

Bourgoisie liebäugeln & handeln, & sehr national &
patriotisch gesinnt sind. Wird Später mehr antworten darauf; in den vorgelegten Beschlüssen seien
Phrasen, ihre Basis sei das kommunistische Manifest,
liest 10 Forderungen desselben; fragt, ob das nicht
dasselbe sei, was sie in Basel gefordert; (wird aufgefordert
weiter zu lesen), finden darin den Grund für die Eroberung politischer Macht, „die Bemächtigung des Staats,
der Staatsgewalt", um selbst Bourgeois zu werden!
Wir weisen die Eroberung politischer Macht im
Staate zurück & verlangen dagegen die vollständige
Zerstörung des Staats als Ausdruck politischer Macht.
Marx macht dem flämischen Uebersetzer (van den Abeel)
Vorwürfe. Longuet sagt, dass Guillaume den
Proudhon & viele andere Socialisten, welche er täglich
angreift, nicht gelesen hat; schildert den Zustand
des Proletariats, als Proudhon nach Paris zurück-
kehrte. Das Proletariat hatte eben gar keine politische
Organisation, bildete nur den Schweif der Bourgeois-
intriguanten; daher kam es, dass am 4 Sept. 1870
die Gewalt in die Hände der Junischlächter, der un-
verbesserlichsten Bourgeois fiel; darum musste Proudhon
1863 den Arbeitern Enthaltung von der Politik
predigen; denn die einzige Politik wäre eigentlich

91

Bewaffnung gewesen; später lieferte uns die I. A. A.
Mittel zur Debattirung der ökonomischen Frage;
wären wir besser als politische Partei organisirt gewesen, so wäre J. Favre & Gen. nicht an's Ruder gelangt, & die Kommune wäre nicht blos in Paris,
sondern auch in Berlin & a. O. proklamirt worden
& siegreich gewesen; Hepner irrt sich indessen, wenn
er den Fall der Kommune dem Mangel an Autorität
zuschreibt; die Kommune fiel durch Mangel an
Organisation, an politischer Organisation; —
wo bleibt der Kollectivismus Guillaume's ohne eine
gewisse Centralisation der Kräfte. Die Arbeiter müssen
sich des ökonomischen Kampfes wegen als politische
Partei organisiren, sonst bleibt Nichts von der
Internationalen übrig, & Guillaume, dessen
Meister Bakunin ist, kann mit solchen Ansichten
der I. A. A. nicht angehören. — Es entsteht wieder
Unruhe während der Uebersetzungen; man verlangt
Abstimmung über den neuen Statuten-Artikel;
Joannard macht Lärm & die Störungen werden so
arg, dass der Vorsitzende die Sitzung schliesst um
11 Uhr Nachts. —

Sonnabend, den 7 Sept., Morgens 9½ Uhr, wird
die Sitzung eröffnet. Es wird ein Schreiben des Vorsitzenden
Ranvier verlesen, worin er seine Abreise anzeigt.

92

Auf Beschluss der Versammlung übernimmt
Sorge den Vorsitz & verliest zuerst Briefe von B. Becker,
Schumacher, Arnoud, Barry, Cournet, Heim, Lessner,
Sexton, Vaillant, welche ihre Abreise anzeigen & fast
sämmtlich das Verlangen stellen, ihre Abstimmung
für den neuen Statutenparagraphen & die Wahl eines
General Raths etc. in's Protokoll eintragen zu lassen.
Von Gießen läuft eine Glückwunsch-Depesche ein.
Der Kongress schreitet zum 3ten Punkt des gestern
angenommenen Seraillier'schen Antrags, zur Wahl
des neuen General Raths. Soura ergreift das Wort
gegen die gemachten Vorschläge, 8 Mitglieder des
nordamerikanischen Föderal-Raths als G. R. zu
ernennen, wiederholt seine früheren Erklärungen
darüber, & behauptet, dass in diesem Föderal Rath
eine deutsche Majorität sei. (Sorge unterbricht
ihm mit: „Das ist nicht wahr.") Sorge gibt den Vorsitz
an J. Ph. Becker ab & beweist durch Soura selbst
& Dereure, dass sich im nordamerik. F. R. nur drei
Deutsche befinden & überhaupt nur zwei Mitglieder
des alten provisorischen Föderal-Raths vom
10 Ward Hotel; zeigt darin, was die Behauptungen
der Gegner überhaupt werth sind, auf welche er
jetzt nicht erwiedern will, um nicht die kostbare

93

Zeit des Kongresses zu verkünden. — Marx schildert
die 3 Parteien <u>der Internationale</u> in Amerika: 1, die wirkliche Arbeiter-
Partei; 2, die Bourgeois, oder kleinbürgerliche Hum-
bugspartei; & 3, die Partei der „weisen Männer", die
nie wissen wohin sie gehören & darum den meisten
Schaden anrichten; zu ihnen gehören Saura, der
merkwürdige Umwandlungen durchmache,
erst in London & auf der Herreise sich gänzlich auf
die Seite des Generalraths stelle & hier auf Seiten
der Föderalisten, Jurassier & Allianceisten stehe.
Was die Abmachungen Dereure's mit Saura be-
treffe, so thäte es ihm leid, dass Dereure sich dazu
hergegeben, — Saura's Urtheil in dieser Frage sei ihm
Nichts werth, obwohl er auf Dereure's Meinung Mehr
geben würde. —
  Der ursprüngliche Vorschlag — Kavanagh, St. Clair,
Cetti, Laurel, Leviele, Bertrand, Bolte & Carl zum G.R.
zu wählen mit der Befugniss, sich bis zur Zahl von
15 zu ergänzen — wird hierauf angenommen mit
19 Ja gegen 4 Nein & 19 Enthaltungen Es wird
heftige Einsprache erhoben gegen Gültigkeitserklärung
dieser Abstimmung, weil keine Mehrheit der
Stimmenden dafür gewesen sei, & Anträge allerlei Art

94

laufenein, (Dupont & Serailler verlangen Einschaltung des Namens von Pillon) bis Marx den
Antrag auf Wiedererwägung der letzten Abstimmung stellt, welche auch genehmigt wird.
Der Antrag der spanischen Delegirten, den G. R.
durch die einzelnen Föderationen zu erwählen (p. 2)
wird vom Kongress abgelehnt. Auf Lafargue's
Vorschlag beschliesst jetzt der Kongress zwölf (12)
Mitglieder des neuen General Raths zu wählen,
welche sich bis zur Gesammtzahl von 15 ergänzen
dürfen; & zum Behuf der Wahl Fünf (5) Minuten
Pause zu machen. Sorge erklärt in der Zwischenzeit, dass er mit den Abmachungen zwischen
Dereure & Saura Nichts zu thun habe; macht
Dereure auf den Misstand aufmerksam, dass er
4 Franzosen auf die zwischen ihm & Saura ver-
abredete Liste gestellt & nur 3 Deutsche; will
Dereure annehmen, aber unter keinen Umständen
Saura & fordert wenigstens noch einen Deutschen;
weigert sich entschieden, die Wahl für sich selbst
anzunehmen; macht die Kongressmitglieder
darauf aufmerksam, dass ihm selbst, wie den
New Yorkern, die Verlegung des G. R. nach New York
vollständig unerwartet gekommen sei, dass man

95

den New Yorkern eine schwere Last aufbürde & Sie
ihnen nicht noch schwerer machen solle dadurch,
dass man ihnen Leute zur Seite stelle, mit denen
sie nicht arbeiten könnten. Bei der nun folgenden
Wahl werden erwählt als G. R. für das Jahr 1872-1873
mit der Vollmacht, sich bis zur Zahl von 15 zu ergänzen,
S. Karanagh, E T. St. Clair Tomacieri, Laurel, Lerille,
David, Dereure, Carl, Bolte, Bertrand, Ward & Speyer.

Der Kongress beschliesst, dass jede Föderation
1 Mitglied zu bestimmen habe, um die Kassenab-
rechnungsablage des Generalraths zu prüfen. —
Es erfolgt nun die gestern Abend unterbrochene
Abstimmung über Einschaltung des Paragraphen
über die politische Thätigkeit der Arbeiterklasse
in die Statuten & wird derselbe mit 27 Stimmen
gegen 4 Nein & 9 Enthaltungen angenommen,
ist somit gesetzmässiger Statutparagraph. — Es wird
der Antrag gestellt, die Beiträge zu erhöhen, worauf Brismée auseinander setzt, wie unpraktisch
& unthunlich das sei, dass vielmehr eine Er-
niedrigung der Beiträge geeigneter & mehr am
Platze wäre. Fränkel spricht für Erhöhung
der Beiträge unter Hinweis auf die dem G. R.
obliegenden Arbeiten & Schilderung Dessen, was die

G. R. beigefüllter Kasse, Alles thun könne x sollte.
Nachdem Dupont nach Frankel erwiedert hat,
wird mit grosser Mehrheit beschlossen, die Beiträge
bei dem bisherigen Betrag zu lassen. —
Seraillier stellt den Antrag: „Alle von dem bisherigen General Rath ausgestellten Vollmachten
an Personen, Sectionen, Komité's x s. f. einzuziehen
x für nichtig zu erklären, x dem General-Rath zu
New York die Ausstellung neuer Vollmachten zu
überlassen". Dieser Antrag wird einstimmig
angenommen. — Lafargue, Sorge x Andere bringen
den Antrag ein: „Der G. R. soll die Bildung
von internationalen Gewerksgenossenschaften
(international Trades Unions) in die Hand
nehmen, binnen einem Monat eine Vorlage
darüber machen, diese in die verschiedenen Sprachen
übersetzt an alle Gewerksvereine aller Länder,
soweit sie erreichen kann, zur Einholung
ihres Gutachtens versenden; die eingelaufenen
Gutachten zusammenstellen x vergleichen; eine
Abstimmung über das Ergebniss veranlassen x
dem nächsten allgemeinen Kongress die ganze
Sache zur endgültigen Genehmigung x Entscheidung unterbreiten."

97

Dieser Antrag wurde ohne Widerspruch genehmigt.

Von den Pariser Sectionen läuft eine Erklärung ein gegen die Sectirerei, besonders gegen die sogenannten Blanquisten, während sie vor Blanqui selbst die grösste Achtung besitzen & bezeugen.

Der Kongress beschliesst, morgen, Sonntag, früh (9) Neun Uhr nach Amsterdam zu gehen, um der Einladung des holländischen F. R. zu folgen.

Pehl von Kopenhagen verliest eine Erklärung der dänischen Parteigenossen zu Gunsten des Generalraths.

Es wird festgesetzt, dass die nächste geschlossene Sitzung um 5 Uhr beginne, dass von 7–9 Uhr öffentliche Sitzung sei, in der besonders holländisch gesprochen werden solle, & dass nach 9 Uhr wieder geschlossene Sitzung gehalten werde. Schluss um 3½ Uhr Nachmittags.

Die Sitzung wird um 5½ Uhr wieder eröffnet. Engels berichtet, dass die Finanz-Komission noch nicht ganz fertig sei; dass aber bereits 8 Föderationen nach Einsicht in die Bücher den Kassabericht des General-Raths richtig befunden & durch Unterzeichnung so

bescheinigt hätten. – Auf Verlangen giebt
er dem Kongress den ausführlichen Kassenbericht
des General-Raths, welcher zeigt, dass die Associat.
Mitgliedern des General Raths & andern noch eine
Summe von über (£.25.-) fünfundzwanzig Pfund
Sterling schuldet. Eccarius weist auf die
Rechnungslegung hin, um zu zeigen, wie
vorsichtig wir mit Eintreibung & Festsetzung
von Beiträgen sein müssen, & an eine Erhöhung
gar nicht denken dürfen, ohne sämmtliche
Gewerkvereine vor den Kopf zu stossen. Auch
könnten wir daraus sehen, wie wenige ihre
Schuldigkeit thun, da aus dem Bericht hervorgehe,
dass nur Spanien, Frankreich & Amerika
vollständig ihren Pflichten nachgekommen
seien. – Marx macht darauf aufmerksam,
daß, während laut dem Finanzbericht die
einzelnen Mitglieder des G. R. ihre Taschen
& Beutel für die Organisation leerten, ihnen die
Lüge nachgesagt würde, dass sie von den Arbeiterpfennigen lebten.
Der Finanzbericht des Generalraths wird
einstimmig vom Kongress angenommen. –
Dereure beantragt einen Tadel gegen die

99

verläumderischer Blätter; Lafargue beantragt
Ausstossung der Redacteure derselben. Joannard
erklärt diejenigen für Feiglinge, welche solche
verläumderische Andeutungen immer machen,
ohne je den Muth zu haben, dergleichen Anklagen
offen zu erheben; wenn wir Marx's Knechte wären,
wie Jene behauptet, so redienten sie gepeitscht
zu werden wie die Hunde. – Alerini erhebt
sich zur Vertheidigung seines Freundes
Guillaume, den man in seiner Abwesenheit
hier anklagt. Wenn man hier Ausstossungen
beantrage, so beantrage er vor allen Dingen
Ausstossung der Urheber & Verfasser des infamen
Schriftstücks: ‚Les pretendües Scissions'; wendet
sich persönlich gegen Longuet. Lafargue & Longuet
geben den Wortlaut die in dem bulletin seiner
Zeit enthaltenen Beschuldigungen & Anklagen
gegen den G. R. & einzelne seiner Mitglieder,
welche mit Entrüstung von der Versammlung
angehört werden. – Alerini sagt, er habe
den Finanzbericht in gutem Glauben unterzeichnet,
würde vielleicht doch Etwas Unrichtiges gefunden
haben, wenn er gesucht hätte. – Guillaume
erklärt, daß nach dem Erscheinen der „pretendües
scissions"

100.

welche sie nur mit der grössten Mühe erlangen
konnten, die Redaction des bulletin den dort
Angegriffenen ihre Spalten angeboten habe zu
Erklärungen, für die sie keine Verantwortlichkeit
übernehmen, sondern sich nur bereit erklärten,
Erwiderungen aufzunehmen; übrigens wären
sie bereit, zu widerrufen, wenn man ihnen den
Nachweis führe, dass jene Behauptung etc
falsch seien. Longuet & Dural gerathen in
heftige Diskussion mit Guillaume; Dural
erzählt den Hergang des Lyoner Aufstand-
versuchs sehr zum Nachtheil von Bakunin,
Joukowski, Gaspar Richard, Blanc etc &
zieht Guillaume als den Freund & Vertheidiger
dieser Leute mit hinein & macht ihn dafür
mitverantwortlich, während Guillaume die
Verantwortlichkeit dafür ablehnt mit dem
Bemerken, dass sie Richard & Blanc, sobald
sie dieselben erkannt, selbst als Spione ge-
brandmarkt hätten, also nicht für dieselben
einzustehen hätten, wogegen ihm erwiedert wird,
dass sie eben diese Leute gross gezogen hätten. —
Auf Antrag Sorge's wird beschlossen, den nächsten
allgemeinen Kongress in der Schweiz abzuhalten,

103.

aber dem G. R. die Wahl des Ortes zu überlassen.
Dereure bringt den Antrag ein: Eine Kommission
von fünf Mitgliedern, in London wohnhaft,
zu ernennen, welche die Protokolle dieses
Kongresses sichten & übersetzen, sowie die Ueberführung der Papiere & Dokumente an den
neuen General Rath leiten soll. — Wird einstimmig angenommen & als solche Kommission
ernannt: Marx, Engels, Seraillier, Dupont
& Fränkel. Sorge hinterlegt bei dem Schriftführer
Anträge der amerikanischen Föderation auf
Regelung der Kongress-Vertretung & Vereinfachung
der Benennungen der zugehörigen Gesellschaften
Da es 7 Uhr Abends ist, wird eine Pause von
10 Minuten gemacht, um Vorbereitungen
für die abzuhaltende, öffentliche Sitzung
zu treffen. — Während der Pause werden zwei
Sammlungen unter den Kongress-Mitgliedern
veranstaltet 1, Um einige Haager Parteigenossen
für ihren Zeitverlust zu entschädigen; 2, um
die Druckkosten der Mitgliederliste zu decken.
Um 7¼ Uhr wird die öffentliche Sitzung
eröffnet, es sprechen nach einander Dave, van den Hout,

102

van den Abeel & Brismée über Ziele & Zweck
der Internationalen Arbeiter Association, die
drei ersten holländisch, der letzte in französischer
Sprache. — Um 9 Uhr wird die öffentliche
Sitzung geschlossen & Pause erklärt, um den
Saal frei zu machen.

Nach 10 Uhr wird die geschlosse Sitzung
mit Namensaufruf wieder eröffnet. Es wird
Bericht über die Sammlungen gegeben & der
Kongress beschliesst, jetzt den Bericht der
Untersuchungskommission über die Alliance
zu empfangen & zu verhandeln. Vorher gibt
Walther schriftlich & mündlich seine Entlassung
als Mitglied des Untersuchungskomites, worin
er sagt, dass Zeit zur gründlichen Untersuchung
gefehlt habe & dass Guillaume verweigert habe,
gewisse Fragen zu beantworten. Der Bericht
wird verlesen & lautet:

&   Bericht der Kommission zur Untersuchung
„ über die Gesellschaft „Alliance":
„ Da es der Kommission an Zeit gebrochen, um
„ einen vollständigen Bericht einzureichen, so
„ kann sie nur eine Beurtheilung liefern, gestützt
„ auf die ihr mitgetheilten Schriftstücke & die ihr

103

„gemachten Aussagen.

„ Nachdem sie auf der einen Seite die Bürger Engels,

„ Marx, Wroblewski, Dupont, Seraillier & Swarm für

„ die Anklage gehört hat; und

„ auf der anderen Seite die Bürger Guillaume, Schwitzguebel,

„ Joukowski, Morago, Marselau & Farga Pelicer, welche

„ angeklagt sind, der geheimen Gesellschaft „Alliance"

„ anzugehören. Erklärt die Kommission:

„ 1., dass die geheime Alliance, gegründet mit denjenigen

„ der I.A.A. vollständig entgegengesetzten Statuten,

„ bestanden hat; dass es aber nicht genügend erwiesen ist,

„ dass sie noch besteht;

„ 2., dass es durch einen Statuten-Entwurf & Briefe,

„ gezeichnet „Bakunin" bewiesen ist, dass dieser

„ Bürger versucht hat, & es ihm vielleicht gelungen

„ ist, in Europa eine Gesellschaft, benannt „Alliance",

„ zu gründen mit Statuten, welche von denjenigen

„ der I.A.A. im socialen & politischen Gesichtspunkte

„ vollständig verschieden sind;

„ 3., dass Bürger Bakunin sich betrügerischer

„ Kunstgriffe bedient hat, um sich einen grösseren

„ oder geringeren Theil des Vermögens Anderer an-

„ zueignen, was die Thatsache des Schwindels

„ ausmacht;

„ dass ferner, um nicht seinen Verpflichtungen

„ nachkommen zu müssen, er oder seine Agenten zur

„ Einschüchterung gegriffen haben;

„ Aus diesen Gründen

„ verlangen die Mitglieder der Kommission vom Kongress:

„ 1, den Bürger Bakunin aus der I. A. A. auszustossen;

„ 2, gleicherweise die Bürger Guillaume & Schwitzguébel

„ auszustossen, in der Ueberzeugung, dass dieselben

„ noch immer der Gesellschaft Alliance angehören;

„ 3, da es im Lauf der Untersuchung bewiesen wurde,

„ dass die Bürger Malon, Bousquet (dieser letzte Sekretär

„ des Polizeikommissärs zu Béziers in Frankreich) &

„ Louis Marchand (welcher in Bordeaux, Frankreich,

„ gewohnt hat) Umtriebe gemacht haben, welche die

„ Zerstückelung (désorganisation) der I. A. A. zum

„ Ziele haben — verlangt die Kommission gleicher

„ Weise deren Ausstossung aus der Gesellschaft;

„ 4, Betreff der Bürger Morago, Farga Pelicer,

„ Marcelau, Joukowski & Alerini hält sich

„ die Kommission an deren förmliche Erklärung,

„ dass sie der genannten Gesellschaft Alliance

„ nicht mehr angehören, & verlangt, dass der Kongress

„ die Genannten ausser Anklage stelle.

„ Um ihre Verantwortlichkeit zu decken, verlangen

„ die Mitglieder der Kommission, dass die ihr mit-

„ getheilten Schriftstücke & die gemachten Aussagen

„ in einem officiellen Organ der Association ver-
„ öffentlicht werden.

Haag, 7 Sept. 1872
 Die Kommission:

Der Vorsitzende: Th. F. Cuno,
 Delegirter von Stuttgart &
 Düsseldorf

Der Sekretär: Lucain, Delegirter
 von Frankreich

Mitglied der Kommission: Paul Vichard,
 Delegirter für Frankreich

„ Ich protestire gegen den Bericht der Untersuchungs-
„ Kommission über die „Alliance" & behalte mir vor, meine
„ Gründe vor dem Kongress geltend zu machen. Ein
„ einziges Ding scheint mir aus den Debatten hervorge-
„ gangen zu sein, das ist der Versuch des Herrn
„ Bakunin, im Schoofe der I.A.A. eine geheime
„ Gesellschaft zu stiften. Bezüglich der durch die
„ Mehrheit der Untersuchungskommission beantragten
„ Ausstossungen erkläre ich mich unfähig, als Mit-
„ glied der genannten Kommission einen Spruch zu fällen,
„ da ich keinen Auftrag (Mandat) für diese Angelegen-
„ heit erhalten habe & bin entschlossen, jene Ent-
„ scheidung vor dem Kongress zu bekämpfen.
 Rox Splingard.

„ Die Mitglieder der Kommission erklären dem Kongress,
„ dass der Bürger Walther es für nöthig erachtet hat,
„ diesen Morgen einen Brief an den Vorsitzenden
„ der Kommission zu richten. In diesem Brief entschuldigt

106

» er sich, nicht länger an den Arbeiten der Kommission
» Theil nehmen zu können wegen höheren (zwingende)
» Ursachen (cause majeure)
» Der Vorsitzende : Th. F Cuno
» der Sekretär : Lucain
» die Mitglieder : Rox Splingard
                        Paul Vichard.

Cuno nimmt das Wort & sagt : es ist ganz sicher,
dass Umtriebe in der I. A. A. stattgefunden; Lügen,
Verläumdungen & Betrügereien sind erwiesen worden,
die Kommission hat übermenschlich gearbeitet, heute
hintereinander 13 Stunden Sitzung gehalten, & verlangt
jetzt ein Vertrauensvotum vom Kongress. Alérini
meint, das Komité habe nur moralischen, keinen
materiellen Beweis; er sei Mitglied der Alliance gewesen & stolz darauf, denn sie habe die I. A. A. in
Spanien gegründet, verbreitet & befestigt, so dass jetzt
in Spanien 84 Föderationen bestehen; ihr seit nur
eine heilige Inquisition; wir verlangen öffentliche
Untersuchung. Joannard ist vollständig überzeugt
von der Richtigkeit des Kommissionsbericht glaubt
aber doch eine Ausnahme machen zu müssen mit
der Ausstossung Malon's, dem er keine Andere
als politische Vorwürfe zu machen hat. Ueber
Bakunin, Guillaume, Schwitzguebel & s. w.

verlässt er sich ganz auf den Kommissionsbericht,
& hofft nur, dass die Kommission äusserst vorsichtig
verfahren sei; denn die Ausstossung aus der I.A.A.
ist die schlimmste, entehrendste Verurtheilung,
welche einen Menschen treffen kann, & die ausgestossenen können nie wieder einer ehrenhaften
Gesellschaft angehören, gibt zuletzt zu, dass das Komite
auch mit Bezug auf Malon Recht habe. —

Splingard verlangt mehr Auskunft & zu wissen,
auf welche Weise Marx sich die Dokumente ver-
schafft habe, da das nicht ehrlich zugehen könne;
Engels habe wohl Beweisstücke beigebracht, Marx
aber nur Behauptungen gemacht; Bakunin
habe nur ein Versprechen nicht gehalten, Marx Werk
zu übersetzen, weil man ihm davon abgerathen
habe; die Alliance bestand in Genf & Spanien
vor der I.A.A.; in Genf habt ihr sie selber anerkannt; beweiset doch, dass sie noch besteht, aber
nicht mit Statuten, Briefen & dergleichen, sondern
mit Protokollbüchern & Sitzungsberichten müsst
ihr es beweisen!

Marx (von Splingard unanständig unterbrochen)
sagt, dass Splingard wohl als Advokat, aber nicht
als Richter handelte; Splingard sagt falsch (verbessert)

108

„uncorrect") aus, dass Marx keine Beweisstücke beigebracht, während er sehr genau wusste, dass
Marx fast alle seine Beweisstücke Engels übergeben
hatte; der spanische F. R. hat selbst Beweisstücke ge-
liefert; er (M.) hat andere beigebracht aus Russland, darf
aber natürlich den Namen des Absenders nicht nennen;
übrigens hatte das Komité sich das Ehrenwort gegeben,
nicht von dem Verhandelten laut werden zu lassen; er
(M.) habe sein Urtheil über die Sache; Splingard möge sie
anders haben; die Schriftstücke seien nicht auf un-
ehrliche Weise erlangt, sie seien ungefragt eingesandt
worden. Lucain fragt Splingard, ob die Mehrheit
der Kommission nicht ebenso gewissenhaft & intelligent sei, wie er; Splingard gibt selbstzu, dass
Bakunin den Versuch gemacht, die geheime „Alliance"
zu stiften; will er nun etwa warten, bis die J. A. A.
zerstört ist, ehe er einschreitet? Wir nicht! wir treten
dem Uebel entgegen, wo wir es finden & thun damit
unsere Pflicht. Morago ergreift das Wort & hält in
spanischer Sprache eine längere Rede zu Gunsten der
Alliance, gegen die Beschlüsse der Kommission u.
s. w.: Es ist spät nach Mitternacht, man den Abel
überbringt dem Vorsitzenden Botschaften, dass das
Lokal geräumt werden muss. Der Kongress verzichtet

auf die Uebersetzung der Morago'schen Rede, um so
mehr, als er & seine spanischen Mitdelegirten nicht
in Anklage stehen, & es wird beschlossen, nur noch die
Angeklagten, Guillaume & Schwitzguebel, anzuhören
& dann zur Abstimmung zu schreiten — Guillaume
erhält das Wort & sagt: Splingard's Stellung ist die einzig
richtige. Das ganze Verfahren ist eigentlich ein Tendenz-
process, & man will die Minorität, d.h. die eigentl.
Majorität, mundtod machen; man hat mich während
der letzten Tage in den Diskussionen stets in der
Rednerliste vorangestellt & sprechen lassen, um durch
meine Auslassung am Sonnabend zu zeigen, daß
hier das föderalistische Princip verurtheilt wird
(Rufe: Nein! Nein!)
Schwitzguebel sagt, er sei überzeugt, dass seine Verurtheilung von vorn herein beschlossen war; erklärt,
dass er der Arbeiterpartei treu bleiben, die Arbeiter =
Sache verfechten & der I. A. A. angehören werde,
selbst wenn er ausgestossen werden sollte.
Vichard wendet sich gegen Splingard & gegen
das eigenthümliche Verfahren Walther's, der sich
zurückgezogen um abzureisen, & jetzt doch hier sei. —
Walther giebt Erklärungen darüber & stellt sich ganz
auf Seite der Kommission, indem er noch weitere
Enthüllungen macht über einen von der jurassischen

Föderation ausgesandten Agenten, Mentschikoff, 110
der versucht habe, die Pariser auf ihre Seite zu bringen.

Dave nimmt das Wort, sagt, dass sie, die sogenannte
Minderheit, das Verfahren der Mehrheit genau beobachtet
habe, sich deshalb öfters zu besonderen Ver-
sammlungen vereinigt habe, welche hiermit die
folgende Separaterklärung abgeben:

Wir unterzeichnete Mitglieder der Minderheit
des Kongresses in Haag, Anhänger der Autonomie
& der Föderation der Arbeitergruppen, Angesichts
der entscheidenden Abstimmung, welche uns gegen
die Principien gerichtet scheint, die in von uns
auf dem verflossenen Kongress vertretenen Ländern
anerkannt sind; aber mit dem Wunsche, jede
Art von **Spaltung** im Schoope der I. A. A. zu vermeiden, ─ machen die folgenden Erklärungen,
welche wir der Genehmigung der Sectionen unterbreiten werden, welche uns abgeordnet haben:

1, Wir werden fortfahren, mit dem G. R. unsere
geschäftl. Beziehungen betreff Zahlung der Beiträge,
   Korrespondenz & Arbeits-Statistik zu unterhalten.
2, Die durch uns vertretenen Föderationen werden
   unter sich & mit allen regelmässig eingesetzten
   Zweiggesellschaften der Internationalen directe
   & regelmässig fortgesetzter Berichte einreichen &

erhalten;

3, Sollte der G. R. sich in die inneren Angelegenheiten einer Föderation einmischen wollen, so verpflichten sich die durch die Unterzeichneten vertretenen Föderationen solidarisch, ihre Autonomie aufrecht zu erhalten, soweit diese Föderationen nicht eine den auf dem Genfer Kongress angenommenen allgemeinen Statuten der J. A. A. direct entgegengesetzte Bahn betreten werden.

4, Wir fordern alle Föderationen & Sectionen auf, sich von jetzt an bis zum nächsten allgemeinen Kongress vorzubereiten auf den Triumph der Principien der föderativen Autonomie als Grundlage der Organisation der Arbeit im Schoße der Internationalen.

5, Wir weisen laut zurück jede Beziehung mit dem sogenannten Universal-Föderal-Rath zu London, oder mit jeder anderen ähnlichen, der Internationalen fremden Organisation.

Haag, 7 Sept. 1872

P. Flues, Delegirter der Föderation des Vesdu-Thales.

Thomas Gonzales Morago, Delegirter der Spanischen Landes-Föderation

Alerine, Delegirter von Spanien

Adhémar Schwitzguébel, Delegirter der Jura-Föderat.

James Guillaume, " " " "

H. Van den abeele, Delegirter der Section von Gent
(Belgien)

112

Ph. Coenen,   Delegirter von Antwerpen.

N. Eberhard,   „   „   Brüssel.

H. Gerhard,   „   des holländischen F. R.

D. Brismée,   „   der Brüsseler Section

J. S. Van der Hout,   „   „   Amsterdamer Section

Victor Dave,   „   von Haag

(Erklärung von V. Cyrille wieder ausgestrichen)

N. Alonso Macclau, Delegat der spanischen Föderat.

R. Farga Pellicer,   Delegirter der   „   „

A. Saura, Delegirter der Sect. 29 & 42 Nordamerika.

Roch. Splingard,   „   von Belgien.

     Herman   „   „   „

Der Kongress schreitet zur namentlichen Abstimmung
über die Vorschläge der Untersuchungskommission.
Die Ausstossung Michael Bakunin's aus der J. A. A.
wird vom Kongress beschlossen mit 29 Ja gegen 7 Nein
& 8 Enthaltungen. —
     Die Ausstossung James Guillaume's aus der
J. A. A. wird vom Kongress beschlossen mit 25 Ja
gegen 9 Nein & 9 Enthaltungen.
     Die Ausstossung Adhémar Schwitzguébel's wird
vom Kongress verworfen mit 15 Ja gegen 16 Nein
& 10 Enthaltungen.
Auf den Antrag von Fr. Engels beschliesst der
Kongress mit grosser Mehrheit, die Abstimmung
über Punct 3 der Kommissionsvorschläge (weitere

113

Ausstossungen) auszusetzen, dagegen die anderen
Vorschläge der Kommission, Punct 4 u. s. w, zu
genehmigen. — Angenommen. —

Laura übergibt dem Bureau verschiedene Anträge & Mittheilungen seiner Wähler.

Auf Vorschlag des Vorsitzenden beschliesst der
Kongress, dem neuen G. R. die Vollendung der
unbeendigten Arbeiten zu übertragen.

Der Vorsitzende erklärt, wohl seine Stimme
(er war heiser geworden), aber nicht seine Zuversicht in die Sache verloren zu haben, (J'ai
perdu ma voix, mais non pas ma foi) & schließt
den fünften allgemeinen Kongress der Internationalen-Arbeiter-Association mit einem
Hoch auf die Arbeit um 12½ Uhr Nachts. —

Nachtrag: Vor Beginn der Abstimmung
über die Kommissions-Vorschläge sandte N. A.
Marcelau die folgende Erklärung ein:

Ich erlaube mir dem Kongress mitzutheilen,
dass eine Untersuchung im Gange ist in den
meisten spanischen Föderationen, um zu entscheiden,
ob wir recht oder unrecht gehandelt haben; ich
erkläre hiermit mein eifriges Verlangen nach
einer solchen Untersuchung, da ich rechtlich

117

gehandelt zu haben glaube, z den Schuldigen zu verdammen wünsche, wenn ich betrogen oder zum Werkzeug irgend Jemands gemacht worden bin.

Haag, 7 Sept 1872   Nicola Alonso Marselau.

Es stimmten für die Ausstossung

	von Bakunin,	von Guillaume,	von Schwitzguebel,
J. Ph. Becker		do	do
J. F. Cuno		do	
Dumont		do	do
Dupont		do	
Dural		do	
Dereure			
Engels		do	do
Fargas		do	do
Friedländer			
Fränkel		do	
Hepner		do	do
Heim		do	do
Journard		do	
Marx		do	do
Kugelmann		do	do
Lucain		do	
Lafargue		do	
Longuet		do	
Le Moussu		do	do
Mc Donnell			
Pihl		do	do
Swarm		do	

115

Sorge	—	do. —	—	do.
Seraillier	—	do.	—	Splingard
Walther	—	do.	—	do
Wroblewski	—	do.	—	do
Vichard	—	do.	—	do
Vilmot	—	do.	—	

Es stimmten gegen die Ausstossung

von Bakunin; von Guillaume, von Schwitzguebel;

Brismée	—	do	—	do
Coenen	—	do	—	do
Cyrille	—	do	—	do
				Dupont
Dave	—	do	—	do.
				Dereure
Flues	—	do	—	do
				Fränkel
Herman	—	do	—	do
				Joannard
				Longuet
				Swarm
		Saura		do
		Splingard		
Vandenabeele		do		Seraillier
				do
				Vilmot

116

Enthalten sich der Abstimmung im Falle

von Bakunin, von Guillaume, von Schwitzguebel

	von Bakunin	von Guillaume	von Schwitzguebel
Alèrini	—	do	do
		Dereure	Cuno
Farga Pelicer	—	do	Dural
		Friedländer	do
Guillaume	—	do	do
			Lucain
			Lafargue
Morago	—	do	do
Marselau	—	do	do
		Mc. Donnell	do
Saura			
Splingaud			
Schwitzguebel			

Es stimmten für die Vollmachten des G. R.

	Artikel 2	Artikel 6
Arnoud	—	do
B. Becker	—	do
J. Ph. Becker	—	do
Baary	—	do
Cournet	—	do
Cuno	—	do
Dupont	—	do
Dural	—	do
Dereure	—	do
Engels	—	do
Fargas	—	do
Friedländer	—	do
Fränkel	—	do

117

Für			Gegen	
Artikel 2	Artikel 6		Art. 2.	Artikel 6
Hepner	— do.		Brismée —	— do
Hein —	— do.		Flues —	— do
Jvanard —	— do.			Coenen
Marx —	— do.		Gerhard	
Kugelmann —	do.			Herman
Lissner —	— do.		Splingard —	— do
Lucain			vander Hout —	
Lafargue —	— do.			Saura
Longuet —	— do.			
Le Moussu —	— do.			
Milke —	— do.			
Pihl —	— do.			
Ranvier —	— do.			
Roche				
Swarm —	— do.			
Saura				
Sorge —	— do.			
Seraillier —	— do.			
Sexton —	— do.			
Schumacher —	— do.			
Walther —	— do.			
Wroblewski —	— do.			
Vaillant —	— do.			
Vichard —	— do.			
Dumont				
Mc. Donnel —	— do.			
Ludwig —	— do.			
Vilmot				

Nachdem die Verlegung des Generalraths-Sitzes beschlossen war, stimmten für Uebersiedlung nach New-York:

B. Becker.	Le Moussu
J. Ph. Becker	Pihl.
Brismée.	Roche.
Barry.	Swarm
Cuno	Splingard
Coenen	Seraillier
Dupont.	Sexton
Dave.	Wroblewski
Flues.	Vandenabeele
Fargas.	Vichard.
Friedländer	Dumont.
Engels.	Mc. Donnell.
Herman.	
Lucain	
Marx.	
Kugelmann	
Lissner.	
Lafargue	
Longuet	

118

Sonntag, 8 Sept, Morgens 9 Uhr 10 Minuten
fuhren die Meisten der Delegirten nach Amsterdam,
wo sie von dortigen Parteigenossen herzlich empfangen & zu einer Volksversammlung geleitet
wurden, in welcher Marx, J. Ph. Becker, Duval,
Wroblewski, Lafargue, Dupont, Sorge & van der
Hout über Ziele & Zwecke der J. A. A., die Arbeiten
des eben geschlossenen Kongresses & die Zukunft
der Association enthusiastisch aufgenommene
Reden hielten. —

An die nordamerikanische

Federation der

Internationalen-Arbeiter-Association.

Bericht über die Delegation

zum fünften allgemeinen Kongresse

im Haag,

2ten bis 7ten September 1872

An die nordamerikanische Föderation
der Internationalen Arbeiter Association.

Bericht über die Delegation zum
fünften allgemeinen Kongresse im Haag,
2ten bis 7ten September 1872.

Der Unterzeichnete langte nach kurzer Seereise
Montag, 19 August, um Mitternacht in
London an & suchte am nächsten Morgen
sofort Karl Marx auf. Wir wurden sehr
herzlich empfangen & von Marx, ein von
anderen hinzukommenden Parteigenossen,
— Fränkel, Longuet, Engels, Le Moussu,
Jones von Manchester & Andern — von der
Lage der Dinge im General Rath, in den
einzelnen Ländern Europa's u. s. w.
ziemlich genau unterrichtet. —
Am Abend desselben Tages gingen wir
mit in die Sitzung des General Raths,
wo wir von den meisten Mitgliedern desselben
freundschaftlich empfangen & durch einen
besondern Beschluss ermächtigt wurden,

den Sitzungen des G. R. beizuwohnen.
Eccarius & Hales hielten sich fern von
uns. Fast die Mehrzahl des G. R. bestand
aus Franzosen, d. h. Flüchtlingen,
Mitgliedern & Anhängern der Kommune.
Damit war dem G. R. wie auch später
dem Kongress, der Stempel der franzöz.
Nationalität aufgedrückt, & litt derselbe
darum an grosser Redseligkeit & über-
triebener Lebhaftigkeit, die mitunter
schwer zu zügeln war. Natürliche Folge
des Exils ist immer Hader & Zwist, unter
den Verbannten, die sich gegenseitig grössere
oder geringere Schuld am Misslingen bei-
messen, ein ander mehr oder minder
berechtigte Vorwürfe machen, — &
Zersplitterung der Flüchtlingschaft in
kleine Gruppen (Kliquen) welche sich unter
einander heftig bekämpfen, anstatt den
gemeinsamen Feind anzugreifen. Man
mache mir nicht den Vorwurf der Parteilichkeit,

weil ich von Franzosen rede. Wir müssen
einander die Wahrheit sagen & ich stehe
keinen Augenblick an zu erklären, dass
die deutsche Flüchtlingschaft von 1848-1849
kein Haar besser, sondern womöglich
noch demoralisirter & zerklüfteter war,
als die französische Flüchtlingschaft v. 1871.

Ich theile nur thatsächliches mit. Diese
vorgenannten Zwistigkeiten blieben natürlich nicht ohne Einfluss auf den so viele
Franzosen enthaltenden G. R. & es bedurfte
der ganzen Geschicklichkeit & des vollen
Ansehens weniger alter, deutscher Partei-
Genossen, um den G. R. vor Ausbruch
offnen Haders in seiner Mitte zu bewahren.

Der Kampf wüthete mit den sogenannten
Föderalisten, Proudhonisten, Allianzisten,
Bakunisten. Diese Leute predigen die
Revolution ohne Organisation, die Associat-
ion ohne Gesetze, den Kampf ohne Führer,

die Gesellschaft ohne Zusammenhang, den Körper ohne Haupt, als auch ohne Gedanken. Denn die von Ihnen über alles gestellte Autonomie d. h. Selbstherrlichkeit, führt in ihren natürlichen Folgerungen zur vollständigen Auflösung der Association, der Gesellschaft in ihre Atome, die kleinsten Bestandtheile, d. h. zur gänzlichen Desorganisation. Das selbstherrliche Ich wird dann, wenn stark genug, das selbstherrschende Ich; aus der verschämten Autonomie entspringt so die nackte Autokratie & es lässt sich das Räthsel der pomphaft angekündigten persönlichen Freiheit auf in die allerordinärste Tyrannei, wie es sich auch gezeigt hat, dass die Vertreter dieser Autonomie & individuellen Unabhängigkeit die grössten Despoten sind in ihren Forderungen & den Mitteln sie zu erlangen.

Es ist wenig Gefahr vorhanden, daß
der praktische, nüchterne Arbeiter sich
von diesen Redensarten täuschen lasse.
Darum finden wir auch in den
Ländern mit stark entwikelter
Industrie, in England, Frankreich
& Deutschland, wenig sogenannter Föd-
eralisten oder gar keine Anhänger dieser
Richtung; dagegen zählt sie eine nicht
unbedeutende Zahl Schüler in denjenigen
Ländern, wo die Industrie & das Proletar-
iat weniger entwickelt, die Arbeiterklasse
also dem Bewußtsein ihrer Lage noch
ferner gerückt ist, wie z. B. in Italien &
Spanien. Bezeichnend ist, was
Bakunin selbst in einem Briefe
von seinen Anhängern in Italien sagt:
„Heruntergekommene oder enterbte Bürgers-
söhne, Advokaten, junge schwärmerische
Studenten, überhaupt Leute ohne Zukunft

und Mittel" — von Arbeitern ist keine
Rede dabei. — Dass die Belgier sich
jener Richtung so sehr zu neigen, hat
seinen Grund in der Eifersucht, mit der
dieselben über ihre Nationalität, ihre
Unabhängigkeit, wachen, ein Gefühl,
dessen Uebermass besonders bei kleinen
Völkern { Nationen gefunden wird.
Uebrigens gehen sie in ihren Forderungen
nicht so weit, wie die Italiener { die Anderen.
Ich sagte oben: der Kampf wüthet!
Die alten treuen Mitglieder { Gründer
der I. A. A. sahen diese Organisation
gefährdet durch die Umtriebe Bakunin
{ seiner Helfershelfer, welche sich mittelst
einer geheimen Gesellschaft, genannt
Alliance, der Internationalen zu bemächt-
igen, dieselbe zu beherrschen suchten.
Ich habe die Beweisstücke dafür, von
Bakunin's eigner Hand geschrieben, in

meine Hand gehabt & gelesen. Der
G. R. hatte daher wohl Recht, wenn er
in seiner letzten Mitheilung an den
New-Yorker F. R. sagte:, Es handle
sich auf diesem Kongress um die
Existenz der J. A. A.", & demgemäss
alle Anstrengungen machte, um den
Gegnern auf dem Kongress zu begegnen.
Die Italiener hatten ungeschickter
Weise die Maske abgeworfen & einen
Gegenkongress nach Neuenburg be-
rufen. Die Jurassier & Spanier waren
klug genug, diesen Schritt zu missbiligen
& ihre Delegirten nach dem Haag zu
schicken.
Dieser Kampf bildete einer der auf dem
Kongress zuentscheidenden Hauptfragen,
& beschäftigte den G. R. ganz ausserordentlich.
Während & inmitten dieses Kampfes
hatten sich in unzweideutiger Weise die

Unzulänglichkeit der Befugnisse des G. R.
selbst herausgestellt. Mit ordentlichen
Vollmachten ausgerüstet, hätte der
G. R. eine Sectirerei, wie die obenbezeichnete,
gar nicht aufkommen lassen können
zu einer jetzt ernstlich zu bekämpfenden
Macht. — Auch war durch die grossen
Zeitereignisse der letzten Jahre & durch die
lange Zwischenzeit zwischen dem Kongress
zu Basel & dem in Haag die Disciplin
in der Partei überhaupt sehr gelockert
worden, & es war nothwendig, die
Bande neu zu knüpfen. Daraus ergab
sich als zweite Hauptfrage für den
Kongress die Vermehrung oder Stärkung
der Befugnisse des Generalraths. —
Als dritter Hauptpunkt musste der
Kongress die Bestätigung der Arbeiten
& Beschlüsse der Londoner Konferenz betracht-
en. Das Wichtigste darunter war der

Beschluss über die politische Thätigkeit
der Arbeiterklasse, & es musste dieser von
den Jurassiern, Bakunisten & Gen.
so heftig angefochtene Satz die Genehmigung des Kongresses & damit Statut-
Gültigkeit erhalten.

Hiezu kam nun als vierte nicht minder
bedeutende Frage die Entscheidung des
Kongresses über die Streitigkeiten &
Spaltungen in Amerika & freut es
mich, meinen Wählern mittheilen zu
können, dass der G. R. sich fast aus-
nahmlos & entschieden auf unsere
Seite stellte & der Erfolg daher für uns
ein durchaus günstiger war.

Mögen unsere Parteigenossen bedenken & sich vorstellen, welch un-
geheure Mühe die Organisation eines
seit mehreren Jahren unterbrochenen
Kongresses verursacht, welch grosse

Anstrengungen zur Bewältigung der oben angeführten Hauptfragen gemacht werden mussten — so werden sie schon desshalb zufrieden sein mit dem Erreichten & sich nicht wundern, dass manche kleine Wünsche & besondere Anträge nicht berathen nicht berücksichtigt werden konnten. — Der Kongress, mögen das unsere amerikanischen Parteigenossen glauben, hat seine Pflicht in vollem Maaße gethan! Thun wir jetzt unsere Pflicht, so wird der nächste Kongress leicht das Fehlende nachholen! Und vergessen wir nicht, dass der Haager Kongress in grossen Grundzügen unverkennbar die Richtschnur unseres künftigen Verhaltens angegeben hat.

Der unausgesetzte Kampf in den letzten Jahren & die lange Amtsthätigkeit

hat mehrere unserer bewährtesten Partei-
Genossen wie alten G. R. wohl nicht
mürbe, aber müde gemacht; ihre der
Bewegung so unendlich wichtigen & nütz-
lichen theoretischen Arbeiten sind liegen
geblieben im Drange der kleinen admini-
strativen Arbeiten, deshalb, wie auch in
Hinblick auf die schon erwähnten Friste,
erklärten mehrere ältere Mitglieder des
Generalraths, besonders Karl Marx & Fr.
Engels, unter keinen Umständen die
Wiederwahl in den G. R. anzunehmen.
Gerade diese ältesten & thätigsten Mitglieder
des alten G. R. machten nach reiflicher Ueber-
legung den wohl begründeten Vorschlag,
den General-Rath nach New-York zu
verlegen, & nachdem der erste Schreck
über diesen gänzlich unerwärteten Antrag
vorüber war, fand sich die grosse Mehrheit
des Kongresses im Einverständniss damit.

Die von Engels im Namen der Antrag-
steller — lauter Mitglieder des alten
G. R. — angeführten Gründe sind

1, Der G. R. muss von London verlegt werden;
2, die meisten älteren Mitglieder nehmen
keine Wiederwahl an;
3, Der G. R. & seine Papiere sind nirgends
auf dem Kontinente sicher (die Belgier
& Schweizer bestätigen dies)
4, Bleibt also nur New York übrig.
5, Für alle Nothfälle & besondere Um-
stände kann der G. R. Vollmachten
an Personen & Delegationen ausstellen.
6, Ist New York mehr international,
als jeder andere Ort.
7, Haben wir tüchtige Parteigenossen
& Kräfte dort & anderes mehr.

Euren beiden Delegirten kam der Antrag
ebenso unerwartet, wie wahrscheinlich Euch.
In Kürze noch die folgenden Notizen: Laura
wurde bei seinem Erscheinen in G. R.
zu London mit dem Mandat der Sect. 2

15

zurückgewiesen, aber mit dem hinter=
rücks erlangten Mandat der Section 42
zugelassen. — West wurde bei seinem
Erscheinen im G.R. zu London zurück=
gewiesen. — Ich gehe jetzt über zu meinem
gedrängten Bericht über den Kongress.

Wir langten Sonntag, den 1 September,
Nachmittag in Haag an.

Der Haag hat fast gar keine industrielle
oder Arbeiterbevölkerung. Der Hof & sein
Tross, Beamte & Bediente machen
die Einwohnerschaft aus. Die Einwohner
begafften uns wie Ungeheuer & Wunder=
thiere; es fehlte nicht an Beleidigungen,
wiewohl sie gegen den Schluss der Kongress-
Woche Etwas anständiger wurden.

Für billiges Quartier, für Quartier
überhaupt war keine Sorge getragen
worden. Wir hatten im Anfang Mühe,
unterzukommen; mussten durchgängig
Alles theuer bezahlen. —

Der Sitzungssaal war sehr weit von
unseren Quartieren entfernt, hatte
schlechtes Licht, keine Ventilation.
Es waren 65 Delegirte erschienen,
nämlich: 18 Franzosen, 15 Deutsche,
7 Belgier, 5 Engländer, 5 Spanier, 4
Holländer, 4 Schweizer, 2 Oesterreicher,
1 Däne, 1 Ungar, 1 Australier, 1
Irländer, 1 Pole. Sie vertraten 95
Mandate, davon hatte gesandt Belgien
17, Deutschland 15, Frankreich 14,
Schweiz 11, Amerika 7, der General-
Rath 6, Spanien 5, England 5,
Holland 4, Dänemark 2, Irland 2,
Ungarn 2, Portugal 1, Polen 1,
Oestereich 1, & Australien 1. —
Angefügt ist die vollständige Liste im
Druck.
Das Auftreten der Delegierten im
Allgemeinen war ein würdiges,

selbstbewusstes & Achtung gebietendes.
Das Vorherrschen der französischen Nationalität unter den Delegirten, sowie
die Thatsache, dass die Verhandlungen
vorzugsweise in französischer Sprache geführt wurden, gaben dem Kongress übrigens den Anstrich französischer Lebhaftigkeit, Redelust & Ungebundenheit.

Sonntag, 1 Sept, Abends ½ 2 Uhr fand
die sogenannte Vorversammlung statt,
in der durchaus nichts vorkam, als
Begrüssung Seitens der Holländer, da
man von mehreren Seiten den Einwand
machte, der Kongress sei nicht auf den
1 ten, sondern auf den 2 ten Sept. einberufen.

Doch wird beschlossen, Montag,
2 Sept., Morgens 9 ½ Uhr die Sitzung als
geschlossen zu eröffnen & nur Mitglieder
zuzulassen.

Montag früh 9 Uhr wird die Sitzung
durch den holländischen F. R. eröffnet,

der später den Vorsitz an Van den Abeel
von Gent in Belgien abtritt. Es wird
beschlossen, keine Berichterstatter
zuzulassen; Dupont, Fränkel & Eccarius
werden zu Uebersetzern ernannt. Auf
Antrag von Engels wird beschlossen,
ein Vollmachtsprüfungskomitee von 7
Mitgliedern einzusetzen, während
Laura & die Jurassier 1 Mitglied aus jeder
Föderation verlangen. Die Spanischen
Delegirten zeigen an, dass sie bestimmte
Weisung haben, nicht eher mitzustimmen,
als bis der Abstimmungsmodus nach
Zahl der vertretenen Mitglieder geregelt
sei. In das Mandatkomitee wurden
gewählt Marx, Ranvier, Roach, Mc Donnell,
Dereure, Gerhard & Fränkel. Schluss der
Sitzung um 3 2 Uhr Nachmittags.
   Die Abendsitzung beginnt erst um

8½ Uhr, da das Mandatsprüfungs=
Komité nicht früher erscheint. Dasselbe
verwirft das Mandat von W. West – Sect. 12
§ 19. –, dasjenige Laura's von Section 2,
dasjenige Alerini, von einer Marseiller-
Section, dasjenige Joukowski's von der
Genfer Section de la propagande revolut. etc
& beanstandet die Mandate der Span=
ischen Delegirten wegen Nichtzahlung
der Beiträge; auch verlangte es weitere
Auskunft über die Mandate von Flues
& Dave. Alle Uebrigen wurden zur Zu=
lassung empfohlen; darunter Laura
mit Mandat von 42. & 29, die ihm noch
nachgesandt worden sind. Nach
längerer Verhandlung werden Flues &
Dave als in Ordnung erklärt, Dereure,
& Sorge beanstandet durch Laura,
Laura's angefochten durch Sorge, Vaillant
durch Schwitzguebel, Lafargue dch. Alerini;

Barry dch. Hales. Mit Ausnahme dieser
& der vom Mandatkomite Beanstandeten
werden die Uebrigen auf einmal zugelassen. — Kaum war dies geschehen,
als Hales protestirte gegen das Recht
Sorge's zu sprechen. — Die Sitzung wird
um 9½ Uhr geschlossen.

Dienstag, 3 Sept., Morgen's 9½ Uhr wird
die Sitzung wieder eröffnet, & 4 Sekretäre
erwählt für die deutsche, französische,
englische & holländische Sprache. Nach
längerer Debatte, besonders durch Saura
hervorgerufen, wird beschlossen, 2 Redner
auf jede Seite zu hören & dann abzustimmen.

Vaillant's Mandat von La chaux de fonds,
angefochten von Schwitzguebel, wird einstimmig anerkannt; ebenso die Mandate
Derewe's & Sorge's gegen die einzige
Stimme Saura's, der in seiner Anfecht-
ung verschiedene falsche Behauptungen
aufstellte; Saura's Mandat von Sect. 29

§ 42 wird von Sorge angefochten, der nachweis't, dass es nur eine List sei, Saura in den Kongress zu bringen, was durch Saura's eigene Aussage erhärtet ist, doch wird wegen Mangels possitiver Beweise, die der F.R. nachzusenden versäumt, Saura als Delegirter von Sect. 29 & 42 endlich zugelassen mit 30 gegen 20 Stimmen, Dereure enthielt sich der Abstimmung & Saura hatte sich also in den Kongress hineingeschlichen. Lafargue's Mandat, angefochten von Alerini, wird anerkannt. — Marx bringt Anträge ein auf Ausstossung der "Alliance" & Einsetzung einer Untersuchungs-Komission Schluss um 2 Uhr.

Wiedereröffnung um 4 Uhr. Es wird beschlossen, von jetzt an die Namens-Liste zu verlesen & die Fehlenden bei ihren Wählern anzuzeigen. Barry's Mandat war angefochten von Hales, in dessen Abwesenheit war Saura so gefällig, es anzufechten, aber ohne Erfolg, denn es wurde anerkannt gegen die einzigen Stimmen von Saura & Motterhead. Alérini's Mandat von Marseilles wird verworfen; Joukowski's Mandat von Genfer Propaganda Section wird zurückgestellt bis zur Entscheidung der Frage der „Alliance". Das Mandat der spanischen Delegirten ruft lange Erörterungen hervor, wird aber endlich anerkannt, nachdem dieselben an den Vorsitzenden Zahlung von Beiträgen geleistet. Das Mandat der Section 2 (New-York) für Saura wird vom Mandatskomité verworfen, nach längerer Debatte vom Kongress für nichtig erklärt mit 39 Stimmen gegen 9 & 11 Enthaltungen; also mit vollen zwei Dritteln. — Schluss 10 Uhr Nachts.

Mittwoch, 4 Sept. Eröffnung um 9¼ Uhr Morgens. Auf Antrag Vilmot's wird

das Rauchen im Saale verboten. Das
Mandat von Section 12 (New York) für
W. West kommt zur Berathung. Auf
Laura's Antrag wird die Geschäftsordnung
für diesen Fall geändert; die Redezeit
nicht beschränkt. (31 gegen 8 Stimmen).
Marx verlangt im Namen des Mandats-
prüfungskomité, daß das Mandat West's
für nichtig erklärt werde, weil West Mitglied
der Section 12, des Philadelphia-Kongresses
& des Prince-Street-Councils sei oder gewesen
sei. Er schildert die Bestrebungen der
der Section 12, ihren "appeal" u. s. w.
& macht auch Andeutungen über deren
Beziehungen zu den Jurassiern, kommt
auch auf die Entscheidung des G. R.
die ⅔ Lohnarbeiterfrage u. s. w. West
antwortet in einer ungefähr andert-
halbstündigen Rede, die durch häufiges
Gelächter unterbrochen wurde wegen
des darin enthaltenen Pathos & Unsinns.

& zuletzt wurde der Kongress ungeduldig.
Sorge erwiedert West. Saura sagt, er wolle
nicht für Sect. 12 reden, hält aber eine
Lobrede auf Frau Woodhull & Sect. 12.
Guillaume versucht eine Diversion zu
Gunsten West's zu machen, sagt, die
Jurassier haben nie officiell nach
Amerika geschrieben; er selber habe
aber privatim an Verpillieu geschrieben;
er verliest die Antwort Verpillieu, voller
Anschuldigungen gegen Sorge & Section 1.
Sorge verlangt Abschrift. Saura tritt
ein für die Wahrheit des Verpillier'schen
Behauptungen. — Brismée stellt den
Antrag, dass der Kongress keine aus
Bourgeois gebildete Section anerkenne.
Angenommen in namentlicher Abstim-
ung mit 47 gegen 9 Enthaltungen.
Das Mandat West's wird in namentlicher
Abstimmung für nichtig erklärt mit

23.

49 gegen keine einzige Ja & 9 Enthaltungen (darunter Eccarius, Guillaume
& Schwitzguebel) Eccarius erklärt seine
Enthaltung damit, dass er immer
Geschäftsbeziehungen mit den Secessionisten gehabt & noch habe, dass die
Berichte an den G. R. gelogen seien &
dass Sorge der einzige Urheber der ganzen
Spaltung sei. — Es wird beschlossen,
um 7 Uhr Abends wieder geschlossene
& morgen, Donnerstag, öffentliche Sitzung
zu halten. Schluss der Sitzung um 4 Uhr
Nachmittags.

Abends 7½ Uhr wieder eröffnet.
Es werden gewählt zu Präsidenten
Ranvier, zu Vicepräsidenten Gerhard
& Sorge, zu Schriftführern Hepner,
Le Moussu, Mc. Donnell, van der Hout
& Marcelau. Ein Antrag von J. Ph. Becker
& Gen. wird nach langer Debatte angenommen,

welcher bestimmt, dass der Kongress
sofort zur Berathung des Nöthigsten, Vollmachten des G. R., Sitz desselben,
Statutenaenderung u. s. w. schreite.
Dem spanischen Antrag auf Aenderung
der Abstimmung wird die Dringlichkeit
abgesprochen. — Geschlosse Sitzung morgen
früh um 8 Uhr, öffentliche Sitzung um
10 Uhr. Schluss der Sitzung nach Mitternacht.

Jetzt waren 3 volle Tage des Kongresses
verflossen, von denen West's Mandat
eine ganze Sitzung verbraucht, während
Saura mindestens die Hälfte der
ganzen Zeit bisher in Anspruch genommen hatt. —

Donnerstag, 5 Sept., Morgens 8 Uhr
geschlossene Sitzung.

Marx theilt mit, dass der Bericht des
G. R. für die Oeffentlichkeit bestimmt
sei.

Es wird beschlossen, einen Ausschuss
von 5 Personen zur Untersuchung der
„Alliance" niederzusetzen. Die Jurassier
& Spanier verlangen, dass man ihnen
wenigstens *ein* Mitglied (Splingard)
darin zugestehe. Genehmigt & werden
als Ausschuss gewählt Cuno, Splingard,
Walther, Lucain & Vichard. — Dasselbe
Komité soll die von den Jurassiern
& Spaniern erhobenen Anklagen gegen
den G. R. untersuchen. —
Um 10 Uhr öffentliche Sitzung. Namens-
aufruf ergibt nur 3 Abwesende. Der
Präsident hält Anrede an das Publikum
zur Vertheidigung der I. A. A. & der
Kommune gegen die gewöhnlichen
Beschuldigungen. —
Sexton verliest jetzt den Bericht des
G. R. in englischer, Longuet in französischer,

Marx in Deutscher, Van den Abecle in flämischer Sprache. Derselbe schildert besonders die von Wien ausgegangene, über den ganzen Kontinent verbreiteten Verfolgungen gegen die J. A. A., hebt hervor wie das Proletariat aller Länder sich für die Kommune erklärt, & die J. A. A. sich ausgebreitet habe besonders in Portugal, Holland, Dänemark, Island, Australien, Neu-Seeland & Buenos Ayres. Den Verfolgten aller Länder wird die Sympathie & der brüderliche Gruss des Kongresses ausgesprochen. — Schluss um 3 Uhr Nachmittags.

Wiedereröffnung um 4¼ Uhr. Es zeigen mehrere deutsche Delegirte ihre Abreise an. Es wird ein Komité niedergesetzt zur Prüfung aller Eingaben. — Dupont, Hepner, Fränkel, Derevre, Lafargue & Brismée. Folgt Debatte über den G. R.

& seine Vollmachten. Lafargue & Sorge sprechen für den G. R. & ausgedehnte Befugnisse desselben, Guillaume & Morago dagegen. — Schluss um 11 Uhr. —

Jetzt kam der fünfte Tag heran & noch war Nichts gethan, die deutschen Delegirten waren gezwungen bald abzureisen & die Kasse der meisten Delegirten ging auf die Neige. Da rafften sich die Deutschen zusammen & brachten am folgenden Tage die wichtigsten Beschlüsse ein & mit Hülfe der Franzosen durch. Es ging nicht länger so, wenn wir nicht unverrichteter Sache nach Hause gehen wollten, & den langen Redereien & absichtlichen Verzögerungen musste ein Ende gemacht werden.

Freitag, 6 Sept., Morgens 9 Uhr Namensaufruf & 7 Abwesende.

28

Der Untersuchungsausschuss erhält Erlaubniss, während der Kongressver=
sammlungen Sitzung zu halten.
Ein Antrag von Becker, Sorge & Gen.
wird genehmigt mit 34 gegen 4 Stimen,
sofort zur Berathung der Generalraths-
vollmachten etc zu schreiten, je
einen Redner für & gegen zu hören
& dann zur Abstimmung überzugehen.
Von denselben Antragstellern werden
eingebracht die folgenden Artikel über
den General-Rath in den Verwaltungsregeln,
Artikel 2. „Der Generalrath hat die
        Kongressbeschlüsse auszuführen
        & darauf zu sehen, dass in jedem
        Lande die Grundsätze, Statuten
        & allgemeinen Regeln der J.A.A.
        genau beobachtet werden.
Artikel 6. Der General-Rath hat eben-
        falls das Recht, Zweiggesellschaften,
        Sectionen, Föderal-Räthe oder Komités

29

& Föderationen der J. A. K. bis zum
nächsten Kongress zu suspendiren.

Bei Sectionen, welche einer Föderation
angehören, soll er dieses Recht nicht
ausüben, bevor er den betreffenden
Föderal-Rath um Rath gefragt hat.

Bei Auflösung eines Föderal-Raths
oder Komites soll der G. R. sofort die
Wahl eines neuen Föderal-Raths oder
Komites durch die Sectionen der betreffenden Föderation binnen 30 Tagen
ausschreiben.

Im Falle der Suspension einer
ganzen Föderation soll der G. R.
unmittelbar allen andern Föderationen davon Nachricht geben.
Wenn die Mehrheit der Föderationen
es verlangt, soll der G. R. eine ausserordentliche Konferenz berufen, welche
aus einem Delegirten jeder Nationalität bestehen, einen Monat nachher
zusammentreten & den Streitfall

30

endgültig entscheiden wird. —

Dabei ist aber ausdrücklich verstanden,
dass diejenigen Länder, wo die J. A. A.
verboten ist, dieselben Rechte ausüben,
wie die regelmässigen Föderationen."
Artikel 2 wird in namentlicher Abstimmung
mit 40 Ja gegen 5 Nein & 11 Enthaltungen
angenommen; — Artikel 6 ebenfalls in
namentlicher Abstimmung mit
36 Ja gegen 6 Nein & 15 Enthaltungen.
Marx, Engels, Le Moussu, Serraillier,
Dupont & A. bringen den Antrag ein:
"Der Sitz des General-Rath's für 1872-1873
ist New-York; der G. R. besteht aus
den Mitgliedern des dortigen Föderal-
Raths & darf sich ergänzen bis zur Zahl
von 15." Der Antrag wird getheilt
& beschlossen: 1, den Sitz des G. R.
von London wegzuverlegen; 2, denselben nach New-York zu verlegen;
der erste Theil mit 26 Ja gegen 23 Nein,

31

der zweite Theil mit 31 für New-York,
14 für London, 1 für Barcelona, 1 für
Brüssel & 10 Enthaltungen. —
Schluss 2½ Uhr.

Abends 6 Uhr öffentliche Sitzung
& Diskussion über Einfügung des
folgenden Artikels in die allgemeinen
Statuten:

„ In dem Kampf gegen die verbündete
„ Macht der besitzenden Klassen kann
„ das Proletariat als Klasse nur handeln,
„ indem es sich selbst als besondere
„ politische Partei im Gegensatz zu
„ allen alten von den besitzenden Klassen
„ gebildeten politischen Parteien
„ bildet & auftritt. — Dieses Auftreten,
„ Stellung des Proletariats als politische
„ Partei ist unerlässlich, um den
„ Triumph der socialen Revolution
„ & ihres obersten Zieles, der Aufhebung
„ der Klassen zu sichern. —

„ Die in den ökonomischen Kämpfen
„ schon erlangte Vereinigung der
„ Arbeiterkräfte muss in den Händen
„ dieser Klasse auch als Hebel in
„ ihrem Kampfe gegen die politische
„ Macht ihrer Ausbeuter dienen.
„ Da die besitzenden Klassen, Grund-
„ herren & Kapitalisten, sich ihrer
„ politischen Vorrechte stets bedienen,
„ um ihre ökonomischen Monopole
„ zu vertheidigen & zu verewigen, &
„ die Arbeit zu unterjochen, — so
„ wird die Eroberung der politischen
„ Macht die grosse Pflicht & Aufgabe
„ des Proletariats. "
Vaillant, Hepner & Longuet sprechen
dafür, Guillaume dagegen. Die Abstimmung wird durch den Lärm
des Publikums unterbrochen und
die Sitzung Nachts 11 Uhr aufgehoben.

Sonnabend, 7 Sept, Morgens 9½ Uhr wird die Sitzung eröffnet & Sorge übernimmt den Vorsitz an Stelle des abgereisten Ranvier. Man schreitet zur Wahl des G. R.. Saura sagt daß im F. R. eine deutsche Mehrheit sei. Sorge beweist ihm, dass das nicht wahr ist. Nach längeren Eröterungen wird der ursprüngliche Antrag von Marx, Engels & Gen. angenommen mit 19 Ja gegen 4 Nein & 19 Enthaltungen. Es wird Widerspruch gegen diese Abstimmung erhoben & auf Vorschlag von Marx die ganze Abstimmung in Wiedererwägung gezogen. Pereure händigt Sorge eine Liste ein, welche von Saura angenommen ist. Sorge weist dieselbe zurück. Der Kongress erwählt hierauf als General-Rath mit dem Recht, sich bis zur Zahl von 15 zu ergänzen, die folgenden Personen, [54] nachdem Sorge ausdrücklich erklärt hat, die Wahl durch den Kongress nicht anzunehmen: S. Kavanagh, E. P. St. Clair, Fornacieri, Laurel, Levièle, David, Dereure, Carl Bolte, Bertrand, Ward & Speyer. —

Es wird beschlossen, dass jede Föderation ein Mitglied zu dem Ausschuss zu ernennen habe, welcher die Kassenabrechnung des General-Raths zu prüfen hat. — Die gestern Abend unterbrochene Abstimmung über den Artikel von der politischen Handlung der Arbeiterklasse wird jetzt vorgenommen & ergibt 27 Ja, 4 Nein & 9 Enthaltungen, als Aufnahme des Artikels in die Statuten der J. A. A.

Den Mitgliedern des Ausschusses wird gestattet, ihre Abstimmung eintragen zu lassen. —

35

Die Erhöhung der Beiträge wird abgelehnt.

Auf Antrag Seraillier's wird beschloss-
en: „Alle vom bisherigen G. R. ausgestellten Vollmachten an Personen,
Sectionen, Komites & dgl. sind
hiermit eingezogen & nichtig. Dem
G. R. zu New York ist die Ausstellung
neuer Vollmachten überlassen."

Der Kongress genehmigt einstimig
den folgenden, von Lafargue, Sorge &
Gen. eingebrachten Antrag:

„ Der G. R. soll die Bildung von inter-
„ nationalen Gewerksgenossenschaften
„ in die Hand nehmen; binnen
„ einem Monat eine Vorlage darüber
„ ausarbeiten, dieselbe in die ver-
„ schiedenen Sprachen übersetzt
„ an alle zu erreichenden Gewerks-
„ Vereine der verschiedenen Länder
„ zur Einholung ihres Gutachtens

36

„ versenden; die eingelaufenen Gutachten
„ zusammenstellen ß vergleichen, eine
„ Abstimmung über das Ergebniss
„ veranlassen ß das Ganze dem nächsten
„ allgemeinen Kongress zur endgült-
„ igen Genehmigung ß Entscheidung
„ unterbreiten."

Es wird beschlossen, morgen,
Sonntag, früh 9 Uhr nach Amsterdam
zu fahren. — Um 5 Uhr geschlossene,
von 7-9 Uhr öffentliche, nach 9 Uhr
wieder geschlossene Sitzung, Schluss 3½ Uhr.

Wiedereröffnung um 5½ Uhr.
Engels berichtet, daß bereits 8 Föderationen den Finanzbericht unterschrieb-
en ß genehmigt haben. Auf Verlangen
theilt er den Gesammtbericht mit,
woraus hervorgeht, dass nur wenige
Föderationen ihre Beitrags-Pflicht
erfüllt haben, ß dass die Association

37

Mitgliedern des G. R. z andern noch gegen 25 Pfund Sterling schuldet. Der Finanzbericht des G. R. wird einstimmig angenommmen. Marx, Dereure, Lafargue, Joannard, Longuet z A. machen darauf aufmerksam, dass der Finanzbericht nachweise, wie einzelne Mitglieder des G. R. nicht bloß Zeit, sondern auch ihre Geld= mittel der Sache geopfert hätten, während man sie von gewisser Seite beschuldigt z öffentlich verläumdet habe (bulletin de la féd jur.), von den Arbeiterpfennigen zu leben. Guillaume vertheidigt sich sehr lahm damit, dass sein Blatt auch den Gegenerklärungen offen stehe. Zwischen Dural z Guillaume entsteht ein heftiger Streit, worin Dural die schwersten Anklagen gegen Guillaume z seine Freunde z früheren Anhänger

58

ausspricht.

Der Kongress beschliesst, den nächsten allgemeinen Kongress in der Schweiz abzuhalten & die Bestim= ung des Ortes dem G. R. zu überlassen. Ferner werden Marx, Engels, Serailler, Dupont & Fränkel als Ausschuss ein- gesetzt, um die Protokolle dieses Kon- gresses zu sichten, zu übersetzen & zur Veröffentlichung vorzubereiten, sowie um die Ueberführung der Papiere & Dokumente an den neuen General-Rath zu leiten. — Von Sorge werden verschiedene Anträge auf dem Bureau niedergelegt. — Um 7 Uhr wird das Publikum zu- gelassen & die Delegirten Dave, van der Hout, Vandenabeele & Brismée halten Ansprachen an Dasselbe. Während dessen werden unter den

39

Delegirten zwei Sammlungen veranstaltet 1, zur Schadloshaltung derjenigen Haager Sectionsmitglieder,
welche Zeit & Arbeit in die Kongresswoche
opfern mussten; & 2, zur Deckung der
Druckkosten der Delegirtenliste. —

Gegen 10 Uhr wird die geschlossene
Sitzung wieder eröffnet. Walther gibt
seine Entlassung als Mitglied der
Alliance-Untersuchungskommission,
sagt dass zu wenig Zeit zur gründlichen
Untersuchung da sei & dass Guillaume
sich geweigert, gewisse Fragen zu beantworten. — Die Untersuchungskommission berichtet:

Dass die geheime Allianz, gegründet mit denjenigen der J.A.A.
vollständig entgegengesetzten Statuten,
bestanden hat, dass es aber nicht
genügend erwiesen ist, dass sie noch

besteht;

dass durch Schriftstücke & Briefe seiner eigenen Hand bewiesen ist,

dass Bakunin, vielleicht mit Erfolg, versucht hat, in Europa eine Gesellschaft Alliance zu gründen, deren Statuten vom Socialen & politischem Gesichtspunkte aus gänzlich verschieden sind von denjenigen der I. A. A.

Dass Bakunin betrügerischer Weise versucht hat, sich fremde Gelder anzueignen, & sogar zu Einschüchterungen gegriffen hat. —

Die Kommission schlägt daher vor:

1, Bakunin aus der I. A. A. auszustossen;

2, Guillaume & Schwitzguebel ebenfalls auszustossen;

3, Malon, Bousquet & Louis Marchand auszustossen;

4, Morago, Farga Pelicer, Marcelau,

41

Joukowski & Alérini ausser Anklage
zu stellen.
5., die Beweisstücke & Aussagen zu
veröffentlichen.

Splingard von der Kommission protestirt gegen diese Vorschläge & gibt
blos zu, dass Bakunin versucht
habe, eine geheime Gesellschaft zu
bilden. — Dave macht die Mittheilung, dass die sogenannte Minderheit, oder Opposition besondere Ver-
sammlungen abgehalten & zu
folgender Erklärung sich geeinigt
habe:

1, Wir werden fortfahren mit dem
G. R. zu verkehren wegen Beitrags-
zahlung, Korrespondenz & Arbeits-
statistik;

2, Die von uns vertretenen
Föderationen werden unter sich
& mit den Andern regelmässige

42

directe Berichte & Verbindung her-
stellen.

3, Sollte der G. R. sich in die inneren
Angelegenheiten einer Föderation
mischen wollen, so verpflichten sich
die durch die Unterzeichneten vertretenen Föderationen solidarisch,
ihre Autonomie aufrecht zu erhalten, soweit diese Föderationen
nicht einen Weg betreten, welcher dem
auf dem Genfer Kongress angenommenen
allgemeinen Statuten der I. A. A
direct entgegengesetzt ist;

4, Wir fordern alle Föderationen
& Sectionen auf, sich zum nächsten
allgemeinen Kongress vorzubereiten
auf den Triumpf der Principien der
föderativen Autonomie als Grundlage der Organisation der Arbeit
im Schoose der Internationale;

43

5, Wir weisen laut zurück jede Beziehung mit dem sog. Universal-
Föderal Rath zu London, oder mit
jeder andern ähnlichen, der Internationalen fremden, Organisation.
gezeichnet von Flues, Morago, Alerini,
Schwitzguebel, Guillaume, Vandenabeele,
Coenen, Eberhard, Gerhard, Brismée,
van den Hout, Dave, Marcelau,
Farga Pelicer, Saura, Splingard &
Herman.
Nach längeren Debatte schreitet
der Kongress zur namentlichen Abstimmung über die Anträge des
Ausschusses:
Michael Bakunin wird ausgestossen mit 29 Ja gegen 7 Nein &
8 Enthaltungen, James Guillaume
wird ausgestossen mit 25 Ja gegen
9 Nein & 9 Enthaltungen. Die Ausstossung Adhémar Schwitzguebel

44

wird verworfen mit 15 Ja gegen 16
Nein & 10 Enthaltungen.

Auf Antrag von Fr. Engels beschließt
nun der Kongreß, die Abstimmung
über Punct 3 (Ausstossung v. Malon &)
auszusetzen, & die anderen Vorschläge
der Kommission (Punct 4 u. s. w.)
zu genehmigen.

Der General-Rath wird daher auf
Grund der stattgehabten Untersuchung immer das Recht haben, gegen
die Betreffenden vorzugehen, wenn
er es für angemessen erachtet.

Auf Vorschlag des Vorsitzenden
wird dem neuen G. R. den Auftrag
ertheilt, die unbeendigten Arbeiten
zu vollenden. Laura hinterlegt verschiedene Schriftstücke & Anträge,
ebenso J. Ph. Becker.

Der Vorsitzende erklärt, wohl seine

45

Stimme, aber nicht seine Zuversicht in die Sache verloren zu haben; schliesst 12½ Uhr nachts mit einem Hoch auf die Arbeit den fünften allgemeinen Kongress der Internationalen-Arbeiter-Association.

Sonntag, 8 Sept., morgens 9 Uhr fuhren die Meisten der Delegirten nach Amsterdam, wurden von den dortigen Parteigenossen herzlich empfangen; zu einer Volksversammlung geleitet, in welcher Marx, J. Ph. Becker, Dural, Wroblewski, Sorge, Lafargue, Dupont; van der Hout über Ziel & Zweck der I. A. A., die Arbeiten desselben geschlossenen Kongresses & die Zukunft der Association enthusiastisch aufgenommene Reden hielten.

An Bord des Dampfers Atlantic,
20 Sept. 1872   Sig. F. A. Sorge
                                  Delegirter

Minutes of the

Fifth General Congress

of the International Workingmen's Association

at The Hague,

September, 1872

A F T E R an interruption of three years this Congress had the task of strengthening again the somewhat loosened organization and of bolstering it against external and internal attacks. During the three years since the previous Congress many diverse views had naturally come to the fore and manifold attempts had been made to weaken the Association, to divide, to destroy it, or to alienate it from its ends.

Great historic events had occurred which did not fail to influence the internal life of the Association. These points must always be considered when judging the work of this, the Fifth Congress, a report of which will now be given.

There were 65 delegates present: 18 Frenchmen, 15 Germans, 7 Belgians, 5 Englishmen, 5 Spaniards, 4 Dutchmen, 4 Swiss, 2 Austrians, 1 Dane, 1 Hungarian, 1 Australian, 1 Irishman, and 1 Pole.

They held 95 mandates of which

Belgium had sent	17	Holland	4
Germany	15	Denmark	2
France	14	Ireland	2
Switzerland	11	Hungary	2
America	7	Portugal	1
The General Council	6	Poland	1
Spain	5	Austria	1
England	5	Australia	1

Among the delegates were

5 tailors	1 commercial employee
4 printers	1 instrument maker
4 teachers	1 weaver
4 writers	1 jeweler
3 shoemakers	1 lithographer
3 physicians	1 gold miner
2 draftsmen	1 flower maker
2 cabinetmakers	1 porcelain painter
2 tanners	1 engraver
2 machinists	2 engineers
1 chemist	1 last maker
1 brushmaker	

and the trade of about 20 was not given.

In the main, business was transacted in French, but translations were always given in two, three, even four languages.

The predominance of the French nationality imparted to the Congress an atmosphere of great and at times unpleasant liveliness.

Sunday, September 1, at 7:00 P.M., the first session, the so-called preliminary meeting, was held. The delegates had to push their way through gaping crowds into a hall which was neither favorably located nor otherwise comfortable.[1] A committee of the Dutch Federal Council was present and opened the meeting. Nonmembers had to leave the hall, and Gerhard of the Dutch Federal Council addressed the delegates, gave them a cordial welcome, and made it plain that we enjoyed the hospitality of the Netherlands not *as a favor* but by the laws of the land, and that an official deviation from these laws would provoke the sharpest opposition of all parties. He asks what to do next.

Eccarius says that in accordance with the precedent of previous congresses this preliminary assembly was merely of a social nature, that the credentials committee would be appointed the next morning and thereupon work would begin.

Longuet requests that the agenda for the next day be determined, Engels, that the delegates submit their names.

Fränkel demands that the credentials committee be formed at once

[1] The Congress met at Concordia Hall on Lange Lombard Straat.

and that the delegates be not required to state the place of their sections since this would be a source of danger for the members who come from countries where the I.W.A. is outlawed, and we are surrounded by spies.

Sorge claims for such delegates the right to use a different name. Both points are held to go without saying.

Ranvier moves to meet tomorrow, Monday, at 9:00 A.M., with the Dutch Federal Council in the chair in order promptly to establish the credentials committee, etc.

Marx adds that the session should be closed [to all] except for the members of the Hague Section.

Hales demands that all members of the I.W.A. be admitted and Marx accepts this amendment provided that membership is to be proved.—

These motions of Ranvier, Marx, and Hales are unanimously carried, whereupon the meeting adjourns until Monday, 9:00 A.M. The delegates separated for their lodgings, stared at like monsters and oddities.

Monday, September 2, at 9:30 A.M., the first session of the Congress is opened.—

Engels requests that no reporter be allowed to report the closed sessions. (This applies to delegates who also act as newspaper reporters.)

Dupont demands that all nondelegates leave the hall, and if they are members of the I.W.A., move to the balcony.

Guillaume moves to appoint provisional official translators. Dupont, Fränkel, and Eccarius are appointed.—

Longuet is against admitting any newspaper reporters.

Ranvier requests a vote on this, and a prolonged debate takes place over the reporters, etc. It is decided that all [reporters] who are not delegates have to leave the hall—with two votes opposed.

Engels then moves to elect a committee of seven to examine the credentials. Sauva proposes against this to choose one (1) member from each federation.

Vaillant [moves] that it consist of only five (5) persons, and that the mandates of countries where the I.W.A. is forbidden be invalidated.

Sauva requests the right to elucidate and defend his motion. This is granted him. He says one should not allow the suspicion to arise that only adherents of the General Council serve on the committee, and therefore one member from each federation should be chosen for the committee.

Thereupon Engels' motion ([to form] a credentials committee of seven) is unanimously carried.

Sauva takes up his motion again and demands that it be put to the vote. (The president disregards this.)

The committee is authorized to reach an agreement with the delegates from countries where the I.W.A. is forbidden and persecuted. Like Sauva, Guillaume demands one member from each federation [on the committee]; Seraillier argues against this: "We have more than seven federations, in some countries several, in others none," etc.; hence one could not vote by federation.

After Seraillier's statement Longuet comes out against Sauva's motion, but wishes that not only adherents of the General Council shall form the committee, although he personally defends [the Council].

Guillaume says that the I.W.A. consists of federations and that therefore the federations must be represented in the committee. He regrets that Longuet wishes to represent the General Council—he (Guillaume) represents the International.

Dupont declares that we are representatives of the labor movement, not of a country. Closure of the debate is moved and accepted.—Seraillier's motion to elect the committee members without exception from the floor is carried with 48 against 9 votes and 4 abstaining.

Morago states that he and his fellow delegates from Spain are specifically instructed to abstain from voting until voting proceeds by numbers of members represented.

Lafargue declares that, though also a delegate for Spain, he has not received this instruction.

A recess of ten minutes is taken to prepare the ballots.

After the session is resumed, Joannard's motion to consider the relative majority sufficient for this vote is carried, and the counting of the ballots begins; fifty-eight ballots were cast, while three (Spaniards) abstained from voting.

Elected were Marx with 41 votes, Ranvier with 44, Roch with 41, McDonnell with 39, Dereure with 36, Gerhard with 50, and Fränkel with 22.

Upon Sorge's motion the Committee is instructed to withdraw and set to work immediately while the Congress will adjourn until 7:00 P.M. when it will hear the Committee report.—
Dereure demands that all motions be submitted in writing and that the delegates report their names, occupations, and places of residence to the Credentials Committee.
The session closed about 3:00 P.M.—

The evening session did not begin until 8:30 since the Mandate Committee did not appear earlier.
Since this morning van den Abeel, delegate of Ghent (Belgium) has been in the chair.—The Credentials Committee reports the following as in good standing with the General Council and entitled to seat and vote:

Swarn [Swarm]	for a French section	
Lucain	" " "	
Longuet	" " "	
Joannard	" " "	
Ranvier	" " "	
Vaillant	" " " and	
	the section at La Chaux-de-Fonds	
Fränkel	for a French section	
Walther	" " "	
Vichard	" " "	
Vilmot	" " "	
Cyrille	" " "	
Dereure	" the American Federation	
Sorge	" " " "	
Marx	" Section I New York	
	and " the Leipzig section	
	and " the General Council	
Guillaume	" the Jura Federation	
Schwitzguebel	" " " "	
H. Scheu	" a Vienna section	
	and " an Esslingen section	
	and " a Koenigsberg section	
G. Ludwig	for a Mainz section	

Sauva	for	Sections 29 and 42 in America
C. Farkas	"	two Hungarian sections
Heim	"	a Bohemian section
McDonnell	"	an Irish "
B. Becker	"	a Brunswick section
" "	"	" Chemnitz section
Le Mouson [Moussu]	"	" French section in London
Dr. Sexton	"	the General Council
B. Splingard	"	sections at Charleroi
" "	"	" " Coureilles
" "	"	" " Depents
Pihl	"	Denmark
Gerhard	"	the Dutch Federal Council
Roch	"	the British Federal Council
"	and "	the Stratford section
G. Schuhmacher	"	the section at Solingen
Eberhard	"	the Belgian Federal Council
"	"	shoemakers, painters, etc.
Lafargue	"	the Madrid Federation
"	"	another Spanish federation
"	"	the Lisbon (Portugal) "
Dr. Kugelmann	"	a section at Celle [Hanover]
Dietzgen	"	" " " Dresden
A. Hepner	"	" No. 8, New York
Cournet	"	the Danish Federal Council
"	"	the General Council
Dupont	"	the General Council
Arnoud	for the section at Carouge	
Wroblewski	" " Polish section at London and the General Council	
van den Hout	" " section at Amsterdam	
Harcourt	" " " " Victoria (Australia)	
Barry	" " " No. 3, Chicago	
Seraillier	" the General Council	
Hales	" the section at Hackneyroad	
Brismée	" " " " Brussels	
F. Engels	" " " " Breslau	
"	" " " No. 6, New York	

Milke	"	"	"	at Berlin
"	"	"	"	" Crimmitschau
Mottershead	"	"	"	" Bethnal Green (London)
Lessner	"	"	German section at London	
Cuno	"	"	section at Düsseldorf	
"	"	"	"	" Stuttgart
Eccarius	"	"	moulding makers (London)	
Coenen	"	"	[section] at Antwerp	
J. Ph. Becker	"	"	section at Basel, Geneva, Lucerne,	
van den Abeel			etc., and for the Romance Federal Council	
	"	the section at Ghent		
Friedländer	"	"	"	" Zürich
Herman	"	"	"	" Liége

Moreover, the Committee reports that Flues appeared as the delegate for the Vesdre valley (Verviers), but does not possess correct credentials; that charges have been raised against V. Dave, delegate of the Hague section, which must first be cleared; that Alerini has not been admitted as the delegate of a section at Marseilles, nor Joukowski as the delegate of the Section *de la propagande et action révolutionaire* at Geneva; [the Committee proposes] to delay the admission of Morago, Marcelau, Farga Pelicer, and Alerini as delegates of the Spanish Federation until they have cleared matters with the General Council; [the Committee proposes] to annul the mandate of Section 2 at New York, because this section has been expelled from the American Federal Council and is not in good standing with the General Council; also to reject the mandate of W. West because West is and has been a member of Section 12, of the Philadelphia Congress, and of the Prince Street Council.[2]

[2] Section 2 of New York had been organized in 1870 and represented mainly French immigrants and refugees. Together, Section 2, F. A. Sorge's Section 1—mainly Germans—and a Czech section formed a "Central Committee of the International Workingmen's Association in the United States." By October, 1871, twenty-seven sections had affiliated with this Central Committee.

Among these sections, Section 12 of New York proved troublesome to Marx's followers. Section 12 was led by Mrs. Victoria Woodhull (1838–

Meanwhile an additional mandate has arrived for J. Ph. Becker and several for Herman from Belgium.—

Splingard withdraws his comments on V. Dave, and Flues gives the latter a good recommendation.

Ranvier proposes a vote on those not contested.

Schwitzguebel requests that the names of all against whom no objection is raised be read over and that they be admitted; but the remaining ones should be reserved for discussion.

Eccarius and Sorge oppose this.

After several statements of Belgian delegates the Committee accepts Dave and Flues as fully qualified.

Engels declares himself for Schwitzguebel's motion as does Sauva who requests an immediate decision.

Ranvier demands the vote as a vote of confidence for the Credentials Committee and prompt action since otherwise we will not be finished with the mandates before Wednesday and will have no time for other work.

Lafargue [is] for Schwitzguebel's motion and for an immediate vote.

1927), who had come to New York from Ohio with her younger sister Tennessee Claflin. In 1870, after two years of residence in New York, they founded *Woodhull and Claflin's Weekly*. The *Weekly* carried the first translation of the *Communist Manifesto* (1872), advocated "advanced ideas," exposed Henry Ward Beecher, and appealed to reformist sectarians of all sorts and conditions: "all persons are desirable." Sorge and the German Marxists considered Section 12 "a motley gathering of bourgeois reformers, evangelists of free love, atheists and deists," etc. They wished to build strictly along class lines. Socialist intellectuals and workingmen should unite. Socialism must be joined to wage labor, not to a "general public."

When Section 12 and its following threatened to take over the organization, Section 1 brought matters to a head, the Central Committee split, and under Sorge's and Bolte's leadership fourteen sections seceded and reorganized a "provisional Federal Council of the International Workingmen's Association." From the meeting-place of their representatives, a room in the 10th Ward Hotel, they were referred to as the "Ward Council." A few days later Section 12 and its following met in No. 100 Prince Street, New York, and organized a rival federal council; hence its name, Prince Street Council. From another location it also became known as the Spring Street Council. This Council called together a congress of sections at Philadelphia. In July, 1872, thirteen sections met there and claimed to represent "The American Confederacy of the International Workingmen's Association."

Perhaps the best source for these disputes is Hermann Schlüter, *Die Internationale in Amerika* (Chicago, 1918). See pp. 157, 160 ff.

Alerini demands that all credentials should be given to a committee member so that everybody can inspect them.

Barry asks why the Committee was appointed in the first place.

Marx says that the Committee had only two things to investigate: 1. whether the credentials were made out correctly; and 2. whether the mandators were in good standing with the General Council and hence qualified as mandators.

Schwitzguebel's motion, supported by Sauva, Lafargue, and others, to suspend for the time being all those contested and after another reading of the list to accept the rest en bloc, is carried against [the votes of] Alerini and Sorge.

The reading of names is resumed, and Farga Pelicer asks, after the reading of the first names of French sections, whether they have paid, whereupon Ranvier says that it was the very task of the Committee to investigate this.

Pelicer merely wished to know whether the Committee treated everyone equally.—

During the reading of the list Schwitzguebel raises objections against the mandate of *Vaillant;* Sauva against that of *Dereure* and of *Sorge;* Sorge against that of *Sauva,* Alerini against that of *Lafargue;* Hales against that of *Barry,* and Guillaume against those of the delegates of the General Council.

All others, fifty-one in number, are admitted en bloc, including the delegates of the General Council, although Brismée demands that the question concerning the latter should be discussed later.—

Lafargue summons the contested [delegates] to withdraw to the rear of the hall.—

The chairman suggests that the bureau should now be elected; Sorge and Dereure object.

Hales protests Sorge's right to speak, as does Flues. The session is adjourned at about 9:30 P.M.—

Tuesday, September 3, at 9:30 A.M., the meeting is reopened and the chairman regrets that so many members are tardy.

It is resolved to elect four secretaries: Le Moussu for the French language, Hepner for the German, Roche for the English, van den Hout for the Dutch.—

Engels moves to hear two speakers for and two against each case, with fifteen minutes discussion time, and then to vote.

The Credentials Committee submits further mandates from Belgium for Flues, from France for Servillier [Seraillier], from the Romance Federal Council at Geneva for Duval; they are accepted.

Ranvier wishes to raise Vaillant's case; Schwitzguebel protests.— Sauva objects to the five minutes [time limit] and demands ten minutes so that he can submit all protestations (he has four of them); he considers the motion [for a five-minute speech limit] a maneuver (a puny expedient) of his opponents to silence him.

Dereure calls this an insult, since the five minutes hold for us as they do for you.

Duval cannot understand Sauva.

Eberhardt, nevertheless, sees in it a trick and "prophesies" that it will end badly.

Sauva and Lafargue propose to amend the motion by granting ten minutes to the first two speakers.

Guillaume, Schwitzguebel, and Sauva propose an amendment allowing ten minutes speaking time with no restriction on the number of speakers.

Sauva and Lafargue's amendment is rejected, 24 to 24.

Likewise, the amendment of Guillaume, Schwitzguebel, and Sauva is rejected and then the original motion (of Engels) is carried with a great majority against 6 votes.—

As regards Vaillant's mandate of La Chaux-de-Fonds, Schwitzguebel merely states that this is no French section but simply an affiliate of the Romance Federation.

Vaillant is instructed to defend the Romance Federation against the Jura Federation some of whose leaders advocate principles which serve solely to disrupt the I.W.A.

Guillaume disputes the credentials of Vaillant, whose name was inserted later by someone else.

The section of La Chaux-de-Fonds is allied with the revolutionaries and old royalists of the canton of Neuchatel. They support the royalists as the Genevans support the radicals.—Both go along with and vote with the bourgeoisie. Elsengel was elected with royalist, Grasselin with radical support.[3]—

Vaillant is accepted by the Congress almost unanimously.

[3] The paragraph would seem to be an obscure presentation of Guillaume's argument as later stated by himself in his *L'Internationale, Documents et Souvenirs (1864–1878)* (Paris, 1907), Vol. II, pp. 327 f.

Seraillier demands that the particular case and not general principles should be discussed.

Concerning Dereure's mandate Sauva says that he has many objections but no time to read them, hence he will deposit them with the bureau. Section 2 [he says] thinks that it was a poor idea of the American Congress to proceed with the election of delegates contrary to the rules. This is an indirect election; besides, Sorge and Dereure were authorized by the American Congress to select five members of the General Council to give mandates to. Moreover the American Congress could not elect two delegates as it did not represent 1,000 members, hence one of the two must be excluded. But which one?

Section 42 protests against the election by the American Congress as an arbitrary (authoritarian) act; it will not surrender its sovereignty and also protests the tax of fifty-five cents which the North American Federal Council had no right to raise since the rules permit but fifteen cents.[4]—

The chairman asks whether he should read all documents submitted to him; the Congress answers in the negative.

Dereure regrets their not being read and also the limitation of discussion because of Seraillier's motion, since this concerns questions of principle. Unless indirect election were to be allowed, most of the delegates present would have to withdraw.

The American Congress was expressly summoned for [the purpose

[4] Simon Dereure and F. A. Sorge had been elected representatives of the Provisional Federal Council of the I.W.A. at a meeting in the 10th Ward Hotel. At the same time it was resolved that the affiliated sections of this council should transfer their mandates to proved party comrades in Europe. The cost of Dereure's and Sorge's journey to Europe was to be defrayed by raising a special contribution of fifty-five cents per member. Section 2, which Sauva represented, refused to collect this contribution from its members. Besides, it maintained that only individual sections were entitled to send representatives to the Hague Congress. When Section 2, on August 4, 1872, elected Sauva as its representative, the federal council in New York suspended the section for failure to abide by its resolutions. At the same time it referred matters to the General Council in London. Section 2 claimed complete independence from the Prince Street Council, from which it had seceded after the latter under the leadership of Mrs. Woodhull had staged a convention in New York nominating Mrs. Woodhull for President of the United States.—Hermann Schlüter, *Die Internationale in Amerika*, pp. 176 ff., 182.

of] choosing delegates; consequently the participating sections must submit [to the resolutions of the meeting].

Brismée says that this last argument is decisive for him.

Dereure's mandate is recognized by the Congress with all against Sauva's vote.

Sorge's mandate is disputed again by Sauva because of the insufficient membership (it is not one thousand).

Sorge argues that the correct interpretation of the rules would entitle us to more members. He asks, what election could be more direct than that by a Congress called for this purpose? What mandate more valid than that given by a general congress? Sauva's thesis that Dereure and Sorge are to select five additional members of the General Council is false; the resolution of the American Congress reads: "that the Congress select two delegates and send them at general expense and that the individual sections are asked to forward credentials to proved party comrades." He grants Section 42 its sovereignty but challenges its right to protest resolutions which are passed with its co-operation. He is willing to believe that this section objects to the fifty-five cents because it does not wish to pay. It would be different if it were unable to pay. [The section] should act openly, not underhandedly.—

Sorge's mandate is recognized by the whole Congress with the exception of Sauva.

Sauva's mandate of Sections 29 and 42 is disputed by Sorge, who says that Section 29 belongs nowhere, hence cannot have paid dues; that Section 42 is nowhere to be found (*introuvable*) since the American Congress; it did not pay its contributions to the general costs of the Congress and made out these credentials with fraudulent secrecy in order to make Sauva's admission possible, since it was afraid that the mandate of Section 2 is in for trouble. It is all only a cunningly engineered maneuver.—

Sauva says there exist simply unaffiliated sections in the United States like, for instance, Section 29, which have remained independent because of the existing frictions. It is slander to maintain that Section 42 is in opposition because of the fifty-five cents; they are in opposition because the American Congress wishes to change the general rules. For the rest, Sections 29 and 42 are in good standing with the General Council since they have paid.—

Le Mous[s]u says Sections 29 and 42 knew full well that only the federal council in the 10th Ward Hotel was recognized by the General Council; hence they should have paid via the federal council. Besides, Sauva himself told him that in London he quickly ran to the treasurer, Mr. Jung, in order to forestall such objections; this proves that the sections themselves recognize their weak position and have sought admission by craft.—

Fränkel [says he] would be sorry if cases like that of Sauva should occur later, but now he cannot but recognize Sauva because the rules unfortunately still allow sections to exist outside the central national federations.

(Le Moussu's report of what Sauva himself had said was translated neither by Fränkel nor by Eccarius.)

Sauva declares that Le Moussu made sorry use of his confidence and that he would beware of giving him further information. Le Moussu says that for him general interests have precedence over personal ones.

Marx points out that sections must either belong to the national federations or be directly recognized by the General Council. Section 29 does neither. In certain cases independent sections are quite useful, but they must be recognized by the General Council and must have direct contact with it. He is decidedly against recognizing Sauva.

Dereure moves that Sauva be admitted as delegate of Section 42 if Sections 2, 29, and 42 are willing to pledge themselves to recognize the acts and resolutions of the General American Congress and to act accordingly. Marx agrees.

Sauva does not accept this compromise, for Section 29 is only awaiting the result of the Hague Congress as a guide to further conduct. Dereure withdraws his motion.

To the question whether these sections are in order Engels declares that neither one is in good standing with the General Council.

Voting proceeds in quite a state of confusion and Sauva is admitted as a delegate for Sections 29 and 42, with 30 against 20 votes.

Cuno moves a vote of censure against the chairman for having recognized too many speakers, to which the latter replies that two mandates have been at stake.

Lafargue's mandate of the Madrid and of another Spanish federa-

tion is disputed by Alerini, who says that the editors of the *Emancipacion*[5] only formed sections which were not recognized by the Spanish Federal Council, whereupon they turned to the General Council, who admitted them with the statement "that it is absurd to ask a federal council which consists mostly of members of a secret society hostile to the I.W.A." The Spanish Federal Council protests against the new Madrid Federation because the General Council accepted them against the rules. The other Spanish Federation, represented by Lafargue, is in the same position as is the entire Spanish Federation, which has not yet paid its contributions.—
Guillaume corrects a mistake in the German translation.—
Lafargue reads an article from the *Emancipacion* (acknowledged by Morago), which gave the reason for the expulsion of the editors of the *Emancipacion*, effected by only 15 (out of the 130) members, without giving the accused the least notice or opportunity to defend themselves. The Spanish Federal Council endorsed this illegal expulsion, and hence we had to turn to the General Council. Morago has twice been traitor to the cause, when he fled to Lisbon and when, after Sagasta's decree, he turned his back on the I.W.A.—Those fifteen men always pretend to be autonomous, but they are extremely authoritarian when it suits their purpose. The motives of their conduct are covert; they did what they did because he attacked the Alliance in the *Liberté*.
Morago says that the General Council, in violation of all rules and regulations, reached a decision on the basis of fancied reasons. The Spanish Federal Council has nothing to do with the internal affairs of the sections. The expulsion was regular, as the rules of the sections prescribe regular meetings the resolutions of which are binding on absent members regardless of whether they [the resolutions] have been passed by five, fifteen, or fifty members.
The Spanish Federation is the most militant of all international federations. All discord in Spain arose only after the arrival and intervention of this one person.—They take their stand on the rules which the General Council has no right to violate. We do not wish to introduce personalities, but at the next Spanish congress we

[5] *La Emancipación* was the Marxist paper edited in Spain by Iglesias, Jose Mesa, and Paul Lafargue, Marx's son-in-law. According to Barry, the dispute of Lafargue's mandate "furnished the battle of the day" (see below, p. 261).

shall decide whether the expulsion was justified and in order. Engels says we must decide whether the I.W.A. shall still be administered under democratic principles or be ruled by a clique secretly organized against the rules of the I.W.A. There are six persons present who belong to this secret society,[6] the four Spaniards and Schwitzguebel and Guillaume.—
Guillaume interrupts: "That is false!"
Engels continues: I have the evidence here (he draws it out of his pocket).
Guillaume is compelled to withdraw his remark.
Engels says, further, that the expulsion of the Madrid members was illegal, since no court of honor had been appointed in accordance with the rules. The new section only asserted its right when it seceded from the Spanish Federal Council and affiliated directly with the General Council. Certainly the General Council went beyond the rules but it did so quite consciously and with the intention of saving the I.W.A. in Spain by this means.—The Alliance engages in action in Spain with the funds of the I.W.A., and the Spanish Federal Council counts among its eight members five brothers of the "Alliance." The General Council full well realized its responsibility but had to take action.
(Marcelau says, yes, o yes! when Engels declares that the present Spanish delegates belong to the Alliance.)
Joannard demands continuation of the discussion in order to give the Spaniards complete freedom of speech and to counter the reproach that they were cut short.
Fränkel is against this as the same case will come up again later.
Continuation of the debate is rejected and Lafargue is admitted as delegate of the Madrid Federation with 40 votes against none.—
Marx moves to expel the Alliance from the I.W.A. and requests that a committee be appointed to examine the documents and investigate the entire affair. The meeting is adjourned for two hours.—

[The meeting is] resumed at 4:00 P.M. The roll call shows twenty-two absent and Cuno censures the chairman for not having begun punctually. Duval moves to wait for another fifteen minutes.

[6] This is the first overt reference to the alleged existence of the anarchist secret society operating in the midst of the I.W.A. under orders of Bakunin. See Introduction.

The chairman speaks for some time, thereby provoking protests.

He reads the list of names for the second time.

Marx informs [the assembly] of a letter from a section in P. Mauricio, near Genoa, sending good wishes.

McDonnell is appointed English secretary in place of the absent Roche.

Lafargue's motion to open every session with a roll call, to list those absent, and to inform the respective federations is accepted.—

Barry's mandate is disputed by Hales. As Hales was no longer present, Sauva was good enough to take his place and upon his request to dispute the mandate, without stating a single reason, however.— Sorge asks for reasons whether anybody disputes the right of the section to make out the credentials? Since there is no answer whatever and no reason for the charge is given, he has nothing to defend, but he blames these people for having caused loss of time to the Congress; the working class will hold them accountable for this waste of time which should be devoted to the discussion of labor problems and workers' interests. He turns especially against Sauva.—

Mottershead asks why of all things Barry was elected by a foreign German section whereas at home in England he does not belong to the leaders and is a nobody?—

Marx says it is none of their (?) business whom the section elects. For the rest, it is to Barry's credit not to belong to the so-called leaders of English workingmen, for they have all more or less sold out to the bourgeoisie and the government.[7] Barry was attacked solely because he did not wish to be made Hales's tool.—

Barry's mandate is recognized against Sauva's and Motterhead's votes.—

The Credentials Committee announces that it has received and passed on further credentials for Duval from Switzerland, for McDonnell from Dublin, for A. Hepner from Regensburg.

Alerini's mandate from a section in Marseilles is disputed by the Credentials Committee itself.

Ranvier demands that Seraillier give particulars. Seraillier declares

---

[7] Both Barry and James Guillaume report Marx as having said that "almost every recognized leader of English working men was sold to Gladstone, Morley, Dilke, and others." See Barry below, p. 262.

that he *never* received news from Marseilles, and also no contributions. Consequently it cannot be granted. He has, however, been informed that recently several local sections were organized in order to send delegates to the Congress.—

Alerini is grieved to hear this at the very moment when the Marseilles people profess that they belong to the revolutionary working class of the world. He now relinquishes this mandate. He finds that there are maneuvers going on here to purge the Association in a certain way and to surrender it into the hands of a few. Last year the General Council meant to forward money to the Marseilles people to have them attend the London Conference; but it failed to do so when the Marseilles people did not wish to dance to the tune of the General Council.[8]

Seraillier moves that an instant reply be permitted to these charges. This is accepted. Seraillier as secretary for France declares that throughout the time mentioned he neither wrote any letter to nor received any from Marseilles, hence Alerini's accusation falls flat.—

Duval reports that two people had written from Marseilles to Geneva in order to establish contact with the Romance Federation. A member of the Romance Federation recently went to Marseilles, and people in Marseilles themselves said that it would be impossible to organize a section there.—

Cyrille opines that sections might nevertheless exist without having contact with the General Council.

Alerini wishes to speak again.

Sorge asks whether it is permitted to debate the digressive points.

[8] In September, 1871, a closed meeting of the I.W.A. had been held in London. Intense police activity on the Continent against the International, the Franco-Prussian war, the collapse of the Paris Commune, and the plight of the refugees from the regime of white terror made it inadvisable to stage a public congress as usual. Of the twenty-three delegates who met in London on September 17, no fewer than thirteen were members of the General Council. There were six Belgian, one Spanish, and two Swiss delegates present. Marx and Engels, with the support of the French Blanquists, controlled the situation and confined the discussion to organizational measures strengthening the General Council. The British members of the General Council pressed for establishing a separate British federal council. Marx and Engels, unable to prevent this, agreed to it. The British members of the General Council therewith held dual membership, in the Federal Council, to which Marx and Engels did not belong, and in the General Council.

Alerini says that Combe's mandate of Marseilles was already made out and that Bastelica corresponded with Marseilles in the name of the General Council.

Seraillier demands that it be recorded that Bastelica promised money to the people in Marseilles and that Bastelica never had the right to write even a single letter in the name of the General Council.

Fränkel requests a vote to settle whether or not to recognize the Marseilles section. The vote is taken.

Seraillier abstains from voting lest he declare that false credentials have been submitted by Alerini who perhaps has been deceived. Alerini protests against this.

Alerini's mandate from Marseilles is rejected with 38 votes and 14 abstentions.—

Joukowski's credentials from the Section de propagande d'action revolutionaire et socialiste at Geneva are disputed by the Credentials Committee; its chairman, Ranvier, states that there are federations in Switzerland but that the section represented by Joukowski is recognized neither by the Romance Federal Council nor by the General Council. Hence the section appeals to the Congress and demands to be informed of the reason for its rejection by the General Council.

Duval relates how the French refugees, upon their arrival at Geneva, tried to take over the *Egalité*. Quite a few of them joined the Alliance. Although the latter had indeed been dissolved on August 6, just before the conference, the Alliance was promptly revived under the name of Section de propagande revolutionnaire, etc., which did not affiliate with any other body.

Brismée spoke against the appearance of the French as sections in Geneva, Brussels, and elsewhere. They should only form a group in order to pay their contributions. Probably they did not join the [existing] sections because in the Belgian sections the position and morals of the candidates are investigated lest "operators" are received into membership.—

Marx says that the Alliance was accepted because at first its secret character was unknown. We knew well that it had formed anew, but in view of the official statement of dissolution of August 6, 1871, the General Council could not do otherwise than to pass the familiar resolutions. I speak not against secret societies *per se*—for I have been a member of such—but against secret societies which are inimical and damaging to the I.W.A.—The Romance Federal Council protested vehemently against admitting the section in question, which is why the General Council rejected it in accordance with the rules.

In Brussels things were different. There the French section wrote the General Council that members of the Belgian Federal Council had told them their admission to the Belgian Federation would expose them to the Belgian police. Hence the General Council could not but recognize and accept the independent French section of Brussels and similarly the second French section at Brussels.

Guillaume requests the floor after Joukowski. Engels protests the deviation from the adopted procedure. Guillaume's request is rejected.

Joukowski says that his section did not turn to the Romance Federal Council. In Geneva there is a central section for propaganda purposes in the canton. At first, the French refugees did not know where to turn. A few joined the central section. Since they intended to engage in propaganda, not in the canton of Geneva but in France, they formed this section which has nothing in common with the Alliance to which hardly any member belonged previously. He himself was indeed a member but only as a section of the I.W.A., not knowing it to be a secret society. The members of his section always protest against dealing with the affairs of the Alliance and now request admission as a section of the I.W.A.

Ranvier moves to postpone this business until Marx's motion against the Alliance comes up for discussion. This is accepted.

The Credentials Committee disputes the mandates of Morago, Farga-Pelicer, Marcelau, and Alerini because they failed to meet their obligations to the General Council.

Ranvier requests that decision be deferred until the decision regarding the Alliance [comes up].

Farga-Pelicer says that their sections are somewhat in arrears partly because they are too poor, which should be understood by all of us. Hence they request an extension for [the dues of] the last three months, for they themselves have not yet received [the money].

Ranvier's motion to defer the matter until the issue of the Alliance is decided surprises him since these sections have been censured only for nonpayment of dues. The Spanish sections are quite active in the struggle against capital which they hope to destroy possibly soon.—

Engels finds it strange that the Spaniards keep the money in their pockets instead of depositing it with their credentials as is always done and should be done at conferences and congresses.

The Spanish delegates are astonished that the Alliance is drawn in, yet they themselves admitted their affiliation with the Alliance even today. (Marcelau and the others say that they are no longer members although they were previously.)

Engels believes that they still belong to it though under different names. If they refer to the puffed-up I.W.A. in Spain, one should consider that this growth was the work of the former federal council (i.e., of those expelled in Madrid).—

Marcelau thinks Engels is not exact. They do not wish to keep the money in their pockets but want to exchange their Spanish currency which could not be done before last night. To be sure, they held back somewhat when this unexpected opposition against their mandates arose. He was a member of the Alliance; the Alliance introduced and raised the I.W.A. in Spain. The Alliance consists of devoted friends of the party, true soldiers of the revolution. I do not mind if we are expelled. This question is decided in advance. I speak the truth and do not fear death for so doing. Our discord dates only from the arrival of one man. We members of the Alliance have suffered more for the cause than have all the members of the General Council, etc., who wish to excommunicate us. Just say frankly that we are to be expelled and we shall leave and let you have the money that belongs to you. The Alliance was dissolved at the congress at Saragossa after it had done its work of propaganda and was no longer necessary. Previously it was necessary because we had no right of assembly in Spain.—

Ranvier pointed out that the issue of the Alliance intrudes everywhere and hence must be settled before we can judge the case of the Spaniards. Last night he had told the Spaniards honestly to pay in order to remove this obstacle. We must take up the question of the Alliance.

Coenen speaks for the admission of the Spanish delegates once they have been recognized by the General Council and have paid their dues, which business seems settled to him. His mandate commands him to leave the meeting if the Spaniards are not admitted.

Ranvier objects to the threat of Splingard, Guillaume, and others to leave the hall, which proves only that their mandators prejudged the matter. His wish is that all police sergeants of the world would take leave in this manner.—

Morago says that they are delegates of the Spanish Federation, not of the Alliance, and hence have nothing to do with it. Such violation of justice would destroy the entire Spanish Federation. What is the issue now, the Alliance, the question of authority, secret societies? The Alliance founded, raised, and propagated the I.W.A. All our voters knew that we belonged to the Alliance (for the police had been informed). You need only to investigate whether our credentials are in order, nothing else. We are the representatives of the Spanish Federation, and there are people here who wish to exclude us. Your business is only to see whether seal, dues, etc., are in order.

Lafargue defends himself against the supposition that he is connected with the Spanish police because he attacked the Alliance. They should consider this no danger as they do not engage in politics and hence cannot be dangerous to any government.

Marcelau says that Lafargue established the paper [*Emancipación*] for denunciatory purposes and his present sophisms are but recent inventions. If Lafargue speaks of traitors he cannot refer to him (Marcelau). Lafargue admits this, "but to others!"

Splingard suggests that we discuss only the credentials, not the Alliance, and points to the large membership in Spain.

There are interruptions.

Ranvier is against a vote before the Spaniards have paid their dues and the issue of the Alliance has been settled.

Now Farga-Pelicer hands the chairman the dues of the Spaniards except those for the last three months.

Ranvier is for granting this exception and moves now for their admission without thereby judging the issue of the Alliance.

Thereupon the Spanish delegates are admitted; only Vaillant abstains from voting because the Spanish delegates, though no longer belonging to the Alliance, failed to state whether they will subscribe to and abide by Article IX of the congress resolutions.—

The mandate of Section 2 (New York) is declared null and void by the Committee because this section is nowhere affiliated and belongs nowhere. Sauva finds himself at a loss because of the resolutions of the morning session. Section 2 has paid its dues, hence is in good standing with the General Council; it has 169 members—formerly 235—it has founded sections in St. Louis, Baltimore, Springfield, Chicago, and elsewhere. An adverse decision would have serious consequences for the American Federation. After the *coup d'état* (Eccarius applauds) [Section 2] affiliated with the Prince Street Council and organized the funeral procession against which Section 1 has protested. In the end it turned against the Prince Street Council because the latter refused to obey the General Council and was connected with the Apollo Hall affair.[9]

Eccarius translates and adds his own comments, which calls forth Sorge's censure.

Dereure asks whether a section may disregard the resolutions passed by a congress with [the section's] co-operation. Sorge refutes the charge against Section 1 by stating the facts of the case.

Marx says that Section 2 does not exist for us since it has not, as an independent section, sought contact with the General Council.

[9] The phrase *coup d'état* refers to the splitting of the Central Committee and the separate organization of the Federal Council in the Ward Hotel (see above, Note 2).

The rival Prince Street Council of Mrs. Woodhull exploited the public indignation against the execution of the Communards Ferré, Rossel, and Bourgeois in Paris in November, 1871, by organizing a funeral procession. It was announced for December 10. The police commissioner of New York prohibited the demonstration and announced the prohibition on December 9 through the press. The Prince Street Council met in the evening and shifted the date to December 25. Some delegates, especially those of Section 9, an American section, decided to demonstrate just the same and on Sunday, December 10, came singly with flagpoles. When they tried to march in close formation, they were dispersed by police; some were arrested and brought to trial. The case was dismissed, and the press took the side of the delegates and criticized the police commission. The police reconsidered, and the funeral procession was staged the following Sunday. After the publicity it proved a success. A few trade unions, the Workingmen's Union, sections of the International affiliated with the Prince Street Council, French refugee organizations, Irishmen, and a company of Negro militiamen joined ranks, and their demonstration boosted the prestige of the Prince Street Council.

Herman says that the Belgian Congress, too, has passed majority resolutions but could not, therefore, exclude the minority. There must be no majority in the I.W.A., hence not in America either.

Dereure declares that the delegates of the American Federation will withdraw if Section 2 is admitted.

Brismée relates how one proceeds with recalcitrant sections in Belgium; they are not only suspended but dropped.

Sorge states that he would first have raised the cabinet question, raised by Dereure, with Section 12 where it would become clear what great harm these elements did to the working class and labor movement in America.

Fränkel is decidedly against admitting Section 2 and points to events in the [Paris] Commune where individual sections also agitated against the Federal Council with posters, etc. He argues for centralization, against so-called autonomy and against vanity. Rebellion against every resolution must no longer be tolerated and discipline *must* be maintained.

Eccarius says that Section 2 is the second oldest in the United States and that Section 1 did not behave in a friendly manner at all toward the procession, as he knows from letters which passed through his hands.

Barry objects to the violation of the accepted rules.

Ranvier argues against admitting Section 2, which has broken its ties with all others, including its own family, and suddenly wishes to be represented at this congress; for this purpose it paid its dues to the treasurer on August 26 when actually there was as yet hardly a General Council. This is but an empty pretext and backhanded conduct. If we tolerate such ways in the future the I.W.A. will have no right to continued existence. In that case it [the I.W.A.] should rather be made into free-masonry, etc.

Joannard requests that a document be read which Sauva has submitted and insists on this in the most violent manner. Engels reads it; it is Bolte's letter of August 4 addressed to Section 2.—

Again Ranvier, in the name of the Credentials Committee, takes the floor decidedly against admitting Section 2. Its mandate is declared null and void with 39 Nays against 9 Ayes and 11 abstentions.—

Marx reports that West wishes the question of Section 12 (New York) to be postponed to the next day and that this meets with the

Committee's consent. He brings up the issue of the Alliance and says that he moved to exclude the Alliance only, *not* the Spanish delegates. The session adjourns at 10:00 P.M.

On Wednesday, September 4, at 9:15 A.M., the meeting is called to order, and quite a few members are absent.

Vilmot requests that smoking in the hall be forbidden. Guillaume seconds the motion, even if it were objectionable to but *one*. Barry and Sexton oppose it. Smoking is forbidden with 15 against 13 votes.

Lafargue moves a vote of censure against Hales for having left the Congress but withdraws his motion upon explanations on the part of British delegates.

A further mandate from San Francisco for Vaillant is announced and approved, and the Congress proceeds to the discussion of the mandate of Section 12 (New York) for W. West.

Sauva moves that for this case the five-minute rule be suspended, which is accepted with 31 to 8 votes.

Seraillier protests against Joukowski's right to vote; Guillaume defends it. The Congress decides, with 26 to 10 votes and 6 abstentions, that Joukowski has no right to vote.

Morago requests a change in the voting procedure—by number of members—since they, the Spaniards, are instructed not to vote before this is settled.

The chairman, Joannard, and Ranvier engage in a separate conversation; meanwhile two more credentials arrive for Marx.—

Marx, in the name of the Credentials Committee, proposes that the mandate for W. West be declared null and void because he is or has been 1. a member of a suspended section; 2. a member of the Philadelphia Congress; and 3. a member of the Prince Street Council. West's credentials are signed by Victoria Woodhull, who for years has had an eye on the presidency [of the United States]; she is president of the spiritists, preaches free love, has a banking business, etc. Section 12, founded by V. Woodhull, initially consisted almost exclusively of bourgeoisie; it agitated especially for the women's franchise and released to the English-speaking citizens of the United States the notorious appeal charging the I.W.A. with all sorts of nonsense; this led to the organization of various sections in that country. Among other things in it there was talk of personal liberty, social liberty (free love), dress regulation, women's franchise, universal language, etc. On October 28 they declared that [the phrase] "the emancipation of the working classes by themselves" means merely that the emancipation of the working classes could not be consummated against the will of the workers themselves. They give precedence to the women's question over the question of labor and take exception to the assumption that the I.W.A. is a workingmen's organization.

Section 1 protested against this policy of Section 12 and demanded that at least two-thirds of the members of the section be wage workers, because every labor movement in the United States is spoiled and exploited by the bourgeoisie.

Section 12 took exception to this demand for two-thirds wage workers with the sarcastic question whether it is a crime not to be a wage slave but free.—

Both parties appealed for a decision to the General Council who rendered it on March 5 and 12, and suspended Section 12. That is why West cannot be admitted. Despite its appeal to the decision of the General Council, Section 12 and its adherents refused to accept this decision. West was also a member of the congress at Philadelphia and of the Prince Street Council which refused to recognize the General Council and maintained contact with the Jura Federation; according to press reports the latter advised them not to pay dues so as to leave the General Council high and dry.

West speaks for about one and one-half hours and states that his case has been prejudged, but that he has traveled 4,000 miles in order to meet his obligations to his voters. He will speak only on the three points of the report, not on unproved accusations; he is a member of Section 12 and proud of it, for Section 12 has established English sections, and he demands justice here against the false charges and slander which the other side has leveled against Section 12 by letter. The suspension was illegal, for it was accusation, verdict, and sanction at once, without a hearing for the accused. Section 12 is innocent as a newborn babe, innocent until found guilty. Therefore, my friend Eccarius refused to dispatch the verdict, knowing that not a word of the first argument for suspension is true, for Section 12 has never passed such a resolution but has merely discussed and amended it. Section 12 even wished to recognize the

General Council as judge if it were given fair hearing and tribunal. The second argument, too, is false, for we have done and said nothing that is not contained in and based upon the very rules, congressional resolutions, etc. The labor question is also a women's question, and the emancipation of women must precede that of the workers. Woodhull and others are spiritists and free lovers! Can you forbid it? Can you command love where there is none? (general laughter) That is none of your business. We have strictly followed the rules. First we are men before we are workers or bourgeoisie. The development and solution of the social question takes the following course: first man is a commodity, then he becomes a wage worker, then he becomes a bourgeois—middle-class man, etc., and then man, who has advanced to bourgeois status by means of his higher intelligence, enters into general co-operation, that is, the substitution of society for individual work. The bourgeoisie have and acquire the necessary experience and intelligence which we need in the movement. Certainly, I have been a member of the Philadelphia Congress; this congress, however, has done nothing against the General Council; besides, yesterday you here recognized the mandate of a section (29) which was represented there [at Philadelphia].—

I have indeed been a member of the Prince Street Council, but have withdrawn upon its own request. We have the sacred right to rebel against all despotism. The General Council has twice violated its duties. The Americans could not accept the two-thirds [membership] rule. After all, the General Council might do all sorts of things unless we had the right to rebel. We do not wish other people's brains to think for us, that the General Council lay down the law for us in America. We are for the Commune, for universal (women's) franchise, for direct legislation. We find that our republic has been a failure and wish to found a new one. One should also exclude the Swiss, who have introduced the referendum and other political rights.

Section 12 has certainly paid for the first year as Sorge will testify, and he [West] will affirm under oath that they have paid for the second year, too. He speaks of the Sorge party and the West party. Sorge objects to his name being linked to that of West.

The Congress is restless because West takes up so much time. Brismée and Ranvier especially are vexed about such waste of time.—

Sorge in answer to West says that his task is easy; he relates how Section 12 was recognized through misrepresentation (West declared "that the majority of Section 12 consists of wage workers like himself"); the other side was sufficiently informed of the demands of the opponents of Section 12; the General Council had merely recommended, not decreed, the two-thirds rule; Mrs. Woodhull pursues personal ends in the association as West himself has told him; nobody has ever disputed their right to hold all sorts of opinions about the women's question, religion, etc., but they have no right to make the I.W.A. responsible for them; Section 12 and its adherents have shamelessly laid bare all dissensions before the public; they have failed to pay dues for the current year; they have been pleased to receive the communication from the Jura Federation and the Universal Federal Council in London; they have engaged in backhanded intrigues, have demanded supreme leadership of the I.W.A. in America from the General Council, and have impudently declared adverse decisions of the General Council to be in their favor; they have come out against the French Communists and German atheists; we demand discipline, submission not to persons but to principle, to the organization; we need the [co-operation of the] Irish in America, but we cannot win them unless we rid ourselves of all connection with Section 12 and the free lovers.— The working class in America consists 1. of Irishmen, 2. of Germans, 3. of Negroes, and only 4. of Americans.—Give us free play and a free field, so that we can make something decent out of the International in America!—

Sauva does not wish to speak for Section 12, but defends the accomplishments and good qualities of Mrs. Woodhull and of Section 12.—[He points to] the hundred dollars for the funeral procession; Mrs. Woodhull is a great speaker, has made speeches for the Commune, has established sections, etc. Section 2 believes that the General Council acted with undue haste in suspending Section 12, which has certainly paid its dues. The accusations hurled against the French Communists and German atheists are not official.

Guillaume maintains that the Jura Federation has never written to America; rather, given the contradictory news about the American discord, he (Guillaume) wrote a private letter to Verpillier in New York asking for factual information. The latter replied in a private letter as follows; he reads the letter containing charges against Sorge, right-hand man of Marx, and his creatures, and states that his section (18) could never affiliate with those who caused the split and made the *coup d'état*, of which Sorge informed only his creatures, etc. The letter is dated August 4.—

Sorge requests a copy of Verpillier's letter in order to sue its author in America; he shows how the opponents always engage in slander in the belief that something will stick; he illustrates it by referring to Elliot's case [10] and his letter to [the editor of] the *Star* on December 9, 1871; Elliot never replied to Sorge's rejoinder in which he offered to prove before any committee that he (Elliot) had lied.— Guillaume promises to hand the letter to the bureau.

Le Moussu protests against Langrand's letter, published in the Bulletin of the Jura Federation, and replete with lies and slander.—

Brismée moves that the I.W.A. deny recognition to any section consisting of bourgeoisie.

West wishes to speak about the motion which leads to unrest; meanwhile Cyrille leaves the hall.

Upon Seraillier's motion a voice vote is taken. For Brismée's motion vote:

Arnoud, J. Ph. Becker, Brismée, Barry, Cournet, Cuno, Coenen, Dupont, Dave, Duval, Dereure, Eberhard, Flues, Forkas, Friedländer, Fränkel, Guillaume, Gerhard, Herman, Hepner, Heim, Joannard, Marx, Kugelman, Lessner, Lucain, Lafargue, Le Moussu, Milke, Mottershead, Pihl, Ranvier, Swarm, Sauva, Sorge, Sohen, Seraillier, Sexton, Schumacher, Splingard, Walther, Wroblewski, van den Abeel, Vaillant, Vichard, Dietzgen, Vilmot.

The following abstain from voting: Ec[c]arius, Harcourt, Roche, Schwitzguebel, van den Hout, Farga Pelicer, Morago, Alerini, Marcelau.

Six [delegates] are absent.—

In the vote on West's mandate which now comes up, the following vote in opposition: Arnoud, J. Ph. Becker, Brismée, Barry, Cournet, Cuno, Coenen, Dupont, Dave, Duval, Dereure, Eberhard, Flues, Forkas, Friedländer Fränkel, Gerhard, Herman, Hepner, Heim,

---

[10] J. T. Elliot was a leading member of Section 26 in Philadelphia which belonged to the Prince Street Council of the Woodhull group.—Schlüter, *Die Internationale in Amerika*, pp. 152, 167. See also Barry below, pp. 266–67.

Joannard, Marx, Kugelman, Lessner, Lucain, Lafargue, Le Moussu, Milke, Pihl, Ranvier, Roche, Swarm, Sauva, Sorge, Scheu, Seraillier, Sexton, Schumacher, Splingard, Walther, Wroblewsky, van den Hout, van den Abeel, Vaillant, Vichard, Dietzgen, Dumont, McDonnell, and Vilmot.
The following abstained from voting: Eccarius, Guillaume, Harcourt, Mottershead, Schwitzguebel, Farga Pelicer, Morago, Alerini, and Marcelau.—
Thus, West's mandate is invalidated with 49 Nays against no Ayes, and 9 abstentions.
The Spaniards abstain from voting until the voting procedure is regulated; for the rest, they themselves have already passed similar resolutions.
Harcourt has not understood the question.
Eccarius states that he has had and still has business relations with the secessionists; he himself stands accused in this matter and the letters to the General Council are lies. In Germany Sorge accused him of intrigues, and yet Sorge himself is the very cause of the dispute as he [Eccarius] intends to prove.
Mottershead has abstained from voting because of Barry's mandate.
Roche [has abstained] because, according to the first, [i.e.,] Brismée's resolution, half the members of the General Council would have to resign.
Guillaume [has abstained] because West was not permitted to speak again; for the rest, he feels reassured by Eccarius' statement.—
Schwitzguebel still lacks sufficient information.
It is moved to refer the Alliance affair to a committee to be discussed in closed session. Upon Seraillier's suggestion it is resolved to take this up in the evening session at seven o'clock and to hold a public meeting the next day.
The meeting adjourns at about 4:00 P.M.

The evening session is opened at 7:30. The roll call shows that thirteen members are absent.
Sorge moves to proceed at once with the election of the bureau. Dupont requests that the minutes be read. The chairman deems this unnecessary—and he says that West has no right to be present.

Sorge requests precedence for his motion. [This is] unanimously carried.

The Credentials Committee announces the receipt of a mandate for the delegates of the Jura Federation.

Sorge insists that the bureau be elected.

Herman nominates Brismée, Gerhard, and Dupont.

Hepner nominates Ranvier, Sorge, and Gerhard.

Gerhard declines.

Vilmot requests separate voting for each of the three presidents; Fränkel, a single vote for all three. Fränkel's motion is carried.

In the vote which now follows Ranvier is elected president, Gerhard and Dupont vice-presidents.

Dupont declines in favor of Brismée. Brismée does not accept it, and Sorge is elected vice-president by acclamation.

Upon Kugelmann's suggestion, the president on behalf of the assembly gives thanks to his predecessor, and he (Ranvier) accepts the chairmanship as an honor, not for himself but for the Section Ferré, for the city of Paris, for the Commune.

Cuno, Fränkel, Eccarius, Vilmot, Dave, van den Abeel, Marcelau, and Alerini are elected translators for the various languages.[11]

Upon Sorge's motion the previous secretaries are confirmed by acclamation except Roche who is replaced by McDonnell for the English language, and Marcelau becomes secretary for the Spanish language.

Van den Abeel has notified the press of a public meeting to be held at ten o'clock next morning and that seats will be reserved for the press. The Congress gives its approval.

The Dutch Federal Council invites the Congress for a meeting in Amsterdam at the end of the Congress. [The invitation] is put aside for later discussion.

Joannard requests a closed session for 8:00 A.M. and tickets of admission in order to avoid scandal.

Van den Hout says that various communications have been received from public authorities.

Gerhard demands that one guilder be collected for admission.

---

[11] "The various recording secretaries appointed were as follows: for French, Lemoussu; for English, J. P. McDonnell; for Spanish, Marcelau; for German, Hepner; for Dutch, Van den Hout."—Barry, p. 269.

Friedländer protests against this. Eccarius suggests leaving the matter to the party comrades from The Hague, which is accepted, and the business of the day is taken up.—

J. Ph. Becker and comrades move to discuss at once the powers of the General Council, the selection of its seat, the meeting-place of the next congress, and the revision of the rules.

Sauva wishes first to hear the report of the General Council and to question it; he has many questions to ask the General Council. Moreover, the General Council is to be elected.

Lafargue supports Becker's motion, as the reports, interpellations, etc., are matters for a closed session. And the Germans, who have to leave for Mainz, must have an opportunity [to attend a closed session].

Scheu, who has signed the motion, says that the request [of the Germans] is true to the cause, for the German Labor Congress is important and the Social Democratic Labor party of Germany is a branch of the I.W.A.[12] Give us a chance to do justice to our mandates!—

Brismée [suggests] taking up the rules first, because there might be no General Council left. The Belgians do not wish an increase but a decrease of powers for the General Council; otherwise they would reunite and take measures like the Spaniards, Italians, Swiss, etc. He says, further, that the General Council has not interfered in the affairs of the Belgians, that the Belgians have not complained against the General Council; the American, Spanish, and other stories show, however, that the General Council has too much power and must be deprived of the right to interfere in the internal affairs of a country.

J. Ph. Becker sides with Scheu but is of the opinion that there is a

[12] On September 8, 1872, the Fourth Congress of the *Sozialdemokratische Arbeiterpartei*, the party of Bebel and Liebknecht, was held at Mainz. There were fifty-five delegates present. Bebel, Liebknecht, and Hepner, the editors of the Leipzig *Volksstaat*, had been tried for high treason in March, 1872. Bebel and Liebknecht had been condemned to two years' fortress imprisonment. Bebel received in addition a nine-month jail term for *lèse majesté*. The strength of the organization is indicated by the fact that at the Congress at Dresden in August, 1871, 6,255 members at 81 places were represented by 56 delegates. See Dr. R. Meyer, *Der Emancipationskampf des vierten Standes* (Berlin, 1882), Vol. I, pp. 269 f.

wrong order of business. Sauva's request for the report goes without saying, but the most urgent business is to define the position of the General Council; this must be settled first, as was done twice before. Also we hope to speed up the Congress by this motion. Thus, there are excellent reasons [for the motion]; besides, almost all German delegates are deputies to the Mainz Congress and we certainly should note this fact.

Morago protests that he is not given the floor. Guillaume demands that Morago be permitted to speak.

Hepner explains the motion requesting priority for the most urgent business. Indeed, the opponents should be all the more for it so that they can soon present their charges against the General Council. All year long they had been grumbling and now people would like to hear what they actually are after.

The discussion is closed and the motion of Becker and comrades is carried with a large majority (41 votes).—

The motion of the Spanish delegates is read and submitted for debate; it requests that the Congress henceforth vote by numbers of members represented. Morago supports the motion, [saying that] it would change the voting procedure in a democratic way; they [the Spanish delegates] are instructed not to vote before such a reform has been accepted, lest a delegate of 100 members have as much power as he who represents 2,000 members.—

Engels speaks against it because it represents a change of the rules and hence is now not in order; for the rest, as a pan-German he is for it because it is done that way in Germany; it is not our fault that the Spanish delegates find themselves in such a sorry situation (not to be able to vote); the instruction, by the way, was not given by the federation but by the Spanish Federal Council.

Herman says the Belgians make the same demand as the Spaniards.

Hepner calls attention to the fact that the Congress has just resolved to give certain matters priority and hence must proceed according to the order of the day. Vilmot is opposed.

The president announces that we have to leave the hall because of the advanced hour (11:30).

The urgency of the motion of the Spanish delegates is rejected with 7 votes against a large majority.

Guillaume says that the Jurassians will no longer vote.

The president explains that the rules are not the work of the General Council but of the I.W.A., hence these attacks are directed not against the General Council but against the International.

A closed session is announced for 8:00 A.M. The meeting adjourns after midnight.—

Thursday, September 5, the meeting cannot be called to order at 8:00 A.M. because there is no list of delegates on hand. After some time business begins; the president announces the agenda for the public meeting and communications received.

Guillaume requests that a committee be formed which should compare the original Langrand letter with the printed version in the bulletin of the Jurassian Federation.

Marx declares that Langrand's letter is replete with lies and insults. Le Moussu is against appointing a committee because the Jurassians by publishing the letter have aided and abetted these infamies and lies.

Marx, Joannard, and Lafargue are nominated for such a committee. A telegram is received from Geneva protesting the genuineness of the mandate of the Section de propagande et d'action revolutionaire; a letter is to follow. Joukowski says that the undersigned of the wire are not members of his section.

Engels protests against West's presence in the hall and relates West's utterance that he (West) would have access to the Congress in any case, "if not through the door, then through the window; if not through the window, then through the chimney." West is made to withdraw.

The motion signed by many to form a committee to investigate the Alliance is taken up for discussion.

Sorge proposes that a committee of five members be elected for this purpose, and that the meeting be adjourned for five minutes.—

Marx announces that the report of the General Council is meant for the public only as the General Council must not report about various national organizations, and several federations, for instance, the Jura Federation, have not met their obligations concerning reports, so that the General Council was not even able to give an accurate report. He mentions that the North American Federation is the only one which has carefully met all obligations concerning reports, payment of dues, etc. He adds the wish that a decision be made concerning public and closed sessions.—

As regards Sorge's motion, Guillaume remarks that the minority thus far has not succeeded in getting a single member on a committee and demands that the members of the Alliance be permitted to designate *one* member of the investigating committee. It is granted, and after consultation with the Spaniards Guillaume announces that R. Splingard is elected by them for this. Marx points out that in order to save time-consuming translations only French-speaking persons should be chosen for the committee.

In the following vote Cuno, Splingard, Walther, Lucain, and Vichard are elected as members of the Committee of Inquiry into the affairs of the "Alliance."

Alerini and Guillaume move that a committee of five neutral members be appointed to investigate the charges against the General Council and its "underground operations" (Leipziger *Hochverrats-prozess*).

Sorge is in favor of it if Eccarius, too, may be investigated in this connection.

Moussu wants this committee to be not elected but appointed by *the accusers themselves*.

Upon Guillaume's motion this investigation, too, is referred ([with] 14 against 4 votes) to the Committee of Inquiry into the Alliance; an intermission is now made to prepare for the public meeting.—

The public meeting is called to order shortly after ten o'clock. A large public fills the reserved rooms; numerous reporters of Dutch and foreign papers occupy the gallery, and the roll call of the delegates shows only three absentees.

The president gives a speech in which he first states the familiar reasons why no general congress could be held during the two previous years, and then discusses the attitude of the I.W.A. to the Commune. He defends the Commune against the usual attacks and demonstrates that the reproaches and charges against the Commune must be laid at the door of the Versailles [government] and gives praise to those countries which have offered asylum to the fugitive Communards and have duly rejected the perfidious extradition demand of the infamous J. Favre. He gives praise also to the Netherlands and concludes with "Long live the International!"

The invitation of the Dutch Federal Council to a get-together in Amsterdam is read and, upon Lafargue's motion, is reserved for discussion in closed session.—

Sexton now reads the report of the General Council in the English, Longuet in the French, and Marx in the German language; van den Abeel then translates it into Dutch. The report describes especially the persecutions to which the I.W.A. is subjected everywhere, in Austria, France, Spain, Germany, Denmark, and elsewhere; [it describes] how the existence of the I.W.A. is viewed in all countries as irreconcilable with modern institutions and is therefore regarded as high treason; how this new conception of justice has spread from Vienna almost across the entire continent; how the I.W.A., the representative of labor, has become all the stronger and has recently gained ground especially in Ireland, Denmark, Holland, Portugal, Australia, New Zealand, and Buenos Aires. The great advance of the proletarian movement is most obvious from the fact that it took years before the workers of the different countries understood the June struggle (1848); but now they hailed the Commune at once in all lands.—

The report of the General Council is unanimously accepted, always with the stereotypic abstention of the Spaniards.

A motion is submitted and unanimously carried to express our sympathy for the persecuted members of the labor party in all countries, and to extend our brotherly greeting to all suffering friends in France, Germany, Denmark, etc.

Upon Brismée's proposal it is resolved to hold closed sessions during the day, and public meetings in the evening.

Sorge now moves an intermission of fifteen minutes, Joannard one of at least one hour. Brismée speaks for Sorge's motion. Joannard's amendment is accepted.

Cuno gives a personal declaration against the former Prussian Consul Schramm at Milan and threatens to call him a cowardly thief unless he will answer him after the meeting.[13]

The Congress of the Geneva Federation sends a congratulatory

---

[13] For this Schramm incident, see Barry's report below, pp. 274 f.

wire, and d'Osten sends a greeting to his comrades of the Commune. The roll call is read and the session adjourns at three o'clock.

At 4:15 the public meeting is reopened with a roll call. Dietzgen announces his departure in writing. Scheu, too, has left.
President Ranvier reads parts of a memorandum of the Section Ferré of Paris which is sharply worded against Bonaparte, Bakunin, Malon, Gaspar Richard, Blanc, and others, as well as against the federation which offers place and shelter, etc., to such elements. Vilmot objects to consideration of this letter, and Guillaume to linking such honorable names as those of Bakunin and Malon to those of such scoundrels as Richard, Blanc, etc.—
Longuet speaks against Vilmot's objections and the Congress takes up the business of the day.—
A resolution is submitted by Arnoud, Cournet, Dereure, Le Moussu, Ranvier, and Vaillant which objects to the abstention from politics and demands that the militant organization of the revolutionary forces of the proletariat and of the political struggle be placed on the agenda of the next congress, and that the General Council be instructed to prepare a comprehensive statement of the question for the next congress.—
Upon Dupont's motion it is resolved to form a committee which shall examine and report on all documents addressed to the Congress. Dupont, Hepner, Fränkel, Dereure, Lafargue, and Brismée are elected to this committee. Herman takes the floor to comment on the agenda, the discussion of the General Council and its powers, and he expresses the view of the majority of the Belgians who wish to retain a General Council but wish to divest it of all power.
Opposed to Herman's comments, Lafargue demands first a vote on the question of whether or not the General Council shall continue to exist.
Dave opposes Lafargue and supports Herman. Longuet requests first a general debate with two [speakers] for and two against the proposal, then special discussion.
Dupont requests the ordinary procedure, which is accepted, whereupon Lafargue speaks for the institution of the General Council, the need for which he attempts to deduce from the economic and social conditions, and he concludes with the statement of the Portu-

guese: "If we had no General Council we would promptly have to invent one!"

Guillaume takes the floor and says that two great ideas run side by side in the movement, that of centralization of power in the hands of a few, and that of the free federation of those whom the homogeneity of the economic conditions in each country has united behind the idea of common interests in all countries. The movement cannot represent the conception of a single brain. For the leadership of the movement there is required no General Council with authority. We want no authority and we in the Jura Federation have none. We speak from experience. Do we need the General Council in the economic struggle (guerre, etc.)? Has it ever organized or conducted a class war? Do we need a General Council for the political struggle? Thus far, the General Council has never built barricades and it will never build any. Of what use has it been anywhere? If it is asked: "Does the I.W.A. require no head?" we answer, "No."

Sorge replies to Guillaume: we, too, have had experiences and we would like to see what the Jurassians have accomplished with these ideas. What results have they to show? Guillaume says that they have no authority in the Jura Federation. If only they hadn't had the authority to publish the lying, infamous letter of Langrand! If the General Council has been of no use during strikes he would like to draw his attention to the case of the Paris bronzeworkers, the English machinists, the New York sewing-machine operators who quickly recognized the advantage of such international ties.[14] Even

[14] From the beginning the International had here and there intervened in strike situations. In 1866 it intervened in a tailors' strike in Edinburgh to hinder the importation of Dutch and Danish workers. In 1867 a collection was made among the members in support of striking bronzeworkers in Paris. In 1868 the building workers of Geneva were on strike, demanding an eleven-hour day and higher wages. They sent a delegation to London to seek the advice and assistance of the General Council of the I.W.A. In 1869 a strike in the Belgian iron industry was put down by troops. There was some bloodshed and the I.W.A. published a manifesto on "The Belgian Massacres." An appeal was made to "the workers of Europe and America" for contributions to aid the families of the victims. Given the chronic lack of funds of the International, given the fact that it had no hold over broad masses, and that on the Continent incipient labor organizations were harassed, such trade union activities could be but modest beginnings. For the British Trade Union members, engaging in such activities was what the International was

if the General Council is no general, it should at least be a general staff to line up and organize the cadres. If Guillaume wishes to have the I.W.A. without a head, he reduces us to animal organisms of the lowest order. We wish to have not only a head, but a head with plenty of brains, and when our enemies shoot with cannons we do not wish to counter with peas.

Morago says he would be in favor of abolishing the General Council, merely retaining a center for correspondence and statistics. The Spanish Federation is absolutely autonomous and demands the true, free, autonomous I.W.A. The General Council should have no power whatever, neither over sections nor over federations. The number of members of the General Council matters less to us. If the Congress wishes to give still *more* power to the General Council, the Spanish Federation will not stand for any impositions, as it is free and autonomous and will not tolerate any domination. Those who wish to augment the power of the General Council will have to bear the consequences.—

Seraillier and Dupont propose to postpone the public meeting until tomorrow at 6:00 P.M.; this is accepted. [The meeting] closed at eleven o'clock.

Friday, September 6, the meeting is opened at 9:00 A.M. with a roll call which shows that seven are absent.

Walther, on behalf of the investigating committee, requests that they be permitted to withdraw in order to begin work. This is accepted.

Sorge, Becker, and comrades introduce a motion of precedence that the rules concerning the powers of the General Council be discussed at once by one speaker each, for and against, for five minutes after which the vote should be taken.

Dave requests that the minutes be read; Dupont [demands] a closed meeting for this purpose.

Van den Abeel objects to the motion [of Sorge]; Vaillant defends it by stating that we came here in order to improve the organization and hence must set to work on it. Sorge's motion is accepted with 34 against 4 votes.

---

meant to do and no more. For Marx, these struggles, though important, were only the beginning, pointing toward the formation of class consciousness, international solidarity, and devotion to the cause of proletarian revolution.

Minutes of the Fifth General Congress

Now the precedence of the following resolution, submitted by the same members, comes up for discussion:

General Rules. General Council.

Article 2: The General Council is bound to execute the Congress resolutions and to see to it that in every country the principles, rules, and general regulations of the I.W.A. are strictly observed. Article 6: The General Council also has the right to suspend branches, sections, federal councils, or committees and federations of the I.W.A. until the next congress.

In the case of a section belonging to a federation, however, [the General Council] will exercise this right only after having asked the advice of the respective federal council.

In the case of the dissolution of a federal council or committee the General Council shall call at once upon the sections of the respective federation to elect a new federal council or committee within thirty days.

In the case of the suspension of an entire federation the General Council shall immediately inform all other federations thereof.

Upon request of the majority of the federations the General Council shall convoke an extraordinary conference, consisting of one delegate of each nationality, which is to meet within a month and will render a final verdict.

It is hereby understood that those countries in which the I.W.A. is forbidden shall exercise the same rights as the regular federations.

Ph. Becker [pleads] for prompt consideration [of the motion]. He says that we really have no need to discuss it further since we already resolved this before; we should feel pangs of conscience for not having resolved or carried out anything by today, the fifth day; even the so-called opposition could not accept the reproach that it engages in opposition for opposition's sake. The [motion] at hand is the main thing; once this is settled we would soon be done with the rest; we all feel the need to go home soon, and our purse certainly is a reminder.—

Vaillant, too, speaks for this; we must get down to business, not indulge in speech-making; first we must settle this main issue, then we may take up the questions of politics and of raising the dues.

Brismée says that it is futile to discuss the powers of the General Council; we (the Belgians) do not wish the General Council to have any power; this is a question of principle about which we in

Belgium all agree; the delegates of the Vesdre valley even demand complete abolition of the General Council; we demand that the General Council be merely the clerk of the I.W.A. and must never interfere in the internal affairs of a country.—

In Longuet's opinion the people cannot be everywhere and must have deputies to perform certain functions which not everybody can perform. [In his eyes] Flues, who demands the complete abolition of the General Council, is more consistent than Brismée since for the tasks which Brismée wishes to leave to it no General Council is needed, for they could very well be taken care of without it.—

Guillaume says: we have already expressed our views and shall not discuss such resolutions; I therefore request a vote at once; may the majority have the courage to come fully into the open; for the rest, he believes that many of the delegates do not represent anybody.—

Seraillier states that he is not tied down here like Guillaume and comrades who are in prior agreement, since they accepted instructions, to withdraw or to vote in a certain manner.

He [Seraillier] throws Guillaume's words back upon him; he declares and offers to prove that he represents France which is better organized now in thirty departments than under the Empire; he fully recognizes the congressional resolutions about politics and the actions of the General Council.

Closure of discussion is accepted with all but five votes.

Sauva believes that one speaker for and one against do not represent all opinions.—

Article 2, cited above, comes up for discussion.

Morago states that the General Council may interpret the congressional resolutions, rules, etc., as it sees fit and that there are no means to check the General Council; what guarantee is available against possible excesses of the General Council? We consider the resolution dangerous and are against conceding any power to the General Council as we refuse to be ruled by anyone.—

Lafargue declares that Morago's argument against the powers of the General Council could likewise be advanced against individual sections which in countries where the I.W.A. is prohibited are occasionally recruited from among spies and police agents; if Morago rants so much against possible despotism of the General Council, I must say to him that his conduct here is most tyrannical as he and his associates demand that [the others] give in, threatening they will withdraw otherwise.—

Article 2 is read and accepted with 40 Ayes, five Nays, and 11 abstentions.—

Dumont requests a vote of censure for the absentees.

Van den Hout criticizes the imperative mandates and wishes that the majority would make greater concessions to the minority.—

The aforementioned Article 6 is taken up.

Sauva says that it has been erroneously maintained here (by Sorge) that the French in the United States favor an increase of power for the General Council; they only wish to retain the General Council; his instructions are that the General Council should have the right to suspend sections and federations only in congressionally stipulated cases, not otherwise.—

Herman attempts to cite cases in which the right of suspension had unpleasant results.—

Marx says: We demand these powers not for ourselves but for the future General Council; we would rather abolish the General Council than follow Brismée's wish and transform it into a letter box; in that case the leadership of the association would fall into the hands of journalists, that is, mainly non-workers.—

He wonders how the Jura Federation (the abstractionists) [15] could support Section 12 which wished to turn the association into an instrument and tool in support of a bourgeois policy; if one disbelievingly smiles about police sections, one should realize that such have been formed in France, Austria, and elsewhere; the General Council was asked by Austrians not to recognize any section which is not founded by delegates of the General Council or the existing [Austrian] organization; Vesinier and comrades, recently expelled from the ranks of the French refugees, are of course for the Jura Federation. The Belgian Federal Council has been as severely attacked before the General Council as any other [group] for abuses of power, nepotism, etc., and indeed by Belgian workers; the respective letters are on hand; fellows like Vesinier, Landeck, and their like might first form a federal council, then afterwards a federation; Bismarck agents might do likewise; therefore the General Council

[15] This should probably read "abstentionists," referring to the Anarchists' policy of nonparticipation in parliamentary elections.

must have the right to dissolve or suspend a federal council or a federation; then follows the appeal to the sections which sometimes may be quite appropriate in order to decide by popular vote whether a federal council still expresses the will of the people; in Austria windbags, ultra-radicals and *agents provocateurs* formed sections in order to compromise the I.W.A.; in France a police commandant formed a section; nevertheless, the Association is best off where it is prohibited, for persecution always produces this result; the General Council, even now, could suspend an entire federation by suspending one section after another; in the case of the suspension of a federal council or a federation the General Council promptly risks criticism and censure, and hence it will exercise the right of suspension only in cases of greatest emergency; however, whether we concede and ascribe to the General Council the prerogatives of a Negro Prince or Russian Tsar, its power is nought once it ceases to represent the majority of the I.W.A.; the General Council has no army, no budget, but only a moral force and always will be impotent unless it has the consent of the entire Association.

Lafargue says the General Council has been accused of having called the Congress to The Hague, in order to secure a majority there; one should just watch how the Dutch always vote with the Belgians against the General Council in order to understand how well prepared the General Council was.

Dave asks why the Congress was called to The Hague.

Marx says that it was done at the suggestion of the Belgians (Brismée confirms this).

Guillaume declares that the Jura Federal Council is the editorial committee of the Bulletin and as such responsible to the federation.—

In the vote which now follows Article 6 as above is adopted with 36 Ayes against 6 Nays and 15 abstentions.—

Vaillant, Arnoud, and Cournet now move to consider the article concerning political action of the working class and increased dues.—

The English delegates lodge a joint protest against the chair for not honoring their right to speak and reproach the French delegates for monopolizing the discussion and for attaining their objective by agility and vehemence.—

Minutes of the Fifth General Congress

The chairman, Ranvier, says that the English have no one to blame but themselves if they are always too late in requesting the floor and promises to have the English translation always given first from now on, which the English delegates accept as satisfactory.— Longuet proposes to place the article concerning the political action of the working class on the agenda of the public meeting.— Consul-General Schramm appears and his protestations cause great unrest until Cuno withdraws with him.— Schwitzguebel requests consideration of the Spanish motion for a change of the voting procedure.— Engels, Marx, and other members of the former General Council propose that the seat of the General Council for the year 1872–1873 be transferred to New York and that the General Council should consist of the following members of the New York Federal Council: Kavanagh, St. Clair, Cetti, Levièle, Laurel, Bertrand, Bolte, and Carl, with the right to increase their number up to a total of fifteen.[16] Joannard argues against London as the future seat of the General Council, but Engels' motion has no precedence and he himself is undecided as to where the General Council should be transferred.— Ranvier proposes the following agenda for the public meeting in the evening: completion of yesterday's business, voting procedure, and third, the political action of the working class. This is accepted; Engels takes the floor [to speak] for the motion of transferring the General Council to New York. The General Council has until now always been in London because only there could it be international,

---

[16] The motion was drafted by Marx in French and reads in English: "We propose that the General Council be moved to New York for the year 1872/73 and that it consist of the following members of the North American Federal Council: Kavanagh, St. Clair, Cetti, Levièle, Laurel, F. J. Bertrand, F. Bolte, and C. Carl. They shall be entitled to add to their number; total membership of the General Council, however, should never exceed fifteen. The Hague, September 6, 1872
>   Signatures: Karl Marx, F. Engels, Geo. Sexton, W. Wroblewsky, Ch. Longuet, A. Serraillier, J. P. McDonnell, Eugene Dupont, F. Lessner, Le Moussu, M. Maltman Barry."
(A facsimile reproduction is to be found in Schlüter, *Die Internationale in Amerika*, pp. 136 ff.) This surprise move of Marx's to "ditch the International," as Daniel Bell put it, came like a bombshell. The dramatic move is brought out by Barry (see below, p. 279 ff.). The writer of the Minutes, a Marxist, was possibly surprised.

there alone papers and documents could be perfectly safe. In New York our papers are at least as safe as in London and in no other place in Europe are they equally safe, not even in Geneva or Brussels as has been shown by certain events. Party frictions have become so bad in London that the seat must be moved. Besides, the allegations and accusations against the General Council have become so vehement and continuous that most of its former members are tired of it and are decided not to accept office again. He can definitely state this, for instance, for Karl Marx and himself. Besides, the former General Council was by no means always unanimous. To this all members could testify. The General Council has been at one place for eight years now and it is a good idea to move it in order to prevent a certain ossification. For similar reasons Marx moved as early as 1870 to transfer the General Council to Brussels, but at that time all federations declared themselves for its continuation in London.— Where should the General Council be moved? To Brussels? The Belgians themselves declare this impossible because there is no security for them there. To Geneva? The Genevans object firmly, partly for the same reason as the people from Brussels, and point to the *Affair Outine*. Thus no other place remains than New York.

There our papers are safe, there we have a loyal, strong organization, there our party is truly international as nowhere else in the world. One should, for instance, look at the New York Federal Council, consisting of Irish, Frenchmen, Germans, Italians, and Swedes, and soon [it] will count among its members native Americans also. The objection that New York is too far away is not sound because it will be a certain advantage for the European federations which jealously [defend themselves] against interferences of the General Council in their internal affairs; this distance will make such interference more difficult and will prevent individual federations from attaining undue influence in the General Council; and for the rest, the General Council has the right and perhaps even the duty to delegate authority in Europe in certain cases and countries as the General Council has until now always done.—

Vaillant takes a stand against transfer to New York; he admits that next to London, New York would be the best place for the General Council; at present, however, dissensions in America are too great and one part of the organization is even entangled in bourgeois politics; New York is too far from the scene of action, too remote from those countries where the I.W.A. is prohibited and therefore is best off (Austria, Hungary, France, Germany). Although he feels it regrettable and a great loss that so many proved men resign and no longer wish to serve on the General Council, still there are so many good internationalists in London that one could easily elect a regular General Council there.—

Sauva speaks for a change of place and personnel of the General Council, but is still undecided whether New York is the best place; [he is] for New York, however, if he has to choose between London and New York; he is against co-optation (supplementing) of members [by the General Council]; the Congress itself should elect the complete General Council but not give it into the hands of a group of people who with excellent intentions (he says this repeatedly) have done great harm; the North American Federal Council with the best intentions cannot do away with personalities, and it represents authoritarianism at least as strongly as, nay, even more so than, the former General Council.—

Closure of the discussion is accepted.

Seraillier requests that the Engels-Marx motion be divided into three parts: 1. Should the General Council be transferred? 2. Where? 3. The election of its members. Vilmot wishes only two divisions. Seraillier's proposal is accepted.—

The first question, Should the seat of the General Council be moved? is voted in the affirmative with 26 Ayes against 23 Nays. Marcelau complains that people laugh when he and his comrades abstain from voting; they have definite instructions to do so.

Ranvier [says] that he has nothing against the delegates but he objects to the strange mandate that brings them into such a peculiar situation.

Alerini says that they freely accepted this mandate and fully approve of it.—

Farga-Pelicer and Alerini move to transfer the General Council to Brussels and to have it consist of two persons for each federation, elected by them [the federations] and responsible only to the federations.—

The vote on the question, Where shall the General Council be moved? results in 31 votes for New York, 14 for London, 1 for Barcelona, 11 abstentions.[17]

Cuno reads a statement from former Consul-General Schramm in which the latter apologizes and [says he] will not mind Cuno's intemperate remark because he is not the person mentioned by Cuno. Engels requests that a committee of one member per federation be formed to audit the financial affairs of the General Council. This is deferred to the public meeting and the meeting adjourns until six o'clock in the evening.

Public meeting at 6:00 P.M.[18] The roll call shows two absent.
Vaillant demands that the discussion of the General Council be closed as it would be quite useless after the resolutions passed in the executive meeting.
Hepner asks whether no reply may be given to what was said yesterday. He and Heim request the floor for this purpose.
Van den Hout addresses a speech to the public in which he refutes with great ardor the insinuations and lies of the *Haager Dagblad*.[19]—
The chairman then reads the resolutions of the morning session concerning the General Council, its powers and its seat.—
Cuno reads the letter of excuse of Consul-General Schramm and publicly withdraws his statement made against him the previous day.—
Guillaume requests a discussion of the voting procedure.
Joannard moves that this take place in a closed meeting, which is accepted by the assembly; then the new paragraphs of the Rules concerning the political action of the working class are submitted for discussion. [The motion is] to insert the following paragraphs between paragraphs 7 and 8 of the General Rules:

"In the struggle against the united power of the propertied classes the proletariat can appear and act as a class only by constituting itself as a separate political party in contrast to all old political parties formed by the propertied classes.

[17] See Barry's comments, p. 281.

[18] Barry gives some idea of the audience situation (see below, p. 282).

[19] Possibly this is a reference to the *Dagblad voor Zuidholland en's Graven-hage*, which demanded that the Dutch government prohibit the Congress.

"This position of the proletariat as a political party is indispensable in order to insure the triumph of the social revolution and its supreme good, the abolition of classes.

"The association of the labor forces already attained in economic struggles must in the hands of this class also serve as a lever in its struggle against the political power of its exploiters.

"As the landlords and capitalists always use their political privileges in order to defend and perpetuate their economic monopolies and to subjugate labor,—so the conquest of political power becomes the great duty and task of the proletariat."

Vaillant pleads for insertion of these resolutions into the Rules. Force is used against us and force can only be driven out by force; the economic struggle must become one with the political struggle, and in the revolution [it] must consummate the abolition of classes through the proletarian dictatorship. We have against us the abstentionists in two divisions; 1. the abstentionists out of ignorance and 2. the abstentionists for reasons of politics who live off politics, who shout and scream and today sit in Versailles; but there is a Versailles everywhere, not merely in France. We must form a party of our own against all parties of the ruling and propertied classes without any connection with the bourgeois classes; even in the Inaugural Address political action of the working class was recommended, and the General Council has never turned from this duty; the London Conference understood this truth perfectly well and assumed the responsibility for the Commune, and the proletarians everywhere adhered to [the Commune].

Hepner [says he] believed that all internationalists understand this question; last night two great ideas were mentioned, those of centralization and of federation, the latter finding expression in abstention. Abstention from political action leads to the police bureau; this was experienced in Germany. This Bakuninist party in Germany [20] was the *Allgemeine Deutsche Arbeiterverein* under Herr von Schweitzer, and Herr von Schweitzer was a notorious police agent. At the outbreak of the war [Franco-Prussian war of 1870] these

[20] Hepner's charges against the "Lassalleans" are unwarranted and reflect the competitive resentment which existed between the two groups, the "Marxists" and the "Lassalleans," before their fusion into the Social Democratic party.

people were highly patriotic; whereas we remained neutral and shouted not only, "Down with Napoleon!" but also, "Down with Bismarck!" our Swiss opponents vilified us as traitors and smashed our windows; that is the result of political abstention; only after the annexation of Alsace and Lorraine did they begin to understand the error of their chauvinism; what comes of political abstention? That with our hands in our pockets we look on complacently as a revolution is made in France, a political action takes place. The international movement knows no political abstention.—There has been talk of the imposition of certain doctrines. None has been imposed upon us. Just name one! If you give no answer you are mere troublemakers. From time to time the General Council released manifestoes, and who among us has not hailed these manifestoes with joy? After having disseminated the address on the *Civil War in France* in more than 4,000 copies in the *Volksstaat*, we issued a separate edition of over 8,000 copies. The German workers welcome such manifestoes of experienced men and proved party comrades; there is talk against authority; we, too, are against all abuse of power; but some authority, some prestige will always be necessary to give cohesion to the party; if they were consistent these so-called antiauthoritarians would have to abolish also the federal councils, committees, federations, and the very sections, since more or less authority is exercised everywhere; they would have to establish absolute anarchy, i.e., reduce the militant international (International Militans) into a narrow-minded, sleepy party of Philistines.

After the Commune, how can one still speak against authority? We German workers, at least, hold that the Commune was overthrown mainly for want of authority and its usage. What curious logic the antiauthoritarians have, by the way! Guillaume accuses the General Council of having done nothing in the economic and political struggle, of not using authority, and in the same breath he demands the abolition of the General Council for its use of excessive authority. Furthermore, the nonsense of the antiauthoritarians shows up glaringly in the charge against the General Council of not having made a revolution. Are these good people so unscientific as to believe that one can make revolutions? Do they still not know that revolutions arise only in a natural way and are stages of historical development? Have these people not even surpassed the barricadology?—

In the course of the translations the public becomes impatient and noisy. Guillaume demands that the hall be cleared (calls of "very authoritarian").

Sorge moves to suspend the session until the hall is cleared. People quiet down again somewhat and Guillaume replies [as follows]:

There is a misunderstanding among us; I have to explain this here for myself and on behalf of my colleagues; it was already obvious at Basel. We take the stand which Hins took at Brussels when he declared we do not wish to mix with present-day governments, in parliamentarianism; we wish to overthrow (*aplatir*) all governments. Unfortunately we allowed ourselves to be called abstentionists, an ill-chosen phrase of Proudhon's. We are adherents of a definite policy, of social revolution, of the destruction of bourgeois politics, of the state; Hepner spoke of the loyalty of the German workers to the General Council and its manifestoes; this is quite natural, for they represented the views of the special party of German Socialists but not of other countries.—The reproach that the Commune has not been sufficiently authoritarian may be answered by the Communards; in France abstention has been preached by Proudhon and Longuet (loud interruptions: Gaspar Richard and Blanc!); to Hepner's reproach that the abstentionists in Germany are chauvinists he answers that with them in Switzerland the political activists and the voters for the *Grossrat* are flirting and cooperating with the bourgeoisie, and that they are quite nationalistically and patriotically minded people. He will say more on this later; the resolutions under discussion contain phrases based upon the Communist Manifesto; he reads its ten demands; he asks whether that is not identical with what they demanded at Basel (he is asked to read on); they see in this the reason for the conquest of political power, "the seizure of the state, of state power," in order to become bourgeoisie themselves! We reject the seizure of political power in the state but demand the complete destruction of the state as the expression of political power.

Marx reproaches the Flemish translator (van den Abeel).

Longuet says that Guillaume has not read Proudhon and many other Socialists whom he attacks daily; he describes the condition of the proletariat upon Proudhon's return to Paris. The proletariat simply had no political organization at all and constituted only the tail of the bourgeois intriguers; that is why it happened that, on September 4, 1870, power fell into the hands of the June butchers, of the irredeemable bourgeoisie; hence, Proudhon in 1863 had to preach to the workers abstention from politics, for the only other policy would have been to arm themselves; later the I.W.A. provided us with the means to debate the economic question; had we been better organized as a political party, J. Favre and his like would not have gained control and the Commune would not have been proclaimed and victorious in Paris alone, but also in Berlin and elsewhere; Hepner, however, errs in ascribing the fall of the Commune to the lack of authority; the Commune fell for want of organization, of political organization;— [21]

What is to become of Guillaume's collectivism without some centralization of forces? Because of the economic struggle the workers must organize into a political party lest nothing remain of the International, and Guillaume, whose master is Bakunin, cannot belong to the I.W.A. while holding such views.—

There is renewed unrest during the translations; a vote concerning the new article of the Rules is demanded; Joannard makes noise and the disturbances become so bad that the chairman closes the meeting at 11:00 P.M.

On Saturday, September 7, the meeting is opened at 9:30 A.M. A letter is read in which the chairman, Ranvier, informs us of his departure.

Upon the resolve of the assembly Sorge takes the chair and first reads letters from B. Becker, Schumacher, Arnoud, Barry, Cournet, Heim, Lessner, Sexton, Vaillant, who announce their departure, and almost all express the request to register their vote in favor of the new article of the Rules, the election of a General Council, etc.

A congratulatory telegram is received from Giessen.

The Congress takes up the third point of Seraillier's motion accepted on the previous day, the election of a new General Council.

[21] This remark of Longuet's is paralleled by Marx's statement at the Amsterdam meeting later to the effect that the Commune of Paris "was doomed to fall because a great revolutionary movement connected with this great rebellion of the Paris proletariat failed to be started simultaneously in all capitals, in Berlin, Madrid, etc." Cf. "Amsterdam Meetings of the First International in 1872," *Bulletin of the International Institute of Social History, Amsterdam* (Leiden, 1951), Vol. VI, p. 4. Cf. also Dr. R. Meyer, *Der Emancipationskampf des vierten Standes*, Vol. I, pp. 160 f. See Barry (p. 282) for somewhat more "color."

Sauva speaks against the proposal to elect eight members of the North American Federal Council as General Council; he repeats his previous statements and asserts that there is a German majority in this federal council. (Sorge interrupts him with: "That is not true!")

Sorge cedes the chair to J. Ph. Becker and proves through Sauva's and Dereure's own statements that there are only three Germans in the North American Federal Council and actually only two were members of the old provisional Federal Council of the 10th Ward Hotel; such, he points out, is the value of the opponents' statements generally, to which he does not wish to reply now lest he waste the precious time of the Congress.—

Marx describes the three parties of the International in America: 1. the true Labor party; 2. the bourgeois or petty bourgeois humbug party; and 3. the party of the "wise men" who never know where they belong and therefore cause the greatest harm; to these belongs Sauva who undergoes strange transformations; first in London and on the journey he takes the side of the General Council and here he takes the side of the Federalists, Jurassians, and Alliance men. As regards the agreements between Dereure and Sauva, he is sorry that Dereure has made himself available.—He cares nothing for Sauva's judgment on this matter; Dereure's opinion would mean more to him.

The original proposal—to elect Kavanagh, St. Clair, Cetti, Laurel, Levièle, Bertrand, Bolte, and Carl to the General Council with the authorization to co-optate others up to fifteen members—is accepted with 19 Ayes against 4 Nays and 19 abstentions. Vigorous objections are raised against honoring this vote as there was no majority of votes for the motion, and motions of all sorts are submitted to the chair (Dupont and Seraillier demand the insertion of Pillon's name), until Marx moves to reconsider the last vote; this is accepted.

The motion of the Spanish delegates to elect the General Council through the individual federations (two [delegates] each) is rejected by the Congress.

Upon Lafargue's proposal the Congress resolves to elect twelve (12) members for the new General Council who may co-optate three more members, and to take a five-minute intermission for the sake of the election.

Meanwhile Sorge states that he has nothing to do with the agreements between Dereure and Sauva; he draws Dereure's attention to the fact that he has placed four Frenchmen on the ticket agreed upon by him and Sauva, and only three Germans; he will accept Dereure but under no circumstances Sauva, and he demands at least one more German; he objects decidedly to his own nomination; he draws the attention of the members of the Congress to the fact that to him, as to the New Yorkers, the transfer of the General Council to New York has come quite unexpectedly, that it lays a heavy burden upon the New Yorkers which should not be aggravated by placing men at their side with whom they could not co-operate.

The following are elected to the General Council for the year 1872–1873 with the authority to increase the number up to a total of 15 members: S. Kavanagh, E. P. St. Clair, Fomacieri, Laurel, Levièle, David, Dereure, Carl, Bolte, Bertrand, Ward, and Speyer.

The Congress resolves that each federation designate one member for auditing the financial statement of the General Council.—

Then follows the vote, interrupted last night, on the insertion in the Rules of the article concerning the political action of the working class. [The article] is accepted with 27 votes against 4 Nays, 9 abstentions, and thus is a legal paragraph of the Rules.—

The motion is made to raise the dues, whereupon Brismée shows how impracticable and unworkable this would be and that rather a lowering of the dues would be more suitable and appropriate. Fränkel speaks for raising the dues considering the tasks of the General Council and what it could and should do with a full treasury.

After Dupont has replied to Fränkel, the great majority resolves to collect the same dues as before.—

Seraillier submits the motion "to declare null and void all credentials given to persons, sections, committees, etc., by the former General Council and to leave it to the new General Council in New York to make out new credentials." This resolution is unanimously carried.—

Lafargue, Sorge, and others move: "The General Council shall take in hand the organization of international trade unions, shall submit a proposal about this within a month, shall forward translations in the various languages to all trade unions in all countries that can be reached in order to gather their opinion; it shall collate and compare the opinions received, hold an election about the result, and submit the entire matter for final approval and decision to the next General Congress." This motion was accepted without dissent.

A statement against sectarianism is received from the Paris sections, directed especially against the so-called Blanquists though they have and express great respect for Blanqui personally.

The Congress decides to go to Amsterdam tomorrow, Sunday, at 9:00 A.M., at the invitation of the Dutch Federal Council.

Pihl from Copenhagen reads a statement of the Danish party comrades in favor of the General Council.

It is decided to begin the next closed session at five o'clock, to hold a public meeting from seven to nine, in which preferably the Dutch language will be spoken; after nine o'clock another closed meeting is to be held. [The Congress] adjourns at 3:30 P.M.

The sitting is resumed at 5:30 P.M.

Engels reports that the finance committee has not quite finished [its work] but that eight federations, after having gone over the books of the accounts of the General Council, have found them in order and have thus witnessed by affixing their signatures.—Upon request he gives to the Congress a detailed financial statement of the General Council which shows that the Association still owes a sum of over twenty-five pounds sterling to members of the General Council and others.

Eccarius points to the financial statement in order to show how cautious we have to be with fixing and collecting of dues, and that we must not think of raising [the dues] lest we offend all trade unions. Moreover, we can see how few members do their duty; the report shows that only Spain, France, and America have fully met their obligations.—

Marx points out that according to the financial statement the various members of the General Council emptied their pockets and purses for the organization while they have been slandered by the lie that they live off the workingman's pennies.

The financial statement of the General Council is unanimously adopted by the Congress.—

Dereure moves a vote of censure against the slanderous press; Lafargue moves to expel their editors.

Joannard declares to be cowards those who continuously engage in such slanderous innuendoes without ever daring to raise such accusations openly; if we were Marx's knaves, as they have maintained, they would deserve to be whipped like dogs.—

Alerini rises in defense of his friend Guillaume, who is being accused here *in absentia*. If expulsions are moved here, he moves that first of all the author of the infamous piece of writing *Les Pretendues Scissions* be expelled; he turns personally against Longuet.

Lafargue and Longuet read the text of the charges and accusations against the General Council and some of its members which at the time were carried in the Bulletin [of the Jurassian Federation]; the assembly listens to them with indignation.—

Alerini says that he signed the financial statement in good faith but that perhaps, if he had searched for it, he might have found a flaw.—

Guillaume says that after publication of the *Pretendues Scissions*, which they were able to get only with the greatest effort, the editors of the *Bulletin* offered to those under attack in the *Scissions* their columns for statements without assuming responsibility for them; they only declared their readiness to print rejoinders; for the rest, they are ready to retract these statements if they are proved false.

Longuet and Duval engage in a vehement discussion with Guillaume; Duval recounts the events of the attempted Lyons insurrection very much to the disadvantage of Bakunin, Joukowski, Gaspar Richard, Blanc, etc., and implicates Guillaume as the friend and defender of these people and holds him co-responsible; Guillaume rejects any responsibility by mentioning that they themselves had branded Richard and Blanc as spies as soon as they had recognized them as such; hence, they must not be held accountable for them; this is countered by the remark that they had raised these people in their midst.—

Upon Sorge's motion it is resolved to hold the next general congress in Switzerland but to leave the choice of the place to the General Council.

Dereure moves to appoint a committee of five members living in London to sift and translate the Minutes of this Congress and transfer the papers and documents to the new General Council. This is unanimously adopted, and Marx, Engels, Seraillier, Dupont, and Fränkel are appointed as such a committee.

Sorge deposits with the recording secretary motions of the American Federation for the regulation of representation at the Congress and simplification of the designations of the affiliates.

As it is 7:00 P.M. the meeting is adjourned for ten minutes to prepare for the public meeting.—

During the intermission two collections are made among the members of the Congress, 1. to compensate some of the Hague party comrades for working-time lost; 2. to cover the printing costs of the membership list.

The public meeting is called to order at 7:15.

Dave, Van den Hout, Van den Abeel, and Brismée make speeches about the purpose and goal of the International Workingmen's Association, the first three in the Dutch, the last in the French language.—

At nine o'clock the public meeting is closed and a recess is announced in order to clear the hall.

After ten o'clock the closed session is reopened with a roll call. The result of the collections is announced and the Congress resolves to hear and discuss presently the report of the Committee of Inquiry into the Alliance. First, Walther submits in writing and orally his resignation from the Committee of Inquiry and declares that there was not sufficient time for a thorough investigation, and that Guillaume refused to answer certain questions. The [following text of the] report is read:

Report of the Committee of Inquiry into the Association 'Alliance.'

"The committee, lacking time for submission of a complete report, can render judgment only on the basis of papers received and statements made before it.

"After having heard on one side the citizens Engels, Marx, Wroblewski, Dupont, Seraillier, and Swarm for the accusation; and on the other side the citizens Guillaume, Schwitzguebel, Joukowski, Morago, Marcelau, and Farga-Pelicer, accused of belonging to the secret society 'Alliance,' the Committee declares:

"1. Considering that the secret Alliance, established with rules entirely opposed to those of the I.W.A., did exist but that there is insufficient proof of its continued existence;

"2. whereas a draft of rules and letters signed 'Bakunin' prove that said citizen has tried to establish, and perhaps has succeeded in establishing, a society in Europe named 'Alliance' with rules entirely different from those of the I.W.A. in social and political respects;

"3. whereas citizen Bakunin has made use of deceptive tricks in order to appropriate a larger or smaller part of other persons' fortune, which constitutes fraud;

"4. whereas, further, he or his agents have had recourse to threats lest he be compelled to meet his obligations;

"Therefore the members of the Committee request the Congress:

"1. to expel citizen Bakunin from the I.W.A.;

"2. likewise to expel citizens Guillaume and Schwitzguebel in the conviction that they still belong to the society Alliance;

"3. as it has been proved in the course of inquiry, that citizens Malon, Bousquet (the latter being secretary to the police commissioner of Beziers, France), and Louis Marchand (who has resided in Bordeaux, France) have engaged in conspiratorial activities with the aim of disorganizing the I.W.A.—the Committee likewise requests their expulsion from the society;

"4. as to the citizens Morago, Farga-Pelicer, Marcelau, Joukowski, and Alerini, the Committee accepts their formal declaration that they no longer belong to the said society Alliance and it requests the Congress to waive charges against them.

"In support of their responsibility the members of the Committee request that the papers and statements communicated to the Committee be published in an official organ of the Association.

The Hague, Sept. 7, 1872   Chairman: Th. F. Cuno, Delegate
       The Committee: from Stuttgart and Düsseldorf
                             Secretary: Lucain, Delegate from
                             France
          Member of the Committee: Paul Vichard,
                             Delegate for France

"I protest against the report of the Committee of Inquiry into the 'Alliance' and reserve the right to state my reasons before the Congress. One thing alone, it seems to me, has resulted from the debates; that is the attempt of Mr. Bakunin to establish a secret society in the body of the I.W.A. As regards the expulsions requested by the majority of the Committee of Inquiry, I declare myself to be unable, as a member of the Committee, to pass judgment as I have not received a mandate for this business and I am resolved to fight this decision before the Congress.

Roz Splingard.

"The members of the Committee declare before the Congress that citizen Walther has deemed it necessary this morning to address a letter to the chairman of the Committee. In this letter he excuses himself for no longer being able to participate in the work of the Committee for compelling reasons (*cause majeure*).

Chairman:	Th. F. Cuno,
Secretary:	Lucain,
Members:	Roz Splingard,
	Paul Vichard"

Cuno takes the floor and declares: it is fully ascertained that there have been machinations in the I.W.A.; lies, slanders, and frauds have been proved; the Committee has done superhuman work, it has been in continuous session today for thirteen hours, and now requests a vote of confidence from the Congress.

Alerini suggests that the Committee has only moral, not substantive, proof; he was a member of the Alliance and is proud of it, for it propagated, established, and strengthened the I.W.A. in Spain so that eighty-four federations exist there now; you are but a holy inquisition; we demand public hearings.

Joannard is fully convinced of the correctness of the Committee report, but deems it necessary to take exception in the case of Malon's expulsion, against whom he has none but political reproaches. As regards Bakunin, Guillaume, Schwitzguebel, etc., he relies completely upon the report of the Committee and only hopes that the Committee has proceeded with the greatest caution; for expulsion from the I.W.A. is the worst and most degrading verdict that can befall a person and those expelled can never again belong to an honorable society; in the end he concedes that the Committee is also right in the case of Malon.—

Splingard requests further information concerning the manner in which Marx managed to get hold of the documents as that could not be done honestly; Engels, to be sure, submitted documentary proof, but Marx only made assertions; Bakunin merely failed to keep a promise to translate Marx's work, because he was advised against this; the Alliance existed in Geneva and Spain before the I.W.A.; in Geneva you yourselves recognized it; furnish proof that it still exists, but you have to prove this not by means of rules, letters, and such like, but by means of books of protocol and minutes of sessions!

Marx (improperly interrupted by Splingard) states that Splingard acted well as an advocate but not as a judge; Splingard states falsely (he corrects himself: 'incorrectly') that Marx has furnished no documentary proof, whereas he knew full well that Marx had handed over almost all his proofs to Engels; [22] the Spanish Federal Council itself has furnished proof; he (Marx) has contributed other pieces from Russia, but naturally must not give the name of the sender; for the rest, the committee members have mutually given their word of honor not to disclose what went on in the discussion; he (Marx) has his opinion about the affair; Splingard might well differ; the documents have not been obtained in a dishonest manner, they were sent without having been requested.

Lucain asks Splingard whether the majority of the Committee are not just as conscientious and intelligent as he; Splingard himself admits that Bakunin made the attempt to establish the secret 'Alliance'; does he want to wait perhaps, before intervening, until the I.W.A. has been destroyed? We do not! We oppose evil wherever we find it and thus do our duty.

Morago takes the floor and speaks at length in Spanish in favor of the Alliance, against the resolutions of the Committee, etc. It is well past midnight; van den Abeel passes word to the chairman that the premises must be cleared. The Congress dispenses with the translation of Morago's speech the more so as he and his Spanish fellow delegates do not stand accused, and it is resolved to give hearing only to the accused, Guillaume and Schwitzguebel, and then to take the vote.—

Guillaume receives the floor and says: Splingard's stand is the only correct one. The entire proceeding actually is a political trial with the desire of silencing the minority, that is, actually the majority;

[22] See Introduction, p. 7.

in the discussions of recent days my name has always been placed at the head of the speakers' list and I had to speak first in order to show by my elimination on Saturday that here the federalist principle stands condemned. (Shouts of Nay! Nay!)

Schwitzguebel declares he is convinced that his conviction had been a foregone conclusion; he says that he will remain loyal to the workers' party, will fight for the cause of labor and belong to the I.W.A. even should he be expelled.[23]

Vichard turns against Splingard and against the peculiar conduct of Walther who withdrew in order to depart, yet is still present.

Walther offers explanations and takes his stand fully at the side of the Committee by making further disclosures concerning Mentshikoff, an agent sent out by the Jurassian Federation, who has sought to win the Parisians over to their side.

Dave takes the floor, says that they, the so-called minority, have closely observed the procedure of the majority and therefore have often joined in separate meetings whose members herewith submit the following separate statement:

"We, the undersigned, members of the minority of the Hague Congress, adherents of autonomy and federation of workingmen's groups, in view of the decisive vote, which appears to us opposed to the principles which are recognized in the countries represented by us at the past Congress; wishing, however, to avoid any sort of split in the body of the I.W.A., make the following statements, which we shall submit for approval to our delegating sections:

1. We will continue to maintain administrative relations with the General Council; relations concerning the payment of dues, correspondence, and labor statistics.

2. The federations represented by us will exchange direct and regularly continued reports among themselves and all regularly established branches of the International.

3. Should the General Council wish to interfere in the internal affairs of a federation, the federations represented by the undersigned assume the joint obligation to maintain their autonomy unless these

---

[23] According to Guillaume, Schwitzguebel confined himself to saying, "We have been condemned in advance; the workers, however, will condemn the decision of your majority."—*L'Internationale, Documents et Souvenirs* (*1864–1878*), Vol. II, p. 348.

federations will take a course directly opposed to the General Rules of the I.W.A. accepted at the Geneva Congress.

4. We summon all federations and sections to prepare from now on till the next general congress for the triumph of the principles of federal autonomy as the organizational basis of work in the body of the International.

5. We emphatically reject all relations with the so-called Universal Federal Council [24] at London or with any other similar organization alien to the International.

The Hague, Sept. 7, 1872
P. Flues, Delegate of the Federation of the Vesdre valley
Thomas Gonzales Morago, Delegate of the Secessionist Spanish Federation
Alerini, Delegate from Spain
Adhémar Schwitzguebel, Delegate of the Jurassian Federation
James Guillaume,   "   "   "   "   "
H. van den Abeele, Delegate of the Section of Ghent (Belgium)
Ph. Coenen,   Delegate of Antwerp
N. Eberhard,   "   "   Brussels
H. Gerhard,   "   of the Dutch Federal Council
D. Brismée,   "   of the Brussels section
J. S. Van den Hout,   "   of the Amsterdam section
Victor Dave,   "   from The Hague
(A declaration of V. Cynille has been crossed out again)
N. Alonso Marcelau, Delegate of the Spanish Federation
R. Farga-Pellicer,   Delegate of the   "   "
A. Sauva   Delegate of Sections 29 and 42 of North America

Roch. Splingard   "   of Belgium
Herman   "   "   "

The Congress makes ready for the voice vote concerning the recommendations of the Committee of Inquiry.

[24] The "Universal Federal Council" (Conseil fédéraliste universel) represented a group which had been established by Pyat and Vesinier in London in opposition to the General Council of the International. See James Guillaume, *L'Internationale, Document et Souvenirs (1864–1878)*, Vol. II, p. 349, note 4; *Sorge Correspondence*, p. 57.

Minutes of the Fifth General Congress

The expulsion of Michael Bakunin from the I.W.A. is passed by the Congress with 29 Ayes against 7 Nays and 8 abstaining votes.—[25]

The expulsion of James Guillaume from the I.W.A. is passed by the Congress with 25 Ayes against 9 Nays and 9 abstaining votes.

The expulsion of Adhémar Schwitzguebel is rejected by the Congress with 15 Ayes against 16 Nays and 10 abstaining votes.

Upon Fr. Engels' motion the Congress resolves by a large majority to table Point 3 of the recommendations of the Committee (further expulsions), to accept, however, the other recommendations of the Committee, Point 4, etc.—This is carried.—

Sauva hands over to the Bureau various resolutions and communications of his voters.

At the chairman's suggestion the Congress resolves to pass on to the new General Council the task of completing unfinished business.

The chairman declares that he has lost his voice (he became hoarse) but not his faith in the cause (j'ai perdu ma voix, mais non pas ma foi) and concludes at 12:30 A.M. the Fifth General Congress of the International Workingmen's Association with a cheer for Labor.

[25] Barry (see below, p. 291) lists 27 Ayes (Friedländer is not listed). The writer of the Minutes actually lists 28 names, not 29. James Guillaume lists 27 votes for the expulsion and states that Friedländer was absent for a moment (p. 350). For the rest, Guillaume and these Minutes are in agreement, whereas Barry fails to mention Cyrille among the Nays, and Farga Pellicer among those abstaining.

Among the abstaining votes in Guillaume's case the Minutes would seem to have omitted Schwitzguebel's name as "9 abstaining votes" are mentioned and only eight names are listed.

The close vote in Schwitzguebel's case is inconsistently reported. Whereas the text speaks of 15 Ayes, the listing gives 16 names. Guillaume does not mention Splingard and criticizes Barry for having listed Splingard instead of Sorge. The Minutes mention both Sorge and Splingard and seem to have listed one too many. The Minutes report that there were 16 Nays counted against Schwitzguebel's expulsion, whereas Guillaume mentions 17. He includes Splingard among the Nays instead of the Ayes as both these Minutes and Barry do. Guillaume would seem to be right.

Whereas Guillaume reports 9 abstentions, the Minutes mention 10 abstentions by including Cuno among them. Barry reports 3 fewer abstentions: he omits Alerini, Cuno, and Friedländer.

Addenda: Before the vote on the Committee recommendations N. A. Marcelau submitted the following declaration:

I take the liberty of informing the Congress that in most of the Spanish federations an investigation is under way to decide whether or not we have acted correctly; herewith I declare my ardent desire for such an investigation, as I believe I have acted justly and wish to condemn the guilty one, if I have been deceived or made someone's tool.

The Hague, Sept. 7, 1872

Nicola Alonso Marselau

Votes for the Expulsion of

Bakunin	Guillaume	Schwitzguebel
J. Ph. Becker	ditto	ditto
T. F. Cuno	do	
Dumont	do	do
Dupont	do	
Duval	do	
Dereure		
Engels	do	do
Fargas	do	do
Friedländer		
Fränkel	do	
Hepner	do	do
Heim	do	do
Joannard	do	
Marx	do	do
Kugelman	do	do
Lucain	do	
Lafargue	do	
Longuet	do	
Le Moussu	do	do
McDonnell		
Pihl	do	do
Swarm	do	

Minutes of the Fifth General Congress

Bakunin	Guillaume	Schwitzguebel
Sorge	do	do
Seraillier	do	Splingar
Walther	do	do
Wroblewski	do	do
Vichard	do	do
Vilmot	do	

Votes against the Expulsion of

Bakunin	Guillaume	Schwitzguebel
Brismée	do	do
Coenen	do	do
Cyrille	do	do
		Dupont
Dave	do	do
		Dereure
Flues	do	do
		Fränkel
Herman	do	do
		Joannard
		Longuet
		Swarm
	Sauva	do
	Splingard	
		Seraillier
Van den Abeele	do	do
		Vilmot

Abstaining Votes in the Case of

Bakunin	Guillaume	Schwitzguebel
Alerini	do	do
		Cuno
	Dereure	

Bakunin	Guillaume	Schwitzguebel
		Duval
Fargo-Pelicer	do	do
	Friedländer	do
Guillaume	do	
		Lucain
		Lafargue
Morago	do	do
Marselau	do	do
	McDonnell	do
Sauva		
Splingard		
Schwitzguebel		

Votes for the Authority of the General Council

For

Article 2	Article 6
Arnoud	do
B. Becker	do
J. Ph. Becker	do
Baary [Barry]	do
Cournet	do
Cuno	do
Dupont	do
Duval	do
Dereure	do
Engels	do
Fargas	do
Friedländer	do
Fränkel	do
Hepner	do
Heim	do
Joannard	do
Marx	do
Kugelmann	do

Against

Article 2	Article 6
Brismée	do
Flues	do

Article 2	Article 6	Article 2	Article 6
Lessner	do		Coenen
Lucain		Gerhard	
Lafargue	do		Herman
Longuet	do	Splingard	do
Le Moussu	do	Van den Hout	
Milke	do		Sauva
Pihl	do		
Ranvier	do		
Roche			
Swarm	do		
Sauva			
Sorge	do		
Seraillier	do		
Sexton	do		
Schumacher	do		
Walther	do		
Wroblewski	do		
Vaillant	do		
Vichard	do		
Dumont			
McDonnel[1]	do		
Ludwig	do		
Vilmot			

After it had been resolved to move the seat of the General Council, the following voted for its transfer to New York:

Article 2	Article 6
B. Becker	Le Moussu
J. Ph. Becker	Pihl
Brismée	Roche
Barry	Swarm
Cuno	Splingard
Coenen	Seraillier
Dupont	Sexton
Dave	Wroblewski
Flues	Van den Abeele
Fargas	Vichard
Friedländer	Dumont
Engels	McDonnell
Herman	
Lucain	
Marx	
Kugelmann	
Lessner	
Lafargue	
Longuet	

Sunday, September 8, at 9:10 A.M., most of the delegates went to Amsterdam, where they were cordially welcomed by the local party comrades and were led to a public meeting; there Marx, J. Ph. Becker, Duval, Wroblewski, Lafargue, Dupont, Sorge, and van den Hout gave speeches which were enthusiastically received on the goals and aspirations of the I.W.A., the labors of the just finished Congress, and the future of the Association.[26]

[26] Unfortunately, the Minutes do not give an account of what was said at this meeting. Some utterances by Marx have played a role in the controversy between Kautsky and Lenin and hence we may briefly point to them here. Two newspapers reported Marx's speech, the *Liberté*, a Brussels paper, and the *Algemeen Handelsblad* of Sept. 10, 1872. The account in *Liberté* has been translated into German by Dr. R. Meyer, who used it in his *Emancipationskampf des vierten Standes* (Vol. I, pp. 159–61). Besides, Hepner, the co-editor of the Leipzig *Volksstaat*, the paper of Bebel and Liebknecht, carried a version of the speech taken from *Liberté*. Although Hepner had been at the Hague Congress, he had not been able to stay until the end as he had to attend the Mainz Congress of the *Sozialdemokratische Arbeiterpartei* on September 8. The account in the *Algemeen Handelsblad* has been published in English by the International Institute of Social History, Amsterdam (see its *Bulletin*, Vol. VI [1951], pp. 10–15, 198 ff.).

Pertinent are the following paragraphs:

"The worker must one day conquer political supremacy in order to establish the new organization of labor. He must abolish the old policy preserving the old institutions, or he will fare as did the early Christians, who despised and neglected to do so and hence never saw their kingdom realized in this world.

"But we do not assert that the attainment of this end requires identical means.

"We know that one has to take into consideration the institutions, mores, and traditions of the different countries and we do not deny that there are countries like England and America and if I am familiar with your institutions, Holland, where labor may attain its goal by peaceful means.

"Whilst this may be so, we must recognize that in most countries of the Continent violence must be the lever of our revolution; in due course an appeal to violence must be made to at long last establish the rule of labor. . . .

"Citizens! let us remind ourselves of the fundamental principle of the International, that is, solidarity. We will attain the great objective of our striving when we establish this vital principle on strong foundations and among all workers of all countries. Solidarity is a must for revolution and the Commune of Paris gives us an example; it came to its downfall because a great revolutionary movement connected with this great insurrection of the Paris proletariat failed to materialize simultaneously in all capitals, in Berlin, Madrid, etc." [translated from Meyer's text].

The general juxtaposition of peaceful means in some cases and violent revolution in the others, hence of "reform" and "revolution," is confirmed by the *Algemeen Handelsblad*.

"The speaker [i.e., Marx] defends the use of violence, where other means do not help. In North America the barricades are unnecessary, because there, if they but want it, the proletariat can win victory through the polls. The same applies to England and some other countries where the working classes have the right to free speech. But in the great majority of states revolution has to be substituted for legality, because otherwise—by a mistaken sense of generosity, by a wrong-headed sense of justice—one will not attain one's ends. Strong, vigorous propaganda will have to prepare and support the revolution. For these reasons too a great centralization of power in the hands of the General Council is urgently needed."

Report to the

North American Federation of the

International Workingmen's Association

Concerning the Delegation

to the Fifth General Congress

at The Hague,

September 2 to 7, 1872

After a brief overseas journey the undersigned arrived in London about midnight on Monday, August 19, and the following morning called at once on Karl Marx. We were received very cordially, and Marx and other arriving party comrades—Fränkel, Longuet, Engels, Le Moussu, Jones from Manchester, and others—informed us rather closely of the situation in the General Council and of conditions in the various European countries, etc.—

In the evening of the same day we went along to the session of the General Council, where we received a friendly welcome from most of the members and by a special motion were allowed to attend the sessions of the General Council. Eccarius and Hales kept aloof from us. Nearly half of the General Council consisted of Frenchmen, that is, refugees, [who were] members and followers of the Commune. This imparted the stamp of the French character to the General Council as well as to the later Congress which suffered therefore from much talkativeness and exaggerated liveliness that occasionally was difficult to restrain. Naturally, exile always results in strife and dissent among the exiles, who blame one another, to some degree, for failure and level more or less justified reproaches at one another,—and refugees split into small groups (cliques), which intensely fight each other instead of attacking the common foe. Do not reproach me for partisanship because I speak of Frenchmen. We must tell each other the truth and I do not hesitate for a moment to declare that the German refugees of 1848–49 were no whit better but possibly even more demoralized and split than were the French refugees of 1871.

I am only reporting facts. Naturally, the aforementioned strife did not fail to influence the General Council, so strongly composed of Frenchmen, and it took all the skill and prestige of a few old German party comrades to prevent open discord in the midst of the General Council.

Fighting raged among the so-called Federalists, Proudhonists, Alliance men, and Bakuninists. These people preach revolution without organization, association without rules and regulations, fight without leaders, society without cohesion, the body without a head, as well as without ideas. For the autonomy, that is, the sovereignty, which they value above all else, leads in its natural consequences to the complete dissolution of the Association, to the atomization of society into its smallest elements, that is, to complete disorganization. The sovereign ego, when or if sufficiently strong, becomes the autocratic ego; thus, naked autocracy emerges from veiled autonomy and the mystery of pompously announced personal freedom dissolves into the most vulgar tyranny; and it has become obvious that the representatives of this autonomy and this individual independence are the greatest despots in their demands and in their methods of realizing them.

There is small danger that the practical, sober worker will allow himself to be deceived by these phrases.

Hence, we find, in countries with strongly developed industry, in England, France, and Germany, few so-called Federalists or no adherents at all of this political current; this current, however, has not a few disciples in those countries where industry and the proletariat are less developed, where the working class is still far from consciously realizing its situation, as, for example, in Italy and Spain. Characteristically, Bakunin himself refers, in a letter, to his followers in Italy as "declassed or disinherited bourgeois sons, lawyers, young enthusiastic students, in general people with no future and means" —in this no mention is made of workers. That the Belgians incline so strongly in that direction is due to the jealousy with which they guard their nationality and their independence, a sentiment which is found in excess especially among small peoples and nations. For

Report to the North American Federation

the rest, they do not go as far in their demands as do the Italians and the others. I said before, the fight is raging! The old loyal members and founders of the I.W.A. saw this organization endangered by the subversive activities of Bakunin and his helpmates, who by means of a secret society, called Alliance, sought to take over and dominate the International.

I have had in my hand and have read evidence of this in Bakunin's own handwriting. Hence, the General Council was quite right when in its last communication to the New York Federal Council it stated: "At this Congress the existence of the I.W.A. is at stake." * Accordingly, it made every effort to counter the opposition at the Congress.

The Italians had ineptly discarded their mask by calling a counter-congress at Neuenberg. The Jurassians and Spaniards were clever enough to disapprove of this step and to send their delegates to The Hague.

This fight constituted one of the main questions before the Congress and it kept the General Council extraordinarily busy.

In the midst of this struggle it had become clear that the General Council lacked sufficient powers. Furnished with proper authority, the General Council could not have allowed such sectarianism as that indicated above to arise and become a force which now had to be fought in earnest.—

Besides, because of the great events of recent years and the long period between the Congresses at Basel and at The Hague, discipline in the party generally had become quite loose, and it was necessary to renew the ties [of the Association]. This led to the second main question before the Congress, that of increasing or strengthening the authority of the General Council.—

The third major point which the Congress had to consider was that of approving the work and the resolutions of the London Conference. Of greatest importance was the resolution concerning the political activity of the working class; this resolution, which the Jurassians, Bakuninists, and comrades disputed so ardently, required the approval of the Congress to become a valid rule.

In addition, the no less important fourth question before the Congress concerned the disputes and schisms in America, and happily

* Apparently a citation from Marx's letter to Sorge of June 21, 1872.— *Sorge Correspondence*, p. 59.

I can inform my voters that the General Council almost without exception decisively took our side, which resulted in decisions favorable to us.

Our party comrades need only consider and imagine the tremendous task of organizing a Congress which had been interrupted for several years, what great efforts had to be made to master the aforementioned major questions,—and they will be satisfied with what has been attained, and not wonder that some minor wishes and special resolutions could not be discussed and considered.—

The Congress—may our American party comrades believe this—has discharged its obligation in full measure! Let us now do our duty and the next Congress will readily make up for what is missing! And let us not forget that the Hague Congress has given us in bold outline unmistakably the directive for our future conduct.

The incessant struggle of the last years and the long tenure of office has tired though not disheartened several of our proved party comrades in the old General Council; their theoretical work, which is of infinite importance and usefulness, has been stalled under the pressure of petty administrative work; for this reason, and in view of the cited disputes, several older members of the General Council, especially Karl Marx and Fr. Engels, have declared that under no circumstances would they accept re-election to the General Council. It was precisely these oldest and most active members of the old General Council who, after mature consideration, made the well-reasoned proposal to move [the seat of] the General Council to New York; after the first shock of this entirely unexpected resolution was over, the great majority of the Congress found itself in agreement with it.

The following reasons were stated by Engels on behalf of the sponsors of the motion—all of whom were members of the old General Council:

1. The General Council must be moved away from London;
2. Most older members will not accept re-election;
3. The General Council and its papers are secure nowhere on the Continent (the Belgians and Swiss confirm this);
4. Thus there remains only New York;
5. In case of emergency and special circumstances the General

Council may grant special authority to persons and delegations;
6. New York is more international than any other place;
7. There we have able party comrades and resources, etc.

This motion came as unexpectedly to both of your delegates as it probably comes to you. I further note the following briefly: Sauva, when appearing in the General Council at London with the mandate of Section 2, was rejected, but he was admitted with the under-handedly obtained mandate of Section 42.—

When West appeared at the General Council at London he was re-jected.—

I shall now proceed to give you my condensed report of the Congress.

We arrived at The Hague in the afternoon of Sunday, September 1.

The Hague has almost no industrial or working class population. The court and its retinue, officials and servants make up its inhabitants. The inhabitants gaped at us as if [we were] monsters and fabled creatures and there was no lack of insults, although people became somewhat more decent toward the end of the week of the Congress.

No provision had been made for reasonable accommodations or any accommodations at all. At first we had difficulty in finding lodgings and we had to pay dearly for everything.

The meeting hall was situated very far from our quarters and had poor lighting and no ventilation.

Sixty-five delegates were present, namely: 18 Frenchmen, 15 Germans, 7 Belgians, 5 Englishmen, 5 Spaniards, 4 Dutchmen, 4 Swiss, 2 Austrians, 1 Dane, 1 Hungarian, 1 Australian, 1 Irishman, and 1 Pole. They represented 95 mandates, of which Belgium had sent 17, Germany 15, France 14, Switzerland 11, America 7, the General Council 6, Spain 5, England 5, Holland 4, Denmark 2, Ireland 2, Hungary 2, Portugal 1, Poland 1, Austria 1, and Australia 1.—

A printed copy of the complete list is attached.

In general, the deportment of the delegates was dignified, self-confident, and demanding respect. The predominance of the French nationality among the delegates, as well as the fact that business preferably was transacted in the French language, imparted to the

Congress French vivaciousness, talkativeness, and lack of restraint.

Sunday, September 1, at 7:00 P.M., the so-called preliminary meeting was held, in which nothing happened except for the Dutch welcome to the Congress. The reproach was made by several that the Congress had not been called for the first but for the second of September.

It was resolved, however, to hold a closed session at 9:00 A.M. on Monday, September 2, and to admit members only.

At 9:00 A.M. on Monday the meeting was opened by the Dutch Federal Council, who later ceded the chair to van den Abeel of Ghent, Belgium. It was resolved not to admit reporters, and Dupont, Fränkel, and Eccarius were appointed translators. Upon a motion of Engels it was resolved to appoint a Credentials Committee of seven members whilst Sauva and the Jurassians demanded [the appointment of] one member from each federation. The Spanish delegates pointed out that they had definite instruction not to vote until voting proceeded by number of members represented. Marx, Ranvier, Roach, McDonnell, Dereure, Gerhard, and Fränkel were elected to the Credentials Committee. The meeting adjourned at 3:00 P.M.

The evening session did not begin until 8:30 P.M. because the Credentials Committee did not appear earlier. [The Committee] rejected the mandate of W. West—Sections 12 and 19—that of Sauva of Section 2, that of Alerini of a Marseilles section, that of Joukowski of the Geneva Section de la propagande revolutionaire, etc., and found fault with the credentials of the Spanish delegates for nonpayment of dues; in addition, [the Committee] requested further information concerning the mandates of Flues and Dave. All other credentials were recommended for acceptance, among them Sauva's mandates of [Sections] 42 and 29, which had just been forwarded to him. After prolonged negotiations Flues and Dave were found to be in good standing, Dereure's and Sorge's credentials were disputed by Sauva, Sauva's by Sorge, Vaillant's by Schwitzguebel, Lafargue's by Alerini, Barry's by Hales. With the exception of these and the ones disputed by the Credentials Committee the others were admitted en bloc.—Hardly had this been done, when Hales protested Sorge's right to speak.—The session was closed at 9:30 P.M.

Report to the North American Federation

Tuesday, September 3, at 9:30 A.M., the meeting was reopened and four secretaries were chosen for the German, French, English, and Dutch languages. After a long debate, provoked especially by Sauva, it was resolved to hear two speakers for each side and then to vote.

Vaillant's mandate of La Chaux de Fonds, which Schwitzguebel had disputed, was unanimously recognized; the mandates of Dereure and Sorge [were] likewise [recognized] against the single vote of Sauva who made several false assertions in dispute. Sauva's mandate of Sections 29 and 42 was disputed by Sorge, who proved that it was only a ruse to bring Sauva into the Congress, which was confirmed by Sauva's own statement; but for want of positive proof which the Federal Council had failed to forward, Sauva was finally admitted as delegate of Sections 29 and 42 with 30 against 20 votes; Dereure abstained from voting and thus Sauva had smuggled himself into the Congress; Lafargue's mandate, disputed by Alerini, was recognized. —Marx made the motion to expel the Alliance and to appoint a committee of investigation.

[The Congress] adjourned at 2:00 P.M.

[The session was] reopened at 4:00 P.M. It was resolved henceforth to take a roll call and report absentees to their voters. Barry's mandate was disputed by Hales; during his [Hales's] absence Sauva was good enough to dispute [the mandate], but without success, for it was recognized against the lone votes of Sauva and Motter[s]-head.

Alerini's mandate from Marseilles was rejected; Joukowski's mandate of the Geneva Propaganda Section was held in abeyance until the question of the "Alliance" was settled. The mandate of the Spanish delegates called forth prolonged discussions but was recognized in the end after they had paid their dues to the chairman. The mandate of Section 2 (New York) for Sauva was rejected by the Credentials Committee and after a somewhat lengthy debate it was declared null and void by the Congress with 39 votes against 9 and 11 abstaining, hence with a full two-thirds [majority]. [The meeting] closed at 10:00 P.M.

Wednesday, September 4, [the meeting] opened at 9:15 A.M. Upon Vilmot's motion smoking in the hall was forbidden. The mandate of Section 12 (New York) for W. West came up for debate. Upon Sauva's motion the rules for business were changed for this case and the time for discussion was not limited (31 against 8 votes).

Marx, on behalf of the Credentials Committee, requested that West's mandate be declared null and void since West was or had been a member of Section 12, of the Philadelphia Congress, and of the Prince Street Council. He described the aims of Section 12, their "appeal," etc., and indicated their relations to the Jurassians, and also dwelled on the decision of the General Council, the two-thirds wage workers issue, etc. West countered in a speech of about one-and-one-half-hours' length, which was interrupted by frequent laughter because of its bathos and nonsense, and finally the Congress became impatient. Sorge replied to West. Sauva said he did not wish to speak for Section 12 but made a speech in praise of Mrs. Wood-hull and Section 12. Guillaume tried to make a diversion in West's favor and said that the Jurassians had never written officially to America; but he himself had written privately to Verpillier; he read Verpillier's answer replete with accusations against Sorge and Section 1. Sorge requested a copy. Sauva testified to the truthfulness of Verpillier's assertions.—

Brismée moved that the Congress do not recognize any section constituted by bourgeois people. This was carried in a voice vote with 47 [Ayes] against 9 abstentions. West's mandate was declared null and void in a voice vote with 49 [Nays] against not a single Aye and 9 abstentions (among them Eccarius, Guillaume, and Schwitzguebel). Eccarius explained his abstention by pointing out that he always had and still has business relationships with the secessionists, that the reports to the General Council are lies, and that Sorge is the sole author of the entire schism.—

It was resolved to hold another private meeting at 7:00 P.M. and a public meeting the following day, Thursday. The session was closed at 4:00 P.M.

At 7:30 P.M. [the meeting] was opened again. Ranvier was elected president, Gerhard and Sorge were elected vice-presidents, Hepner, Le Moussu, McDonnell, van den Hout, and Marcelau for protocol. After a lengthy debate a motion of J. Ph. Becker and comrades was carried to the effect that the Congress take up at once the discussion of the most urgent business, [such as] the powers of the General Council, its seat, the revision of the Rules, etc.

Report to the North American Federation

Priority was denied to the Spanish motion to change the voting procedure.—A closed session [was announced for] the next morning at eight o'clock, a public meeting at ten o'clock. The meeting closed after midnight.

Three full days of the Congress had now passed, an entire session had been spent on West's mandate while Sauva had taken up at least half of the entire time.—

Thursday, September 5, at 8:00 A.M., a closed meeting [was held].

Marx announced that the report of the General Council was intended for the public at large.

It was resolved to appoint a committee of five persons to enquire into the "Alliance." The Jurassians and the Spaniards demanded that at least *one* member (Splingard) be conceded to them on [the committee]. This was granted and Cuno, Splingard, Walther, Lucain, and Vichard were elected to the committee.—The same committee was to investigate the accusations leveled by the Jurassians and the Spaniards against the General Council.—

At 10:00 A.M. a public meeting [was opened]. The roll call showed only three absentees. The President addressed the public in defense of the I.W.A. and the Commune against the usual accusations.—

Sexton now read the report of the General Council in English, Longuet in French, Marx in German, and van den Abeele in Flemish. The Report described especially the persecutions of the I.W.A. which emanated from Vienna and had spread across the entire Continent; it emphasized how the proletariat of all countries had declared itself for the Commune; and how the I.W.A. had spread, especially in Portugal, Holland, Denmark, Ireland, Australia, New Zealand, and Buenos Aires. The sympathy and brotherly greeting of the Congress were extended to the persecuted of all countries.—[The meeting] was closed at 3:00 P.M.

[The Congress] was reopened at 4:15 P.M. Several German delegates announced their departure. A committee was appointed to examine all matters submitted [to the Congress].—[It consisted of] Dupont, Hepner, Fränkel, Dereure, Lafargue, and Brismée. There followed a debate about the General Council and its powers. Lafargue and Sorge spoke for the General Council and pleaded for broader powers; Guillaume and Morago [spoke] against this.— [The meeting] was closed at 11:00 P.M.

The fifth day was now approaching and nothing had been accomplished as yet; the German delegates were compelled to leave soon and the funds of most of the delegates had run low. Thereupon the Germans banded themselves together and next day they submitted the most important resolutions and carried them with the aid of the French. Things could no longer go on that way if we did not wish to go home having accomplished nothing, and an end had to be made to the long talks and deliberate delays.

Friday, September 6, at 9:00 A.M., the roll call [showed] seven absentees. The Committee of Inquiry received permission to hold meetings during the congressional sessions. A motion by Becker, Sorge, and comrades was carried with 34 against 4 votes to debate the authority, etc., of the General Council at once, to hear *one* speaker for and one against, and then to vote.

The same proponents submitted the following article concerning the General Council for inclusion in the Rules of the organization:

Article 2. "The General Council has to execute the resolutions of the Congress and to see to it that the principles, statutes, and general rules of the I.W.A. are closely adhered to in every country.

Article 6. The General Council also has the right to suspend affiliations, sections, federal councils or committees, and federations of the I.W.A. until the next Congress.

"With sections which belong to a federation, it shall not make use of this right before having sought the advice of the respective federal council.

"In cases of dissolution of a federal council or committee the General Council shall arrange at once for the election of a new federal council or committee by the sections of the respective federation within thirty days.

"In the case of suspension of an entire federation the General Council shall notify directly all other federations.

"Upon request of the majority of federations, the General Council shall call an extraordinary conference consisting of *one* delegate from each nationality; it shall meet within one month and bring the dispute to a final decision.—

"It is expressly understood, however, that those countries where the I.W.A. is prohibited have the same rights as the regular federations."

Article 2 was adopted by voice vote with 40 Ayes against 5 Nays and 11 abstaining votes.—

Article 6 was similarly adopted by voice vote with 36 Ayes against 6 Nays and 15 abstaining votes.

Marx, Engels, Le Moussu, Seraillier, Dupont, and others submitted the following motion:

"The seat of the General Council for 1872–1873 is New York; the General Council consists of the members of the New York Federal Council and may co-optate others up to fifteen members." The motion was divided and it was resolved 1. to move the seat of the General Council away from London; 2. to remove it to New York; the first part [of the motion was accepted] with 26 Ayes against 23 Nays, the second part with 31 for New York, 14 for London, 1 for Barcelona, 1 for Brussels, and 10 abstaining votes. [The meeting] was closed at 2:30 P.M.

At 6:00 P.M. a public meeting [was held] and the insertion of the following article into the General Rules [was submitted] for discussion:

"In the struggle against the combined power of the propertied classes the proletariat as a class can act only by constituting itself as a special political party in opposition to all older political parties formed by the propertied classes.—This stand and position of the proletariat as a political party is indispensable in order to secure the triumph of the social revolution and its supreme goal, the abolition of classes.—

"The unity of the forces of labor already attained in the economic struggles, in the hands of this class must serve also as a lever in its struggle against the political power of its exploiters. As the propertied classes, landlords and capitalists, always use their political privileges in order to defend and secure forever their economic monopolies and to subject labor,—the conquest of political power becomes the great duty and task of the proletariat."

Vaillant, Hepner, and Longuet spoke in favor, Guillaume against the resolution. The vote was interrupted by the noise of the public and the session was closed at 11:00 P.M.

Saturday, September 7, at 9:30 A.M., the meeting was opened and

Sorge took the chair after the departure of Ranvier. [The meeting] proceeded to elect the General Council. Sauva stated that the Federal Council had a German majority. Sorge proved this to be untrue. After lengthy debate the original motion of Marx, Engels, and comrades was carried with 19 Ayes against 4 Nays and 19 abstaining votes. Objections were raised against this vote and, upon Marx's proposal, the whole motion was opened again for discussion. Dereure handed a list [of candidates] to Sorge, which Sauva had accepted. Sorge rejected it. After Sorge's explicit statement that he would not accept election by the Congress, the Congress elected the following persons to the General Council with the proviso that they were entitled to co-optate others, up to fifteen members in all: S. Kavanagh, E. P. St. Clair, Fornacieri, Laurel, Levièle, David, Dereure, Carl, Bolte, Bertrand, Ward, and Speyer.—

It was resolved that each federation appoint *one* member to the Committee to audit the financial statement of the General Council. —Then the vote concerning the article on the political action of the working class, which had been interrupted the night before, was taken up and showed 27 Ayes, 4 Nays, and 9 abstaining votes for inclusion of the article in the Rules of the I.W.A.

The members of the Committee were permitted to enter their vote in the record.

[The motion to] raise the dues was defeated.

Upon Seraillier's motion the following was resolved: "All credentials given out by the previous General Council to persons, sections, committees, etc., are herewith null and void. It is left to the General Council at New York to issue new credentials."

The Congress unanimously accepted the following motion of Lafargue, Sorge, and comrades:

"The General Council shall undertake the organization of international trade unions, work out a proposal to this effect within one month, and send copies translated into the various languages to all available trade unions of the various countries to obtain their opinions; it shall collate and compare the incoming opinions, arrange for a vote of the result, and submit the entire matter to the next general congress for final approval and decision."

It was resolved to journey to Amsterdam the next day, Sunday, at 9:00 A.M.—

A closed session [was announced] for 5:00 P.M., a public meeting for 7:00–9:00 P.M. and after 9:00 P.M. another closed session. [The meeting] adjourned at 3:30 P.M.

[The meeting] was opened again at 5:30 P.M. Engels reported that eight federations had already signed and approved the financial report. Upon request he read the entire report showing that only a few federations had paid their dues and that the Association still owed about £25.00 to members of the General Council and others. The financial statement of the General Council was unanimously accepted. Marx, Dereure, Lafargue, Joannard, Longuet, and others drew attention to the fact that the financial statement has shown how some members of the General Council have not only sacrificed their time but also their financial means to the cause while certain quarters (Bulletin de la Federation Jurassien) accused and publicly slandered them of living off the workers' pennies. Guillaume defended himself quite lamely by [pointing out] that the columns of their paper are open for rejoinders. A hot dispute arose between Duval and Guillaume, Duval leveling the most grievous charges against Guillaume and his friends and former followers.—

The Congress resolved to stage the next general congress in Switzerland and to leave the determination of the place to the General Council. Furthermore, Marx, Engels, Seraillier, Dupont, and Fränkel were appointed to a committee to review, translate, and prepare for publication the Minutes of this Congress as well as to direct the transmission of the papers and documents to the new General Council.—

Sorge deposited various resolutions with the bureau.—At 7:00 P.M. the public was admitted and the delegates Dave, van den Hout, Van den Abeele, and Brismée made speeches.

Meanwhile two collections were made among the delegates 1. in order to compensate those members of the Hague section who had to sacrifice time and labor during the week of the Congress, and 2. in order to cover the printing expenses of the list of delegates.—

At about 10:00 P.M. the closed session was reopened. Walther stated his discharge from the Committee of Inquiry into the Alliance and declared that there was not enough time for a thorough investigation and that Guillaume had refused to answer certain questions.—

The Committee of Inquiry reported:

Whereas the secret Alliance, established with rules entirely opposed to those of the I.W.A., had existed, but there was insufficient proof of its continued existence;

Whereas written documents and letters of his own hand prove that Bakunin, possibly with success, had tried to establish a society 'Alliance' in Europe with rules entirely different from those of the I.W.A. in social and political respects;

Whereas Bakunin had fraudulently sought to appropriate other people's money and had even taken recourse to intimidation.

Therefore the committee proposes:

1. to expel Bakunin from the I.W.A.;
2. to expel likewise Guillaume and Schwitzguebel;
3. to expel Malon, Bousquet, and Louis Marchand;
4. to waive the accusations against Morago, Farga-Pelicer, Marcelau, Joukowski, and Alerini;
5. to publish the documentary proofs and hearings.

Splingard, a member of the Committee, protested against these proposals and merely admitted that Bakunin had attempted to found a secret society.—

Dave stated that the so-called minority or opposition had held special meetings and had agreed upon the following statement:

1. We shall continue to communicate with the General Council in matters of payment of dues, correspondence, and labor statistics;
2. The federations represented by us will exchange among one another and with others regular and direct reports, and will establish such connections;
3. Should the General Council wish to interfere in the internal affairs of a federation, the federations represented by the undersigned assume the joint obligation to maintain their autonomy unless these federations take a course directly opposed to the General Rules of the I.W.A. as adopted at the Geneva Congress;
4. We summon all federations and sections to prepare for the next general congress, for the triumph of the principles of federative autonomy as the organizational basis of work in the body of the International;
5. We reject emphatically all relationship to the so-called Universal Federal Council at London or to any other similar organization alien to the International.

Report to the North American Federation

Signed by Flues, Morago, Alerini, Schwitzguebel, Guillaume, Van den Abeele, Coenen, Eberhard, Gerhard, Brismée, van den Hout, Dave, Marcelau, Farga-Pelicer, *Sauva*, Splingard, and Herman.

After a lengthy debate the Congress put the recommendations of the Committee to a voice vote:

Michael Bakunin was expelled with 29 Ayes against 7 Nays and 8 abstaining votes, James Guillaume was expelled with 25 Ayes against 9 Nays and 9 abstaining votes. The expulsion of Adhémar Schwitzguebel was rejected with 15 Ayes against 16 Nays and 10 abstaining votes.

Upon the motion of Fr. Engels the Congress resolved not to vote on Point 3 (the expulsion of Malon and others) and to accept the other proposals of the Committee (Point 4, etc.).

Hence, on the basis of the investigation the General Council will always have the right to proceed against the respective members if it should deem it appropriate.

Upon the chairman's proposal the new General Council was instructed to wind up unfinished business. Sauva deposited various documents and motions, as did J. Ph. Becker.

The chairman declared that he had lost his voice but not his confidence in the cause and at 12:30 A.M. closed with cheers to the work done by the Fifth General Congress of the International Workingmen's Association.

Sunday, September 8, at 9:00 A.M., most of the delegates drove to Amsterdam, were welcomed cordially by the Amsterdam party comrades, and were led to a public meeting where Marx, J. Ph. Becker, Duval, Wroblewski, Sorge, Lafargue, Dupont, and van den Hout made enthusiastically received speeches on the goals and aspirations of the I.W.A., the work of the Congress just closed, and the future of the Association.

Aboard the Steamer Atlantic   Signed: F. A. Sorge, Delegate
September 20, 1872

Report of the

Fifth Annual General Congress of the

International Working Men's Association,

Held at The Hague, Holland,

September 2–9, 1872.

By Maltman Barry.

THE HAGUE, *September* 2.

I DO NOT know that I am quite right in heading this letter as I do. Your readers will, no doubt, recollect that, in consequence of the disturbed state of the Continent, no Congress was held last year, but a private conference in London was substituted. However, the above is the official designation, and, therefore, I use it.

I was greatly surprised, on my arrival, to find how large a space the International fills in the popular mind here. Its Congress, begun to-day, has been the principal subject of conversation in all grades of society for months past, and has been looked forward to with the greatest interest. However flattering this attention may be interpreted by the Society and its friends, I am afraid it was not, at least in some measure, so intended. The Hague, being the place of Royal residence and the seat of the government of the country, may be safely trusted to possess a considerable number of enemies of Revolution. Indeed, so strong is the feeling in some quarters against the Society that the children of the town have been warned not to go into the streets with jewellery or articles of value upon them as "The International is coming and will steal them." On the other hand, I was somewhat surprised yesterday at the table d'hote, by the landlord of our hotel calling upon us to drink "Success to the International;" and still more surprised by the enthusiasm with which the toast was drunk by the numerous and respectable company present.

I had only been in the Hague a few hours when, on Saturday evening, I was invited and conducted to the meeting of the local section. This section is not very strong, numbering only about twenty members; but I am told it is young and growing fast. The members seemed all decent working men, with intelligent faces and quiet decorous manner. Being a delegate to the congress, and also a member of the general council, I was received with every manifestation of friendliness and courtesy.

I had scarcely been five minutes in the room when some one announced that two gentlemen wished to be permitted to be present during the sitting. They were ushered in, and upon interrogation declared themselves to be correspondents of two Amsterdam papers —the *Dagblad* and *Standaard*. Subsequently, one introduced the other as the Secretary to the States Council of Holland. To their reminders of the "reactionary" character of the papers they represented they essayed the "mild answer," which is reputed to "turn away wrath." But neither their credentials nor their blandishments could avert their doom. In a few words, simple and dignified, the chairman gave them their *congé*. I stayed some time afterwards, but not long, as the business being transacted was only interesting to the local members, arranging for the accommodation of the great bulk of the delegates who were to arrive the next day, &c. Their arrival created quite a sensation in the town, considerable crowds following each batch of travellers to their respective hotels, the figure of Karl Marx attracting special attention, his name on every lip.

In the evening a preliminary meeting was held at the Concert Zaal, in Lombard Straat, where the congress will sit. It was almost wholly of a social and convivial nature, the only matters of business determined being the hour (nine o'clock) of meeting on Monday, and that, as the first business would be in connection with purely administrative affairs, the sittings would be open only to delegates and verified members of the International until that part was disposed of.

On reassembling this morning sixty-two delegates were present; Henry Van den Abeele, Antwerp, in the chair. After considerable discussion the appointment of a committee on credentials was proceeded with. Seven was the number determined upon, and those elected were Dureure, Frankel, Gerhard, M'Donnell, Marx, Ranvier, and Roach. The sitting was suspended at two o'clock till seven, in order that the committee might examine credentials and then bring up their report thereon.

September 3.

The reassembling of the delegates last night, appointed for seven o'clock, was delayed till about half-past eight in consequence of some members arriving in the interval whose credentials required examination. The report, which was read by Ranvier, the reporter appointed by the committee itself, recommended the congress to accept and pass fifty-seven credentials, reserving for discussion about eight or nine others. Eccarius, London, proposed the adoption of the committee's recommendation. Guillaume, Bakouninist, proposed that the names be taken *seriatim*, and every credential discussed. Barry, London, supported the motion of Eccarius. If the proposal of Guillaume was adopted the whole matter would require to be gone over again, and the committee's work wasted. Lafargue, Spain, proposed that the entire list be read over; that the uncontested credentials be passed, and those to which there were objections be challenged as they were read, and reserved for discussion. After a good deal of animated debate, the motion of Lafargue was carried. The reporter (Ranvier) then read the list, and each contested credential was challenged by the particular objector in the case, and a separate list made of these. The sitting was then suspended till this morning. About 10 a.m. to-day the sitting was resumed. The first contested mandate was that of Vaillant. Sauva, America, who had challenged it, formally withdrew his opposition. Guillaume, Bakouninist, denounced Vaillant as a Royalist and *bourgeois*. Vaillant briefly replied, and the congress then accepted his credentials. The mandate of Dereure, New York, was next opposed by Sauva, but ultimately accepted by the Congress. Sauva moved the rejection of the credentials of Sorge, New York; but, after hearing Sorge, the Congress passed them. Sorge then opposed the admission of Sauva, who claimed to represent sections 29 and 42 of New York. These sections had not paid their contributions, and had seceded from the local federation. Sauva's credentials were accepted. The next mandate, that of Paul Lafargue, furnished the battle of the day. This man had exposed and denounced Bakounine's secret organisation (L'Alliance) inside the International Society in Spain. For this he was illegally expelled, in his absence, from the federation of Madrid, and now these emissaries of Bakounine had the most imperative orders to prevent his admission if at all possible. Morago, Bakouninist, violently attacked Lafargue, denouncing him as a traitor. Lafargue replied, accusing the Bakouninists of treachery. The excitement and tumult at this point were extraordinary. The Bakouninists, as Lafargue unfolded his evidence, rushing wildly about, shrieking and howling interruptions. One, Cyrille, presenting himself with his hat on before the President, gesticulated dramatically, and, shouting as if he would burst a blood-vessel, rushed out. Finding, however, that nobody followed him, he subsequently slunk in again. Engels, London (Spanish secretary), said the question was really whether the International in Spain was to be either domineered over or disorganised by a secret irresponsible body. The society would not allow either consummation. After some more very warm words, the credentials of Lafargue were accepted by an overwhelming majority. The sitting was then (about half-past one) suspended till half-past three. On reassembling the mandate of Barry was discussed. Sauva opposed, as the section Barry represented (Section 3, of Chicago), was already represented by Sorge. Sorge replied that that was not the case. He (Sorge) represented the federation of New York, while of the three sections in Chicago, each entitled to representation, section 3 only was represented. Mottershead, London, had nothing to say against Barry, nor yet the mandate, but he just wanted to ask a question, and that was, how Barry came to represent a German-speaking section in Chicago. He (Mottershead) asserted that Barry was not a recognised leader of English working men. Also, he had been expelled from the British Federal Council. Marx said no fault had been found in Barry, and the validity of the mandate had not been contested. The question of fitness was one for the section making the appointment. As to the accusation that Barry was not a recognised leader of English working men, that was an honour, for almost every recognised leader of English working men was sold to Gladstone, Morley, Dilke, and others. In regard to the expulsion of Barry from the British Federal Council, every one knew all about that. Barry's credentials

were then accepted, with only three dissentients. The mandate of
Alerini, for Marseilles, was rejected. Joukowski, Geneva, the
Bakouninist delegate from that city, was refused recognition. The
credentials of four Spanish delegates—Alerini, Morago, Farga, and
Marselau—were contested because the Spanish Federation had not
paid their contributions to the General Council. They offered an
instalment of the Spanish contribution; the General Council withdrew its opposition to the Spanish delegates, and they were then
admitted.

THE HAGUE, *September* 4.

My letter of yesterday closed with the admission of the four
Spanish delegates on depositing with the president of the sitting,
Van den Abeele, an instalment of the contributions which they
owed to the general council. This admission did not, in any way,
prejudice the question of the Alliance. That will be treated separately on a motion which Marx will propose for their expulsion
from the Association. The next contested mandate was that of
Section 2 of New York, held by Sauva. Its rejection was moved
by the reporter, inasmuch as the section had been suspended by
the Federal Council of New York. Sauva, in reply, asserted that
as the section had paid its contribution to the General Council, it
was entitled to representation. Dereure, New York, said the section had taken part in the American Congress, and afterwards repudiated the resolutions there passed. He thought, therefore, that
they ought not to be considered members of the society at all. Marx
said the section had no legal existence. It had been turned out of
the federation it belonged to, and since then it had not sought
recognition by the General Council. It was, therefore, out of the
International. After being opposed by Sorge and Frankel, the
credentials of Section 2 were disallowed. The sitting was then
suspended till nine this morning.

The great American question was first on the programme, arising
on the consideration of the mandate of Section 12 of New York,
held by West. A rule, submitted by Engels, had been laid down in
one of the first sittings of the congress, to the effect that only four
speakers—two for and two against—with five minutes each, should
be allowed on each contested credential; but so important was the

American question considered by the members of the general council, and so anxious were they to afford Section 12 every opportunity of justification that the same delegate, Engels, proposed that for this case the aforesaid rule should be suspended. To this the congress assented.

Marx, in the name of the Committee, himself conducted the case. He proposed the rejection of West's mandate for three reasons. Firstly, he (West) claimed to represent a suspended section. Secondly, he had participated in the Philadelphia Congress, which assembly had denied and disowned the authority of the General Council. And, thirdly, Section 12 had not paid its contributions. The whole question of the proper composition of the International, said Marx, would have to be considered in this case. Section 12 was well-known in America as an organisation got up primarily to forward the chances of Mrs. Victoria Woodhull for the Presidency of the United States of America; and, secondarily, to propagate those pet doctrines of her party, such as free love, spiritualism, &c. It was composed exclusively of bogus reformers, middle-class quacks, and trading politicians, and it denied the proposition laid down in the preamble to the general rules, that "the emancipation of the working classes must be conquered by the working classes themselves;" at least it interpreted it in such a way as to amount to a practical denial, for it said the meaning intended was that the working classes could not be emancipated against their own will, it even denied expressly that the International was a working men's organisation. When the division took place between the different sections in America, both appealed to the General Council. Section 12, moreover, privately applied to the General Council, asking to be allowed the lead of the movement in America. To these appeals the General Council replied, recommending union under one federal council, and that in future no section be formed which did not contain a proportion of at least two-thirds wage-paid labourers among its members. Section 12 not only disregarded these recommendations, but made the breach wider by setting forth this mongrel programme, and taking up a position of distinct hostility and rebellion towards the regularly constituted head of the association, the General Council. For these reasons he proposed that the delegation of Section 12 be not accepted. West then rose. He began by saying that he was afraid he was already condemned, but he had come 4,000 miles just to tell the Congress the truth of the matter. There were three counts in the indictment against him, and to these he would address himself *seriatim*. Dr. Marx had introduced much irrelevant matter, making foul accusations which he had no evidence to support. To these he would offer no reply. It was the custom in all countries where liberty existed for an accused person to be informed of the nature of the offence with which he was charged, and permitted to offer a defence before he was condemned. Neither of these conditions had been fulfilled in the case of Section 12. The first charge with which he (West) was assailed was that he was the delegate of a suspended section. It was quite true that he belonged to Section 12; he admitted it; he was proud of it. But Section 12 was illegally suspended; moreover, the suspension, granting its validity, only lasted till the meeting of the Congress. When the Congress assembled the suspension had expired, and the delegate of Section 12 was entitled to take his seat with the others. With respect to the second charge, he denied that the Philadelphia Congress had repudiated the General Council. All they had done was to refuse to support the Council in illegal measures; the legitimate and reasonable jurisdiction of the General Council had never been questioned. As to the third point, the contributions, he could only say that they were sent. True he had no receipts for them, and where the fault lay, or into whose hands the contributions fell, he could not tell, but that they were *sent* he was quite certain. These were the nominal and professed reasons for his rejection, but they were not the real ones. The hostility of the General Council to Section 12 was in consequence of its middle-class composition; because it had not bowed submissively to the despotic commands of the Council in respect of having two-thirds of its members wage-slaves; because its members, in their private capacity, held and advocated views outside the specific programme of the society, the section was to be cast out from the fold. West here entered upon that part of the question relating to Free Love, Woman's Rights, &c., and caused great merriment by his manner of treating it. "The preamble to the general rules lays down as the great aim of the society the emancipation of the working classes. Well, any emancipation of the working classes must comprehend the emancipation of working women. Sexual equality is the first step in the true path of liberty. While women are enslaved, men will never be free. And why should the International bother itself about free love or social freedom? If a woman wished to change her husband and the other parties are agreeable I would like to know what right anybody else has to interfere. Would you pass a law forbidding a woman to have such a wish; and if you did, do you fancy you could enforce it?" As to the two-thirds idea, said West, that is a mistake. The best leaders are not the working men themselves, but those who, mixing more in intellectual society, see with a clearer eye the inequalities and vices of the present condition of things. The foregoing is only a brief summary of West's speech. It lasted over an hour, some say an hour and a half. West, who is a little spare man, apparently about 50, with bald head, thin sharp features, peering eyes, and the usual American billy-goat beard, is in every way a representative Yankee. His delivery is spasmodic and gesticulatory, his voice rising and falling, now a shout, now a whisper, for all the world reminding one of a veritable Stiggins in the pulpit of an indubitable Bethel.

When we had recovered our composure, Sorge, of New York, replied, and in a dry, business-like manner he touched briefly upon all the irrelevant points of West's oration, demolishing each position as he slowly moved along. When West applied to have Section 12 recognised by the New York Council, he assured him (Sorge) that its members were all wage-paid workmen like himself (West). When they were going to be suspended, they were duly informed of the reasons and the fact beforehand, but refused to offer any explanation or defence. Instead of that they dragged the question of the dissensions into the public gaze, and paraded every little personal detail, however trivial or irrelevant, at their meetings and in their papers. But West himself, as if simply and insanely to show his capacity for double-dealing, came to him (Sorge), and privately assured him of his hostility to the Woodhull and Claflin party, at the same time making serious accusations against them. There was a man in that party called Elliot, who had made certain charges against him (Sorge). He wrote to Elliot undertaking to prove him a liar in five minutes before any committee of three, which Elliot might himself appoint. To that he received no response. Woodhull and Claflin's lot (Section 12) were always trying to expose, by their foolish acts, to ridicule and discredit the real Internationalists in America. The French members, according to them, were all Communists (in the vulgar sense of the word), and the Germans Atheists. But they themselves, said Sorge, were all jobbers, loafers, and idlers, thorough Yankees in fact. Every one who knew anything about the character of the population of the United States knew that the working class there was composed of the following elements: first, the Irish; second, the Germans; third, the negroes; last of all came the native-born Yankees. Such being the case, the Irish were the most important element in any labour movement in America. Well, the Irish had a profound distrust of those classes, the middle-men, &c., represented by Section 12, and would not join with them for any purpose whatever. As to the contributions, said Sorge, in conclusion, "West's statement that they have been sent is mere assertion. Not only is there no evidence of the money being received, but there is no evidence of its having been sent." After a few words from Sauva repeating some trivial things West had already treated us to, the credentials were rejected, 49 voting against, eight abstaining, and not one supporting. Approval of its action on the questions raised so unanimous and so thorough, exceeded the expectations of the General Council itself.

After this we were treated to a private letter, which Guillaume, one of the Bakouninists, had received from somebody somewhere. It denounced Marx as a tyrant, and the members of the General Council as his servants. The only explanation of its production was that it served, counting its translation, to waste about an hour of the time of the Congress. These tactics were being pushed to such an extremity by the small knots of malcontents that a check was found to be absolutely necessary if the work of the Congress was to be got through by the appointed time. Irrelevant and disorderly speeches were frequently made, and when translations into English were requested we were told that what had been said was unimportant, irrelevant, &c., and consequently did not merit translation. To this we replied that that which was unworthy of translation ought not to be allowed expression, and appealed to the President to stop at the outset, all such interruptions to the business of the Congress. The President promised compliance and did his best, but some members were literally unmanageable. So Barry drew up the following formal protest, and having obtained the affixed signatures, handed it to the President, by whom it was read:—"To the President of the Congress,—We, the undersigned members of the Congress, protest against the manner in which the majority of the members of the Congress, themselves speaking other languages, disregard the simple rights of those members who only understand English. The difficulty, amounting almost to an impossibility, of obtaining a knowledge of the proceedings or a hearing of any question, renders our delegation a nullity and our presence a farce.—(Signed) BARRY, T. ROCHE, T. MOTTERSHEAD, SEXTON, J. P. M'DONNELL." Sexton said it was not so much the difficulty of knowing what was going on as the difficulty of obtaining the ear of the Congress. He had repeatedly sent up his name to the President when important questions were being discussed, but had not yet been afforded an opportunity of speaking. The President explained that the close of the debate had always been demanded and declared before he got down to Sexton's name on his list; he disclaimed all partiality. Barry was of opinion that against the President no charge of partiality was intended—certainly he had made none. But what he did complain of was, as the protest set forth, the conduct of the majority of the members. The French-speaking members (and this term comprised the Spanish delegates) were always getting up and evading the rules of the Congress by pretending to rise to order, &c., making long speeches, and thus obstructing real business. The subject then dropped, the good effect of the formal protest being very evident for some time after.

With the settlement of the American question the examination of credentials ceased. Other credentials besides those of Section 12 of New York (notably Section 2 of the same city) had been rejected, but as their holders all held other credentials, whose validity was allowed, West was the only individual rejected, he having no other mandate. As one looked up at him in the gallery to which he had been relegated, where he sat among the other non-delegate members of the society, looking wistfully down, one could not help a touch of pity for him in his long and fruitless errand. The credentials being settled, the time had arrived for electing the President and other officers. The rule at these congresses is that the President of the local section presides till the credentials are examined, after which the Congress elects its own functionaries. In the present case Gerhard was consequently nominally President, but being a very quiet, diffident young man, he requested Henry Van der Abeele, of Antwerp, to officiate, while he (Gerhard) sat beside him. The candidates were Ranvier, Sorge, Brismee, Dupont, and Gerhard. The greatest number of votes were recorded for Ranvier. After him, Brismee and Dupont were equal; but both of these, thinking perhaps that they ought to have been President, refused the post of vice-President, whereupon Sorge and Gerhard accepted the office. The various recording secretaries appointed were as follows:—For French, Lemoussu; English, J. P. M'Donnell; Spanish, Marselau; German, Hepner; Dutch, Van den Hout. Kugelmann (Germany) then moved a vote of thanks to the retiring President, which was cordially given and modestly acknowledged. With this Wednesday's sitting ended. On Thursday morning the public were admitted. The number measured by London audiences, was not large, but then the Hague has not a population of three and a half millions, and the meeting, it must be remembered, was held at ten o'clock in the forenoon, when working men are generally in their workshops. As soon as some preliminaries had been got through, the President, Ranvier, delivered a short address. He sang the praises of sacred revolution in a high key, boasted of his delegation (section Ferre, of Paris) and urged the International to establish a permanent committee of barricades. I need not say that he was vehemently applauded. After that came the following general report, written by Marx. It was read first in English by Sexton, next in French by Longuet, than [*sic*] in German by Marx himself, and finally in Flemish by Van den Abeele, and excited the greatest enthusiasm.

"Citizens,—Since our last congress, two great wars have changed the face of Europe—the Franco-German war and the civil war in France. Both of these wars were preceded, accompanied, and followed up by a third war—the war against the International Working Men's Association. The Paris members of the International had told the French people publicly that voting the plebiscite was voting despotism at home and war abroad. Under the pretext of participation in a plot for the assassination of Louis Bonaparte, they were arrested on the eve of the plebiscite, on the 29th April, 1870. Simultaneous arrests of Internationalists took place at Lyons, Rouen, Marseilles, Brest, and other towns. The men of the 4th of September published documentary evidence proving these facts. Ollivier, in a private circular, directly told his subordinates, 'The leaders of the International must be arrested, or else the voting of the plebiscite could not be satisfactorily proceeded with.' The plebiscite over, the men arrested were condemned simply on the ground of being Internationalists. Before war was declared the Internationalists, nothing daunted, denounced the intentions of the Government. They appealed to their 'brothers in Germany' to oppose the war in their country. That appeal was enthusiastically responded to, thus presenting a picture to the world unparalleled in history. This opens the vista of a brighter future. It proves that in contrast to old society, with its economical miseries and political delirium, a new society is springing up, whose international rule will be peace. The pioneer of that society is the International Working Men's Association.

Up to the proclamation of the Republic the members of the Paris Federal Council remained in prison, while the other members were daily denounced to the mob as traitors in the pay of Prussia. With the capitulation of Sedan, when the Second Empire ended, as it had begun, by a parody, the Franco-German war entered upon its second phase. After the repeated solemn declarations to take up arms for the sole purpose of repelling foreign aggression, Prussia now dropped the mask and proclaimed a war of conquest. From that moment she found herself compelled not only to fight the Republic in France, but simultaneously the International in Germany. Immediately after the declaration of war the greater part of the territory of the North German Confederation—Hanover, Oldenburg, Hamburg, Brunswick, Schleswig-Holstein, Mecklenburg, Pomerania, and the province of Prussia were placed in a state of siege. This was done nominally for protection from foreign invasion, but was used only against the Internationals in Germany. On the 5th September the Brunswick Central Committee of the German International issued a manifesto calling upon the people to oppose by all the means in their power the dismemberment of France. The manifesto denounced the proposed annexation of Alsace and Lorraine as a crime tending to transform all Germany into a Prussian barracks, and to establish war as a permanent European institution. On the 9th September, by order of Vogel Von Falkenstein, the members who issued that manifesto were arrested and marched off, a distance of 600 miles, to Lotzen, a Prussian fortress on the Russian frontier, where their ignominous [*sic*] treatment was to serve as a foil to the ostentatious feasting at Wilhelmshohe. As the International continued to extend, despite the incessant persecutions to which its members were subjected, Falkenstein issued an ukase of September 21, interdicting all meetings. Leaving the cares of the war abroad to Moltke, William of Prussia directed that at home. By his personal order of October 17, Vogel Von Falkenstein was to send his Lötzen captives to the Brunswick district tribunal the which on its part was to find grounds for their legal durance, or, failing that, return them to the safe keeping of the dread general."

Falkenstein's proceedings were imitated in various parts of Germany, while Bismarck, in a diplomatic circular, mocked Europe by standing forth as the indignant champion of free speech, a free press, and free meetings on the part of the peace party in France. He imprisoned Bebel and Liebknecht, the representatives of the International in the German Parliament, to get them out of the way during the impending general election. His master supported him by prolonging the state of siege in Germany over the whole of the election period—in fact, for two months after the conclusion of peace with France. The stubbornness with which he was insisting upon the state of war at home proves the awe in which he, amidst the din of victorious arms, and the frantic cheers of the whole middle class, held the rising party of the Proletariat. It was the involuntary homage paid by physical force to moral power.

On the 6th June, 1871, Jules Favre issued a circular to the foreign powers demanding the extradition of the refugees of the Commune as common criminals, and a general crusade against the International as the enemy of family, religion, order, and property, so adequately represented in his own person. Austria and Hungary caught the cue at once. On the 13th June a raid was made on the reputed leaders of the Pesth Working Men's Union; their papers were sequestrated, their persons seized, and proceedings instituted against them for high treason. Several delegates of the Vienna International happening to be on a visit at Pesth were carried off to Vienna, there to undergo similar treatment. Beust asked and received from his parliament a supplementary vote of £30,000 "on behalf of expenses for political information that had become more than ever indispensable through the dangerous spread of the International all over Europe." In its last agonies the Austrian government anxiously clings to its old privilege of playing the Don Quixote of European reaction. On the 27th November, 1871, judgment was passed upon the members of the Brunswick Committee, being sentenced to various terms of imprisonment. At Pesth the prisoners belonging to the Working Men's Union, after having undergone for nearly a year a treatment as infamous as that inflicted upon the Fenians by the British Government, were brought up for judgment on the 22nd April, 1872. In spite, however, of the appeal of the public prosecutor, the Court acquitted them. At Leipsic, on the 27th March, 1872, Bebel and Liebknecht were sentenced to two years' imprisonment in a fortress for attempted high treason. His Holiness Pope Pius IX. said in an allocution to a deputation of Swiss Catholics, "Your government, which is Republican, thinks itself bound to make a heavy sacrifice for what is called liberty, and it affords an asylum to a goodly number of individuals of the worst character. It tolerates that sect of the International which desires to treat all Europe as it has treated Paris. These gentlemen of the International, who are no gentlemen, are to be feared because they work for the account of the everlasting enemy of God and mankind. What is to be gained by protecting them? One must pray for them." Hang them first and pray for them afterwards.

Supported by Bismarck, Beust, and Stieber, the Emperors of Austria and Germany met at Salzburg in the beginning of September, 1871, for the ostensible purpose of founding a Holy Alliance against the International Working Men's Association. "Such an European alliance," declared the *Norddeutsche Allgemeine Zeitung*, Bismarck's private *Moniteur*, "is the only possible salvation of State, Church, property, civilization—in one word, of everything that constitutes European states." Bismarck's real object, of course, was to prepare alliances for an impending war with Russia, and the International was held up to Austria as the red rag. Lanza suppressed the International in Italy by simple decree. Sagasta declared it an outlaw in Spain. Russia found the general hue and cry a pretext for reaction. The Republican government of Switzerland itself has only been prevented by the agitation of the Swiss Internationalists from handing up to Thiers refugees of the Commune. Finally, the government of Mr. Gladstone, unable to act in Great Britain, set forth its good intentions by the police terrorism exercised in Ireland against our sections then in course of formation, and by ordering its representatives abroad to collect information with respect to the International Working Men's Association. But all the measures of repression which the combined government intellect of Europe was capable of devising vanish into nothing when compared with the war of calumny undertaken by the lying power of the civilized world. Apocryphal histories and mysteries of the International, shameless forgeries of public documents and private letters, sensational telegrams followed each other in rapid succession; all the sluices of slander at the disposal of the venal respectable press were opened at once to set free a deluge of infamy in which to drown the execrated foe. When the great conflagration took place at Chicago, the telegraph, round the globe, announced it as the infernal deed of the International, and it is really wonderful that to its demoniacal agency has not been attributed the hurricane that ravaged the West Indies. Since the congress of Basle, in 1871, the International has been extended to the Irish in England and to Ireland itself, to Scotland, Holland, Denmark, and Portugal; it has been firmly organised in the United States, and has established ramifications in Buenos Ayres, Australia, and New Zealand. The difference between a working class without an International and a working class with an International becomes most evident if we look back to the period of 1848. Years were required for the working class itself to recognise the insurrection of June, 1848, as the work of its own vanguard. The Paris Commune was at once acclaimed by the universal Proletariat. Again, the delegates of the working class meet to strengthen the militant organisation of a society aiming at the emancipation of labour and at the extinction of national feuds. Almost at the same moment there met at Berlin the crowned dignitaries of the Old World in order to forge new chains and to hatch new wars.

THE HAGUE, *September* 7.

After the reading of the report Thursday's sitting ended. But before the public retired an incident occurred which I must mention, because of its sequence. Cuno, addressing the gallery, said if Herr Schramm, Prussian Consul at Milan, was present, he would confer a favour on him (Cuno) by coming forward and showing himself. Otherwise he (Cuno) would brand him as a coward. This caused considerable tumult and excitement, but Schramm could not be seen anywhere; order was soon restored. On the following day, however, in the middle of our administrative sitting, Schramm forced his way past doorkeepers and landlord, and stood before us. He is a big, stout man, middle-aged, with typical German face, and the inevitable spectacles. He seemed terribly frightened, and spoke very loudly and rapidly. He said he chanced to be in the Hague just then, and had seen in the *Dagblad* that he been denounced by Cuno, and condemned to death by the society. He was not afraid of death; he had fought before, and would fight again if necessary. But he wished to know what he had done to call down the condemnation of the International, and seeing Marx, he came forward, held out his hand, and appealed to him to clear his character before the congress. Meantime all the delegates had sprung up to their feet, and a Babel of voices ensued. Marx shook hands with Schramm, and told him there was a mistake somewhere; there was no condemnation to death. Ultimately Cuno and Schramm went out together. Before the close of the sitting Cuno returned and read to the congress a declaration, written and signed by Schramm, condemning and disavowing the conduct of which Cuno complained, and acknowledging the justice of Cuno's indignation. Cuno also read a declaration, written and signed by himself, expressing his conviction that Schramm was innocent of the matter. I took an early opportunity of ascertaining from Cuno the particulars of the case, and they are as follows: —Cuno, a German engineer employed at Milan, was very active in the International movement there, on which account the Italian government arrested him and seized his papers and his money. He was subjected to the most brutal and infamous treatment, and after a month's detention brought in chains to the frontier and handed over to the Austrian authorities, who escorted him to the Bavarian frontier where at last he was set at liberty. While in prison he consulted the Milan directory and finding Schramm therein described as Prussian Consul, wrote requesting him to demand the restoration of his money and papers. To this and other succeeding similar requests, Cuno received no reply. Schramm now explained that at that time he was no longer Prussian Consul and absent from Milan, but declared that Cuno's letters ought to have been handed over to his successor, and that Cuno was perfectly justified in his indignation at the shameful treatment he received and at the inaction of his Consulate. It seems Schramm was one of the leaders of the Revolution of 1848; but in 1866, after Sadowa, Bismarck wanted as many old revolutionists as he could get, in order to help him in his manipulation of the people, and Schramm was afterwards Bismarck's consul at Milan.

I think I forgot to tell you that on Wednesday Marx asked for a commission of five to inquire into the secret "Alliance." He said he would prefer this course, as the papers were so voluminous and various that if laid before the whole congress they would never get through their discussion. Guillaume (Bakouninist) assented to Marx's proposal for a commission, but thought that it ought to comprise some members of the accused party. Sauva differed from Guillaume. The commission ought to be composed entirely of neutrals. Sauva's opinion was that of the General Council itself, as briefly expressed by one or two of its principal members, and a commission, fully embodying the principle, was at once appointed. It consists of Cuno, Splingard, Lucain, Walther, and Vichart. This commission is carrying on its labours in the intervals between the sittings, and will lay its report before the congress as soon as all the evidence is examined, and then Marx will propose its expulsion from the society. There is a *sanctum* and a *sanctum sanctorum* in this "Alliance." Bakounine does not initiate all his disciples—in fact, only a few— into the innermost mysteries of the system he has devised. All his men at the congress assert that it was dissolved some time ago, which dissolution Marx declares to have been a sham for the purpose of foiling the hunt. We await eagerly the report of the commission.

My friends of Saturday night, the secretary to the States Council of Holland and his companion, undaunted by their failure upon that occasion, tried their luck at our hotel the other night. A number of us were sitting round the table at supper, when they dropped in quite innocently, and ordering some refreshment, sat down at our table. I whispered to Marx, who sat next me, who and what they were, and passed the word round to prevent an unguarded expression. By and bye the secretary addressed himself to Marx, approaching him, as he no doubt supposed, on his weak side, by talking solely about Marx's great book on political economy, on which he has been engaged twenty-five years, and which was published in Germany in 1867, and is now being published in French. But the secretary is welcome to all he got out of Marx. His companion, recognising me, began to assure me that he had been misrepresented and traduced, but I pretended not to understand him (this was perfectly justifiable, his English was so atrocious), and went out with some others for a walk, in the course of which we were overtaken, passed, and repassed, by these two industriously inquiring young men. These are representative men. The manner in which Marx is pestered by requests for interviews from people of all countries and politics is perfectly ludicrous.

On reassembling yesterday morning a request was handed in from the Spanish delegates, asking the congress to devise some means whereby they might escape from the trammels imposed upon them. They said they were bound by an imperative mandate to abstain entirely from voting on any question whatever, until a new mode of taking the votes, proposed by their constituents, had been adopted by the congress, and they besought the congress to free them. Engels said it was most remarkable to find men coming to a congress with their hands tied. These men had received their credentials from one source and their orders from another, and it was mere childishness to ask the congress to deliver them from authority which they had voluntarily sought and accepted.

An official communication was received from the section at Amsterdam inviting the members of the congress to a public meeting in that city on Sunday. This invitation was, after some conversation, accepted, and the section thanked by the president in the name of the congress.

The alterations in the general statutes proposed by the general council were then discussed. The council proposed that Article 2 should declare that "The general council is bound to execute the resolutions of the congresses, and enforce upon all branches, sections, or federations strict observance of all the rules and regulations of the society." Article 6, as revised, declares "The general council shall have power to suspend any branch, section, or federation till the following congress. Nevertheless, where federal councils exist, it shall be the duty of the general council to consult the same. Where a whole federation is suspended the general council shall apprise all the sections in the various countries of the same, and should a majority of the sections require it, the general council shall, within thirty days, convoke an extraordinary conference, consisting of one delegate from each nationality, to consider the question. And where a federal council is dissolved, any new federal council intended to replace it must be established within thirty days of said dissolution." Brismee (Brussels) led off the attack. There were, he said, seven Belgian delegates in the congress. Some of these desired the total abolition of a general council, thinking the sections and federations could best do their work free from all interference whatever. Others wished to see the powers of the council diminished. None would agree to a continuance, much less such an increase as was proposed, of its authority. Longuet (London) did not think the general council ought to exercise the functions of a government, but he did think it was necessary to have a central authority, empowered to mediate, and, if necessary, arbitrate, whenever and wherever dissensions arose. Guillaume said they all understood each other; discussion was useless. The majority were there with matured plans, and it was idle to oppose them. Serraillier (London) said such a taunt was unfortunate in the mouth of a delegate whose course was marked out for him, and whose hands were tied by an imperative, an irrational mandate. It was the simple duty of the council to mature their plans before submitting them to the congress. Each delegate of the majority was free to follow, upon each question, the dictates of reason and conscience, and was not, as he (Guillaume) was, the supple tool of an unseen and irresponsible power. These abstentionists maintained that the International did not exist in France. He, as French secretary, had the written proofs with him that not only did it exist, but that it was fully organised in thirty out of the eighty-six departments of the country, and was, in fact, now stronger than it had ever been before. This speech was loudly cheered. Morago (Bakouninist) protested against the interference of the general council with the

sections. Lafargue denounced the minority as obstructive and tyrannical. The division on Article 2 was then called, with the following
result:—Ayes, 44; Noes, 5; Abstentionists, 11. The article was
therefore adopted. In support of Article 6, as revised, Marx spoke
next. He said—"The congress would understand that the general
council, of which I am now speaking, and for which the increased
powers are asked, is not the old council. That council's tenure of
office expired simultaneously with the assembling of the congress.
The council of which I now speak is that one whose election for
1872–3 will be one of your duties before you separate. Some have
urged that the general council's powers should be reduced to being
merely a centre of communication. Others recommend its abolition.
Of the two the latter is to my mind preferable. It is, at least, logical;
the other is both illogical and silly. You would constitute the council
a letter-box where no letter-box was required, thus involving unnecessary expense, for what would be more simple and natural than for
the sections and federations to correspond with each other direct;
why pass the letters through the mechanical letter-box? If an attempt was made to conduct the affairs of the association in that way
the result would be that the association would get into the hands of
irresponsible men—the journalists; for every one knows that the
association has newspapers in all countries and in all languages, and
it is clear that these papers would be able to communicate all International news quicker than this could be done by voluminous letters
which the working men have not always the time to write. Thus
there would be a letter-box but no letters at all, or only such containing stale news; the power taken from the responsible general council
would pass over to the hands of the irresponsible journalists. We
have been asked to limit the suspensory power of the council to
foreseen and specified cases. That is impossible; it is just for the
unforeseen that we most require provision. There are some who
chafe under the authority of the general council, who nevertheless
reveal their love of subjection by embracing a jurisdiction that is
both illegal and immoral. Let them remember that the power of the
general council of the International is not one of arms, of soldiers,
nor the law. It is a moral power which shall increase in proportion
as it retains the confidence of the members of the association; with
that confidence the council will be strong; without it, it will be

powerless, even if you armed it with the most despotic attribute. After some unimportant remarks by sundry delegates the article was adopted—Ayes, 36; Noes, 6; Abstentionists, 15.

THE HAGUE, *September* 9.

After the adoption of the two articles in their revised form there was a slight pause. It was the lull before the storm. Knowing what was coming, and whom it would most affect, I stood up and watched the operation. Up got Engels, Marx's right hand, and said he would make a communication to the Congress. It was a recommendation from a number of members of the general council respecting the seat of the council for the next year. "Between two and three years ago, before the Franco-German war broke out, Marx proposed to the general council the removal of its seat to Brussels. To this some members objected, and the federations being asked for an opinion on the matter, the unanimous reply was, 'Stay in London.' There certainly were many reasons, and good ones, for staying. London was, undoubtedly, the only place in Europe where the papers of the society were safe. London, moreover, possessed in its working population greater diversity of nationalities than any other town. This last peculiarity resulted in a truly international composition of the general council. If any one was led to suppose that there had been no discussions and conflicts in the council itself he would be in error. There had been almost all shades of socialist opinion represented in it, and the debates had, at times, been quite as excited as those of the present Congress. Moreover, its members had been so numerous that the council, from a mere administrative and executive body, had sometimes degenerated into a parliamentary assembly. This was especially the case when, after the defeat of the Commune, there was a very large addition of French members. Therefore, the number of the members of the council ought to be limited, and it was proposed to limit it to fifteen. Then, as to the seat of the future council, the continent of Europe is still out of the question. The delegates who have signed this recommendation have come to the conclusion that the interests of the association require the removal of the seat of the council, at least for one year, from London; and taking into account the considerations I have enumerated, they recommend New York." Consternation and discomfiture stood plainly written on the faces of the party of dissension as he uttered the last words. "New York," proceeded Engels, "furnishes the elements of safety and cosmopolitanism possessed by London, and if not in the same degree, at least more approximately than any other place. In going to New York the authority of the general council is not going into the hands of untried men. Although not long in the work, the members there show a capacity and a zeal which amply warrant us in trusting them. The recommendation is signed—Marx, Engels, M'Donnell, Sexton, Longuet, Lessner, Le Moussu, Serraillier, and Barry, members of general council." It was some time before any one rose to speak. It was a *coup d'etat*, and each one looked to his neighbour to break the spell. At length Vaillant rose. He is an extreme Blanquist, and a member of the late general council. He opposed the change. "The International," he said, "had prospered exceedingly under its present leaders, and why should they be changed, even for a year? The appropriate place for the general council was close to the field of battle—France and Germany. If it were moved across the Atlantic its influence in Europe would be lessened. Moreover, there were dissensions in New York as well as in London (as had been amply demonstrated at that very Congress), and what security had the leaders of the society that the natural enemies of the people, the *bourgeois*, which swarmed so abundantly in that country, would not ultimately succeed in gaining possession of the government of the movement, when all hope of the emancipation of the proletariat would be lost. He besought those whose leadership had made the International Society the dread of kings and emperors, to continue their great sacrifices for the cause, sacrifices which, ere long, would surely be crowned with success." Vaillant was followed by Sauva. Sauva, who lives in New York, had no objection to the transfer of the seat of the general council to that city, but he would like the Congress to elect all the members itself, instead of appointing only a portion and leaving to it the filling up of the remainder. I forgot to mention that, besides determining the seat of the council for next year, the proposition suggested that out of the fifteen members eight should be elected by the Congress, these eight to choose the other seven themselves. Serraillier said the recommendation included three questions, which had better be discussed and voted upon separately. He suggested that they consider

—first, should the seat of the council be removed from London; second, to where; and third, the composition of the council. This was discredited by Wilmot, who endeavoured to show the Congress that, if it settled the second point, it settled the first at the same time. He therefore moved as an amendment that the questions be divided into two instead of three. But the Congress had been so thoroughly worried and badgered by idle obstruction that it would not listen to Wilmot's hairsplitting, as it evidently thought it to be, and overwhelmingly voted him a bore, and his amendment a nuisance. The roll was then called upon the question— Should the council be removed from London? with the following result:—Ayes, 26; Noes, 23; Abstentionists, 9. The astonishing number of noes represents Marx's oldest and most devoted followers, men who believe that his personal supervision and direction is absolutely essential. So strong is their conviction on this point that they broke away from his lead in this case, and tried to outvote him. The Ayes, for the same reasons, include a number of his enemies. Marselau (Bakouninist) said he had been pained to hear some members laugh when he and his fellow-abstentionists answered "Abstain." They did not abstain from choice, but because of their imperative mandate, which strictly prohibited them from voting. It was, under these circumstances, he thought, unbrotherly to laugh at them, and he begged that it might not be continued. This man, Marselau, seemed quite different from his companions; serious, conscientious, and quiet, he impressed one, if only by contrast, very favourably. We then proceeded to fix upon a place to which the seat of the general council should be moved. But before this could be done, Johannard wished to speak, protesting that the subject had not been sufficiently discussed. The President pointed out that the discussion had been formally closed, but Johannard is not easily controlled. By-and-bye he consented to resume his seat, handing up to the President a brief speech in writing, to the effect that removal to New York would look like flight. Undaunted by this dreadful contingency, the Congress voted— New York, 31; London, 14; Brussels, 1; Barcelona, 1; Abstentionists, 11. This division shows that the question of removal once decided in the affirmative, those who had opposed [i]t now voted for New York; in other words, if not London, then New York.

The sitting was then suspended till six in the evening, when the public were admitted. If any one was dissatisfied with the numbers of the first public meeting, there was, assuredly, no room for such feelings on Friday evening. An immense crowd blocked the street outside, making the ingress of members a work of no slight difficulty; and whenever the doors were opened it poured in like a flood. Soon every available spot was occupied, and some even that could not legitimately be expected to afford accommodation. Window-sills were not despised, and some lads clustered round the supporting iron pillars. The galleries also were crammed to suffocation. In the course of the evening the crowd in the body of the hall had so increased that its front rank was forced upon the barrier, which had to be shifted several yards forward. Preliminaries over, Van der Hout, a member of a Dutch section, obtained permission to address the public upon a special question. He is a young man, of, perhaps, twenty-five or thirty, with nothing remarkable about him but a good loud voice and a free action when speaking. The *Dagblad*, he said, the organ of the government of Holland, had printed that morning a shameful and scurrilous article on the meeting of the preceding day. It said that the delegates looked and smelt of blood—that they were an ill-looking, unwashed, badly-clad rabble. It did not even keep its ribald tongue off the three ladies present amongst the delegates (Mrs. Marx, her daughter, Madame Lafargue, and another delegate's wife), but called them *tricoteuses*. The people of Holland, he said, knew the value which properly attached to anything the *Dagblad* said, but he thought it was their duty towards the men so foully aspersed and so shamelessly misrepresented to express that night, publicly, their repudiation of the *Dagblad* as the exponent of their views, and their contempt for its unscrupulous falsehoods. Pointing to the delegates, he asked if even in the outward description of these men the *Dagblad* did not stand convicted of a misrepresentation which would be abominable if it was not ridiculous. The time-serving, unprincipled sycophancy of the *Dagblad* would be remembered by the people of Holland long after the delegates of the International Congress had returned to their homes. This oration (for I can call it nothing else) was delivered with great fire and vigour, and evoked the most intense enthusiasm on the part of the audience, who interrupted the orator, from time to time, with great shouts of applause. After this the two declarations of Cuno and Schramm were read to the people. Then several delegates, including Guillaume,

Vaillant, and Longuet, discussed the question of the political action of the working class, but nothing new or worthy of record was said. At the end an unseemly altercation arose between the president (Ranvier) and Johannard. Johannard insisted on making a speech, and although Ranvier reminded him that all those had spoken whose names were inscribed for that purpose on his list, he would and did speak, amid the humiliation of the president, the irritation of the delegates, and the jeers of the audience, which, like all audiences, quickly showed its appreciation of the ludicrous. When he had done some reactionary, in the gallery started the Dutch national air, and, the humour being on them, the bulk of the audience caught it up instanter. To make matters worse, Johannard, of whom the audience had had enough, got on to a table, and, aided by a few feeble voices near him, attempted the Marseillaise. Of course this challenge was answered in such style as to literally drown him and cause an ignominious [*sic*] descent from his "bad eminence." The mob, now thoroughly roused, surged and roared at us, and we had enough to do to get out.

Next morning (Saturday) a considerable number of delegates left the Hague. Some went to a congress which was to open on Monday at Mayence; others returned, for personal reasons, home to London. The last-mentioned batch comprised Ranvier, Cournet, Roach, Vaillant, Sexton, Lessner, and Arnould. A number of these, before departing, left in writing their vote upon the composition of the new General Council. There are three parties in New York—the federal council party, the opposition, and the go-between. The first of these, the really popular section, is the one into whose hands the old General Council proposed to pass its power. This party is represented in the Congress by Sorge, and if it possesses one or two more men like him the affairs of the Association will not suffer mismanagement in consequence of the incapacity of its officers. When the approved list was proposed a hot and angry discussion ensued. Now were linked together all the previously discordant elements of opposition. The Spaniards were more riotously obstructive than ever. The two or three discontented Englishmen who, for their own purposes, wished the Council to remain in London, thought they descried an opportunity of virtually reversing the previous decision of the Congress on that question. And, most curious of all, at least to those who did not know the men, was the spectacle of Dereure, the whimsical and erratic, leagued for once, with the implacable and irreconcilable Sauva in support of a counter "ticket" which comprised both their own names! But all this motley combination was unable to do more than postpone, while they spoke, the action resolved upon. The federal council list was voted almost intact; the only alteration being the elimination of two of the least important names, and the substitution, therefore, of Dereure and another, Sauva being peremtorily [*sic*] rejected. On the motion of Marx it was agreed that the federation, instead of those members of the General Cruncil [*sic*] now elected, as at first proposed, should appoint the remainder of the number (15) specified.

In the evening the Commission appointed to inquire into the secret "Alliance" brought up its report. The evidence of its existence was overwhelmingly conclusive. The documentary proofs submitted by Marx and Engels left no room for further doubt. Even those members of the Commission friendly to the parties implicated acknowledged the completeness of the evidence. Those members of the Alliance, such as Marselau, who honestly believed it to have been dissolved, were let off on a formal renunciation of it and its chief; but with respect to three, Schwitzguebel, Bakounine, and Guillaume, the Committee proposed their expulsion from the Association. The vote was taken. Bakounine and Guillaume were cast out, but Schwitzguebel, about whom some members were in doubt, escaped by the skin of his teeth. So ends a great conspiracy. Unmolested, it would have diverted and broken the course of the International. The ability and persistency with which it was devised and propagated have only been excelled by the power that crushed it.

The next morning (Sunday) we went to Amsterdam to partake of the hospitality of our friends there. Congratulatory speeches were made by Marx, Sorge, Longuet, Lafargue, and Serraillier. There was some carping amongst the Adullamites, because they were not allowed an opportunity of showing the good people of Amsterdam that there were some details on which there was a difference of opinion. But their plaints were addressed to unsympathetic ears. The meeting at Amsterdam was a great success, the people listening eagerly to the enunciation of the principles of the International, and responding enthusiastically to Marx's invitation to membership.

There is nothing more to be recorded. The Congress, which has just ended, has been both eventful and significant. In degree of importance, after the intensely satisfactory spread of the propaganda reported in the branches and sections everywhere, comes the increase of the powers of the General Council, and removal of its seat to New York, and the extinction of Bakounine's secret alliance. Such a record is one of which the late General Council need not be ashamed. Of these the question which will probably most interest the English public is the removal from London of the General Council. This step was found absolutely necessary. The time and thought which the affairs of the General Council exacted of Marx, when added to his labours of translating the various editions of his great book, and general supervision of the Association, were found exhausting and injurious to his health. During the last year or so, since the accession to the Council of a number of "representative" Englishmen, it has taxed all his efforts (and these have sometimes failed) to keep the Council to its legitimate work. If he retired from the Council, and it still remained in London, it would be in great danger of falling into the hands of men who would make it either a pothouse forum or an electioneering machine. Marx is quite certain that somewhere, probably in the provinces, there are Englishmen, not only capable, but honest and well fitted to lead the movement in this country. In the course of a twelvemonth these men may come to the front; but meantime there is not a sufficient number of them in London to protect the organisation from "falling among thieves." However, it is of little consequence where the General Council is. Given freedom of action its work will be done. The principles of the International are independent of geographical conditions; and these will guide the complex forces of the proletariat to their ultimate goal.

I.—Resolution relative to the General Rules.

The following article which resumes the contents of Resolution IX. of the conference of London (September, 1871) to be inserted in the Rules after Article 7, viz:—

Article 7A.—In its struggle against the collective power of the propertied classes, the working class cannot act as a class except by constituting itself into a political party, distinct from, and opposed to all old parties formed by the propertied classes.

This constitution of the working class into a political party is indispensable in order to insure the triumph of the social revolution, and of its ultimate end, the abolition of classes.

The combination of forces which the working class has already effected by its economical struggles ought at the same time to serve as a lever for its struggles against the political power of landlords and capitalists.

The lords of land and the lords of capital will always use their political privileges for the defence and perpetuation of their economical monoplies, [*sic*] and for the enslavement of labour. The conquest of political power has therefore become the great duty of the working class.

Adopted by thirty-six votes against five, and eight abstentions.

Voted for—Arnaud, Barry, J. Ph. Becker, B. Becker, Cournet, Dereure, Dumon, Dupont, Duval, Eccarius, Engels, Farkas, Friedlaender, Frankel, Hepner, Heim, Johannard, Kugelmann, Lafargue, Longuet, Le Moussu, Mottershead, Pihl, Ranvier, Serraillier, Sorge, Swarm, Vaillant, Wilmot, Mac-Donnell.

The Congress having passed the formal resolution to admit the votes of the delegates whom the work of the commissions prevented from being present at the sitting—Cuno, Lucain, Marx, Vichard, Walter, Wroblewski, gave their votes for the article in question.

Voted against—Brismee, Cœnen, Gerhardt, Schwitzguebel, van der Hout.

Abstained—Van den Abeele, Dave, Eberhardt, Fluse, Guillaume, Herman, Sauva, Marselau.

II.—Resolutions relating to the Administrative Regulations.

1. Powers of the General Council.

Articles 2 and 6 have been replaced by the following articles:—

"Article 2.—The general council is bound to execute the Congress resolutions, and to take care that in every country the principles and the general rules and regulations of the International are strictly observed.

Voted for—Arnaud, Barry, J. Ph. Becker, B. Becker, Cournet, Cuno, Dereure, Dumon, Dupont, Duval, Engels, Farkas, Frankel, Friedlaender, Hepner, Heim, Johannard, Kugelmann, Lafargue, Lessner, Le Moussu, Longuet, Lucain, Mac-Donnell, Marx, Milke, Pihl, Ranvier, Roach, Sauva, Scheu, Serraillier, Sexton, Sorge, Swarm, Schumacher, Vaillant, Vichard, Walter, Wroblewski.

Voted against—Fluse, Gerhardt, Splingard, Van der Hout.

Abstained—Alerini, Cœnen, Dave, Eberhard, Guillaume, Herman, Morago, Marselau, Farga-Pellicer, Schwitzguebel, Van den Abeele.

Adopted by forty votes against four; abstentions, eleven.

"Article 6.—The general council has also the right to suspend branches, sections, federal councils, or committees, and federations of the International, till the meeting of the next Congress.

"Nevertheless, in the case of sections belonging to a federation, the general council will exercise this right only after having consulted the respective federal council.

"In the case of the dissolution of a federal council, the general council shall, at the same time, call upon the sections of the respective federation to elect a new federal council within thirty days at most.

"In the case of the suspension of an entire federation, the general council shall immediately inform thereof the whole of the federations. If the majority of them demand it, the general council shall convoke an extraordinary conference, composed of one delegate for each nationality, which shall meet within one month and finally decide upon the question.

"Nevertheless, it is well understood that the countries where the International is prohibited shall exercise the same rights as the regular federations."

Article 6 was adopted by thirty-six votes against six; abstentions, sixteen.

Voted for—Arnaud, Barry, J. Ph. Becker, B. Becker, Cournet, Cuno, Dereure, Dupont, Duval, Engels, Farkas, Frankel, Friedlaender, Hepner, Heim, Johannard, Kugelmann, Lafargue, Lessner, Le Moussu, Longuet, Ludwig, Mac-Donnell, Marx, Milke, Pihl, Ranvier, Serraillier, Schumacher, Sexton, Sorge, Swarm, Vaillant, Vichard, Walter, Wroblewski.

Voted against—Brismee, Cœnen, Fluse, Herman, Sauva, Splingard.

Abstained—Alerini, Cyrille, Dave, Dumon, Eberhardt, Guillaume, Lucain, Marselau, Morago, Mottershead, Farga-Pellicer, Roach, Schwitzguebel, Van den Abeele, Van der Hout, Wilmot.

2. Contributions to be paid to the general council:—With regard to the proposal, on the one hand to raise, on the other to re-

duce, the amount of their contributions, the Congress had to decide whether the actual amount of ld. per annum should be altered or not. The Congress maintained the rate of one penny by seventeen votes against twelve, and eight abstentions.

Voted against the change—J. Ph. Becker, Brismee, Cœnen, Cyrille, Dupont, Duval, Eberhardt, Eccarius, Farkas, Fluse, Gerhardt, Herman, Hepner, Serraillier, Sorge, Swarm, Wilmot.

Voted for—Dumon, Engels, Frankel, Heim, Johannard, Lafargue, Le Moussu, Longuet, Lucain, Mac-Donnell, Pihl, Sauva.

Abstained—Alerini, Dave, Dereure, Guillaume, Marselau, Morago, Farga-Pellicer, Schwitzguebel.

The following delegates, Arnaud, Cournet, Ranvier, Vaillant, having been obliged to leave The Hague before the discussion, left their votes in favour of raising the contributions.

III.—Resolution relating to the Internationalisation of Trades' Societies.

The new general council is entrusted with the special mission to establish International Trades Unions.

For this purpose it shall, within the month following this Congress, draw up a circular which shall be translated and published in all languages, and forwarded to all trades' societies whose addresses are known, whether they are affiliated to the International or not.

In this circular every union shall be called upon to enter into an International union of its respective trade.

Every union shall be invited to fix itself the conditions under which it proposes to enter the International Union of its trade.

The general council shall, from the conditions fixed by the unions, adopting the idea of International union, draw up a general plan, and submit it to the provisional acceptance of the societies.

The next Congress will finally settle the fundamental treaty for the International trades unions.

(Voted unanimously *minus* a few abstentions, the number of which has not been stated in the minutes.)

IV.—Resolutions relating to the admission of Sections.

1. Section 2 (New York French) of the North American Federation.—This Section had been excluded by the American Federal

Council. On the other hand, it had not been recognised as an independent Section by the General Council. It was not admitted by the Congress. Voted against the admission, 38; for, 8; abstained, 11.

2. Section 12 (New York American) of the North American Federation.—Suspended by the General Council.

Section 12 was excluded by 49 votes against 0; abstentions, 9.

Voted for the exclusion—Arnaud, Barry, J. Ph. Becker, Brismee, Cournet, Cœnen, Cuno, Dave, Dereure, Dietzgen, Dumon, Dupont, Duval, Eberhardt, Fluse, Farkas, Frankel, Friedlaender, Gerhardt, Heim, Hepner, Herman, Johannard, Kugelmann, Lafargue, Le Moussu, Lessner, Lucain, Mac-Donnell, Marx, Milke, Pihl, Ranvier, Roach, Sauva, Scheu, Schumacher, Seraillier, Sexton, Sorge, Splingard, Swarm, Vaillant, van den Abeele, van der Hout, Vichard, Wilmot, Wroblewski, Walter.

Abstained—Alerini, Eccarius, Guillaume, Harcourt, Marselau, Morago, Farga-Pellicer, Mottershead, Schwitzguebel.

3. The International Working Men's Association, based upon the principle of the abolition of classes, cannot admit any middle-class Sections.

Voted for—Arnaud, J. Ph. Becker, Barry, Brismee, Cournet, Cuno, Cœnen, Dave, Dereure, Dietzgen, Dupont, Duval, Eberhardt, Fluse, Farkas, Frankel, Friedlaender, Guillaume, Gerhardt, Heim, Hepner, Herman, Johannard, Kugelmann, Lafargue, Le Moussu, Lessner, Lucain, Marx, Milke, Mottershead, Pihl, Ranvier, Sauva, Schen, Schumacher, Serraillier, Sexton, Sorge, Splingard, Swarm, Vaillant, Vichard, Wilmot, Wroblewski, Walter, van den Abeele.

Abstained—Alerini, Eccarius, Harcourt, Marselau, Morago, Farga-Pellicer, Roach, Schwitzguebel, van der Hout.

4. Section of Marseilles.—This Section, quite unknown to the General Council, and to the French Sections in correspondence with the latter, is not admitted. Against the admission, 38; for, 0; abstentions, 14.

5. Section of Propaganda of Revolutionary Action, at Geneva.— This Section, which is but the resurrection of the (public) "Alliance de la Democratique Socialiste," of Geneva, dissolved in 1871, had been recognised neither by the Romand Federal Committee nor by the General Council, which, indeed, had returned its contributions when sent by the Jurassian Federal Committee. The Congress re-

solved to suspend it till after the debate on the second *Alliance*. The suspension was voted unanimously, less a few abstentions not counted.

6. New Federation of Madrid.—The new Federation of Madrid was formed by the members of the previous Spanish Federal Council, after the old Federation of Madrid, in flagrant breach of the rules then in force, had expelled them for having denounced the conspiracy of the secret alliance against the International Working Men's Association. They addressed themselves, in the first instance, to the Spanish Federal Council, which refused to affiliate the new Federation. They then addressed themselves to the General Council, which took upon itself the responsibility of recognising it without consulting the Spanish Council, amongst whose eight members not less than five belonged to the *Alliance*.

The Congress admitted this Federation by 40 votes against o; the few abstentions were not counted.

V.—Audit of the accounts of the General Council.

The Committee appointed by the Congress for the auditing of the accounts of the General Council for the year 1871–72, was composed of the following citizens:—Dumon, for France; Alerini, for Spain; Farkas, for Austria and Hungary; Brismee, for Belgium; Lafargue, for the new Federation of Madrid and for Portugal; Pihl, for Denmark; J. Ph. Becker, for German Switzerland; Duval, for the Romand Swiss Federation; Schwitzguebel, for the Jurassian Swiss Federation; Dave, for Holland; Dereure, for America; and Cuno, for Germany.

The accounts submitted to this Committee were approved and signed by all its members excepting Dave, absent.

The accounts having been read, the Congress approved of them by a unanimous vote.

VI.—Powers issued by the General Council, and by Federal Councils.

The Congress resolved, "To annul all powers issued, as well by the General Council as by any of the Federal Councils, to members of the International in such countries where the Association is prohibited, and to reserve to the new General Council the exclusive right of appointing, in those countries, the plenipotentiaries of the International Working Men's Association."

Adopted unanimously, less a few abstentions not specially counted.

VII.—Resolutions relating to the Alliance.

The Committee charged with the inquiry regarding the (second) Alliance of Social Democracy, consisted of the citizens—Cuno (33 votes), Lucain (24), Splingard (31), Vichard (30), and Walter (29).

In its report to the Congress, the majority of this Committee declared that "the secret Alliance was established with rules entirely opposed to those of the International." It proposed:—

"To exclude from the International Michael Bakounine, as founder of the Alliance, and for a personal affair.

"To exclude Guillaume and Schwitzguebel, as members of the Alliance.

"To exclude B. Malon, Bousquet * (Secretary of Police at Beziers, France), and Louis Marchand, as convicted of acts aiming at the disorganisation of the International Working Men's Association.

"To withdraw the charges against Alerini, Marselau, Morago, Farga-Pellicer, and Joukowski, upon their formal declaration that they no longer belong to the Alliance.

"To authorise the Committee to publish the documents upon which their conclusions were based."

The Congress resolved—

"1. To exclude Michael Bakounine. Voted for, 27; against, 6; abstentions, 7.

Voted for—J. Ph. Becker, Cuno, Dereure, Dumon, Dupont, Duval, Engels, Farkas, Frankel, Heim, Hepner, Johannard, Kugelmann, Lafargue, Le Moussu, Longuet, Lucain, Mac-Donnell, Marx, Pihl, Serraillier, Sorge, Swarm, Vichard, Wilmot, Walter, Wroblewski.

Voted against—Brismee, Dave, Fluse, Herman, Cœnen, van den Abeele.

---

* The Committee was not acquainted with the fact that M. Bousquet, upon the demands of his Section, had already been excluded by a formal vote of the General Council.

Abstained—Alerini, Guillaume, Marselau, Morago, Sauva, Splingard, Schwitzguebel.

"2. To exclude Guillaume. 25 for, 9 against, 8 absentions.

Voted for—J. Ph. Becker, Cuno, Dumon, Dupont, Duval, Engels, Farkas, Frankel, Heim, Hepner, Johannard, Kugelmann, Lafargue, Le Moussu, Longuet, Lucain, Marx, Pihl, Serraillier, Sorge, Swarm, Vichard, Walter, Wilmot, Wroblewski.

Voted against—Brismee, Cyrille, Dave, Fluse, Herman, Cœnen, Sauva, Splingard, van den Abeele.

Abstained—Alerini, Dereure, Friedlaender, Mac-Donnell, Marselau, Morago, Farga-Pellicer, Schwitzguebel.

"3. Not to exclude Schwitzguebel. For exclusion, 15; against, 17; abstentions, 7.

Voted for—J. Ph. Becker, Cuno, Dumon, Engels, Farkas, Heim, Hepner, Kugelmann, Le Moussu, Marx, Pihl, Splingard, Walter, Vichard, Wroblewski.

Voted against—Brismee, Cœnen, Cyrille, Dave, Dereure, Dupon, Fluse, Frankel, Herman, Johannard, Longuet, Sauva, Serraillier, Swarm, Wilmot, van den Abeele.

Abstained—Duval, Lefargue, Lucain, Mac-Donnell, Marselau, Morago, Farga-Pellicer.

"4. To refrain from voting upon the other exclusions proposed by the Committee. Adopted unanimously, minus some few abstentions.

"5. To publish the documents relating to the Alliance. Adopted unanimously, minus some few abstentions."

It is to be noted that these votes upon the Alliance were taken after a great number of French and German delegates had been obliged to leave.

VIII.—Residence and Composition of the next General Council.

1. Vote upon the change of residence of the General Council. Voted for the change, 26; against, 23; abstentions, 9.

Voted for the change—Barry, J. Ph. Becker, Brismee, Cuno, Dave, Dumon, Dupont, Engels, Harcourt, Johannard, Kugelmann, Lafargue, Lessner, Le Moussu, Longuet, Mac-Donnell, Marx,

Roach, Sauva, Serraillier, Sexton, Sorge, Swarm, Vichard, van den Abeele, Wroblewski.

Voted against—Arnaud, B. Becker, Cournet, Dereure, Duval, Farkas, Frankel, Friedlaender, Gerhardt, Heim, Hepner, Herman, Lucain, Ludwig, Milke, Pihl, Ranvier, Schumacher, Splingard, Vaillant, Wilmot, Walter, van der Hout.

Abstained—Cyrille, Eberhardt, Fluse, Guillaume, Marselau, Morago, Farga-Pellicer, Schwitzguebel, Alerini.

2. The seat of the General Council has been transferred to New York, by 31 votes against 14 for London, and 12 abstentions.

3. Voted for New York—Barry, J. Ph. Becker, B. Becker, Brismee, Cuno, Cœnen, Dave, Dumon, Dupont, Engels, Farkas, Fluse, Friedlaender, Herman, Kugelmann, Lafargue, Lessner, Le Moussu, Longuet, Lucain, Mac-Donnell, Marx, Pihl, Roach, Serraillier, Sexton, Splingard, Swarm, Vichard, van den Abeele, Wroblewski.

Voted for London—Arnaud, Cournet, Dereure, Duval, Frankel, Heim, Hepner, Ludwig, Milke, Ranvier, Schumacher, Vaillant, Wilmot, Walter.

Abstained—Cyrille, Eberhhardt, Gerhardt, Guillaume, Johannard, Alberini, Marselau, Morago, Farga-Pellicer, Sorge, Schwitzguebel, van der Hout.

4. The Congress resolved to appoint twelve members, residing in New York, to the General Council, with the faculty of adding them to that number. The following were elected:—

	Votes.		Votes.
Bertrand (German)	29	Carl (German)	28
Bolte (German)	29	David (French)	26
Laurel (Swede)	29	Deureure (French)	26
Kavanagh (Irish)	29	Fornacieri (Italian)	25
Saint Clair (Irish)	29	Speyer (German)	23
Leviele (French)	28	Ward (American)	22

IX.—Place of meeting of next Congress.

The proposition that the new Congress should meet in Switzerland, and that the new General Council should determine in what town, was adopted. There voted for Switzerland 15, for London, 5, for Chicago, 1, and for Spain 1.

X.—Committee to draw up the Minutes.

The following were appointed, without opposition:—Dupont, Engels, Frankel, Le Moussu, Marx, and Seraillier.

Committee $\left\{\begin{array}{l}\text{E. Dupont, F. Engels, Leo Frankel, Le Moussu,} \\ \text{Karl Marx, Auguste Serraillier.}\end{array}\right.$

BIOGRAPHICAL GLOSSARY
INDEX

Abeele, Van den, Henry
A Fleming from Belgium. Outstanding propagandist of international-
ist ideas among Dutch workers.

Alerini, Charles
Professor of physics. Member of the most militant sections of the
French branch of the I.W.A. Follower of Bakunin. In 1870 he lost
his professorship and became editor of the *Rappel de Provence*. In
May, 1870, he was arrested for having participated in the activities
of a secret and conspiratorial association.

Bakunin, Michael (1814–1876)
Russian anarchist, born of an aristocratic family at Torjok, in the
district of Tver. Officer of the Imperial Guard; served in Poland. He
resigned his commission, studied in Berlin, and then went to Paris,
where he met Proudhon, George Sand, and the chief Polish exiles.
From Paris he went to Switzerland, taking an active part in all social-
istic movements. When he refused to obey a government order to
return, his properties were confiscated. In 1848 he returned to revolutionary Paris; in 1849 he fought on the barricades of Dresden. He
was arrested and condemned to death and eventually handed over to
the Russian authorities. He was jailed in Russia and sent to Siberia
in 1855. He escaped via Japan and the United States and went to
England in 1861. He spent the rest of his life in Italy and Switzerland. In 1869 he founded the Social Democratic Alliance which, however, dissolved the same year. He joined the I.W.A. and appeared in
1870 in Lyons to assume leadership in a local *émeute*. He attended

the Congress of Basel of the I.W.A., but could not travel to The Hague in 1872 to defend himself against Marx and Engels. He retired to Lugano in 1873 and died at Bern.

His volcanic personality fascinated plebeian intellectuals, destitute farmers, and rebellious small-shop workers. He projected numerous conspiratorial societies and revolutionary schemes, and always won a devoted following of sectarian rebels. His lieutenants agitated successfully in Italy and Spain. He hated Karl Marx as a disciplinarian Prussian and Jew, whereas Marx hated in him the phantasmagoric and romantic Slav. Whereas Bakunin objected "to all legislation, all authority, and all influence, privileged, patented, official and legal, even when it has proceeded from universal suffrage," Marx hailed the "ten-hour bill," sought to build enduring mass organizations of labor, and relegated the "withering away of the state" to the far distant future.

Barry, Maltman (1842–1909)

A British cobbler and journalist who served many masters at the same time. Despite a resolution against press reports, Barry covered the proceedings of the International at The Hague for the conservative *Standard* which, according to E. H. Carr, "had doubtless defrayed his expenses." Barry was the one English delegate to vote with Marx and Engels for transferring the seat of the International to New York. Later on, Barry attached himself to the Conservatives.

Becker, Bernhard (1826–1882)

German Forty-eighter radical who lived for a time in London and then returned to Germany. He joined Ferdinand Lassalle's socialist group and by designation became Lassalle's successor. His authoritarian manner made him intolerable to the organization, and von Schweitzer displaced him. He wrote a tract against the Paris Commune of 1871 and *Enthüllungen über das tragische Lebensende Ferdinand Lassalles und seiner Beziehungen zu Helene von Dönniges* (1868).

Becker, Johann Philipp (1809–1886)

Leader of the Geneva section of the I.W.A. and editor of its paper *Der Vorbote* from 1866. This paper is one of the important documentary sources for the history of early Socialism in Central Europe. Becker participated as a young man in the big demonstration of South

West German Liberals in 1832, the so-called Hambach Festival. He then moved to Switzerland and became a Swiss citizen. In 1848 he gathered about thirty German rebels around him to form a "German Legion." He became the commander of all civil militias of Badenia during the days of revolutionary insurgence. He returned to Switzerland. Later he participated in Garibaldi's struggle in Italy. Characteristically, Engels in a letter of March 14, 1883, wrote to him, "You and I are now almost the last of the old guard of 1848. Well, we'll remain in the breach!"

Cluseret, Gustave Paul (1823–1900)
General of the army of the Paris Commune, who is described as an "enigmatic figure," as "a boastful and swaggering adventurer." He helped repress the rebellious workers in 1848. In 1871 he was deposed as incompetent. He joined the I.W.A. in 1871.

Cournet, Frederic (1839–1885)
A Blanqui follower. In 1866 he served on the staff of *Révail*. He was jailed in 1869 and again in 1870. During the days of the Paris Commune he represented the 19th district. He fled to London; after the amnesty of 1880 he returned to France and served as a member of the Paris municipal council.

Danielson, N. F. (pseudonym: Nikolai-on) (1844–1918)
Russian economist during the 1880's and 1890's. Translator of Marx's *Capital* into Russian. Theoretical representative of the Narodniki, the Russian populist movement.

Dereure, Simon
Attended the Hague Congress together with F. A. Sorge as a delegate of the North American Federation. He was a shoemaker. During the Paris Commune he had been elected mayor of the 18th *arrondissement* of Paris. He fled to London after the fall of the Commune. After the amnesty of 1880, he returned to France. He was a follower of Blanqui.

Dupont, Eugene (1831–1881)
French musical instrument maker. Lived in exile in London and became a follower of Marx. Member of the General Council of the I.W.A. from 1864. In 1865 he served as corresponding secretary of the General Council for France. He participated in the London Conference of 1865 and the Geneva Congress of 1866. He was a chairman

of the Lausanne Congress in 1867. In 1870 he went to Manchester where he was active in the local branch of the I.W.A. In 1871 he was delegated to the London Conference. After the Hague Congress he abandoned political activity.

Duval, Emile Victor (1841–1871)

Member of the International. Militant fighter for the Paris Commune.

Eccarius, Johann George (1818–1889)

Thuringian tailor. Member of the First International from its beginning in September, 1864. Member of the General Council of the I.W.A. Secretary of the General Council, 1867–71. Participated in the London Conference of 1865 and 1871, the Geneva Congress of 1866, the Lausanne Congress of 1867, the Congresses of Brussels of 1868, of Basel of 1869, and of The Hague. From the 1850's he was influenced by Marx. He wrote several pamphlets. In 1870/71 he served as corresponding secretary for the United States. At the Hague Congress he sided with the Anarchists. In 1873 and 1874 he attended the Anarchist congresses of Geneva and Brussels. He dissociated himself from the Bakuninists, and worked in the trade union movement to the end of his life.

Engels, Friedrich (1820–1895)

Friend and co-worker of Karl Marx from the 1840's. Contributor to the *Deutsch-französische Jahrbücher*, edited by Marx and A. Ruge. From 1845 to 1848 he lived with Marx in Paris and later in Brussels. He contributed to the *Rheinische Zeitung*. In 1849 he participated in the Badenia insurrection and subsequently sought refuge in England. From 1850 to 1869 he managed the branch establishment of the parental textile firm in Manchester. He supported Marx and his family in London, where Engels moved in 1870. His main writings are *Die Lage der arbeitenden Klasse in England* (1845), *Herrn Eugen Durings Umwalzung der Wissenschaft* (1878), and *Naturdialektik* (1925). He edited Volumes II and III of Marx's *Capital* after Marx's death.

Farga-Pellicer, Rafael

Printer and journalist. Follower of Bakunin. Editor of *La Federación* (1869–72) and *El Trabajo* (1872), organs of the Spanish branch of the I.W.A. He attended the Congress of the I.W.A. at Basel in 1869. He was a delegate of the Barcelona section.

Fränkel, Leo (1844–1896)

Hungarian jewelry worker of German extraction. A Versailles police report describes him as of "small stature, brown hair, pale complexion, strong nose, bad face; he wears a pince-nez and blond beard, German accent." He had come to Paris a few years before the Franco-Prussian war. During the days of the Commune he became one of its members and held a leading position despite his youth. He had helped to establish the Lyons section of the I.W.A. He was corresponding secretary of the General Council for Hungary. After the fall of the Commune he escaped to London. Later he returned to Hungary, where he helped found the Socialist party.

Gerhard

Tailor. Delegate of the Federal Council of Amsterdam to the Hague Congress.

Guillaume, James (1844–1916)

Swiss schoolteacher and journalist who wrote the most informative and charming history of the First International. At The Hague he was the undisputed leader and spokesman of the Anarchists. He represented the federation of the Jura workers, largely small-shop watchmakers and followers of Bakunin. In 1878 he retired from the Anarchist movement in Switzerland, then in Kropotkin's hands. He moved to Paris.

Hales, John

General secretary of the I.W.A. in 1871 and at once secretary of the British Federal Council of the I.W.A., Hales had the confidence of the London East End workers. After the demise of the International he carried on and represented the London Commonwealth Club at the Ghent Unity Congress in 1877.

Harcourt

Australian miner representing a section of the I.W.A. at Victoria, Australia.

Hepner, Adolf (b. 1846)

Co-editor with August Bebel and Wilhelm Liebknecht of the Leipzig *Volksstaat*, the leading paper of the early German "Marxists."

Herman

Corresponding secretary of the General Council for Belgium. Delegate of the Liége Federation of mechanics, united carpenters, and stoneworkers.

Jung, Herman

Swiss watchmaker; lived in England. Adherent of Marx; corresponding secretary of the General Council for Switzerland. At The Hague he sided with the Anarchists together with the British representatives.

Kugelmann, Dr. Ludwig

Gynaecologist from Hanover, Germany. Adherent of Karl Marx; during the 1870's one of his most regular correspondents. He attended the Lausanne Congress of the I.W.A. as a spectator, joined the International, and at The Hague represented a section at Celle near Hanover.

Lafargue, Paul (1842–1911)

Son-in-law of Karl Marx, born of French parents in Cuba, educated in Bordeaux, studied medicine in Paris and London. Returned to Paris after amnesty of Communards in 1880. Became a Socialist pamphleteer. His most famous pamphlet was *The Right to Be Lazy*. He was close to Jules Guesde and with him founded a Marxist party.

Lessner, Friedrich

Tailor from Thuringia. Follower of Marx, friend of Engels from the days of the "Communist League." Lived in London. Represented the General Council of the I.W.A. at the Basel Congress.

Longuet, Charles (1833–1901)

Son-in-law of Karl Marx. He studied law in Paris, engaged in journalism, and during the time of the Paris Commune edited the *Journal Officiel*. He fled to London and participated in the London Conference of 1871. After the amnesty of 1880 he returned to Paris, worked as a journalist, became a member of the Paris municipal council in 1886 and editor of the *Egalité* in 1889. He was active in Jules Guesde's *Parti Ouvrier*, a Marxist party.

Lucraft, Benjamin (1809–1897)

British furniture worker and trade unionist. He was elected to the General Council of the I.W.A. at the inaugural meeting in St. Martin's Hall in 1864. He agitated for electoral reform. He represented the General Council at the Brussels Congress of 1868 and at Basel in 1869. He refused to sign Marx's address, *The Civil War in France*, which Marx published in the name of the I.W.A. without prior endorsement of the General Council. Lucraft left the International in 1871.

McDonnell, P. J.

Irishman from Dublin. As a youth he had been active in a national revolutionary society of the Irish. He went to London, where he agitated among Irish workers on behalf of the I.W.A. and organized an Irish section. For a time he was a member of the General Council. At the Hague Congress he supported Marx against Hales. In 1872 he emigrated to the United States. He was co-founder of the United Workers and Internationale Arbeiter Union and became editor of the *Labor Standard*. Later he founded the *Patterson Labor Standard*. He became a professional politician and dissociated himself from labor organizations.

Marx, Karl (1818–1883)

Greatest Socialist thinker and revolutionary of the nineteenth century. He brought the legacy of French Socialist thought, German idealist philosophy, and English economic theory into a fusion and linked the cause of socialism to the emancipatory struggle of the modern labor movement. He studied at Berlin, Bonn, and Jena where he took his Ph.D. in philosophy. In 1842 he edited the radical democratic paper, the *Rheinische Zeitung*, at Cologne. In 1843 he married Jenny von Westphalen (1814–1881). After the suppression of the *Rheinische Zeitung* in 1843, Marx went to Paris, where he met Friedrich Engels, his friend and co-worker for the rest of his life. In 1845 he was expelled from Paris and went to Brussels. In Brussels Marx and Engels were active in radical labor organizations with connections in London, Paris, and Switzerland. In 1848, after a short stay in France, Marx and Engels went to Cologne and founded the *Neue Rheinische Zeitung*, "An Organ of Democracy." Marx agitated for a tax strike and for armed resistance. At the end of the year the paper was suppressed; Marx was put on trial for high treason but was acquitted by a jury. In 1849 he was expelled from Prussian territory and went to Paris. As Paris authorities denied him residence there, he went to London, where he lived for the rest of his life.

When British and French trade unionists in 1864 organized the I.W.A., Marx joined the association after years of withdrawal from organized political life. The congresses of the First International provided a platform for the debate of all mid-century anticapitalist ideas and policy proposals. Marx became in fact though not in name the head of the General Council, and his astutely formulated ideas won out in competition. By linking the tragedy of the Paris Commune to the I.W.A., Marx created the revolutionary myth, which exerted great influence on revolutionary Russian thought. His most famous works include *The Communist Manifesto* (1847), *The German Ideology* (1925), *Poverty of Philosophy* (1847), *Capital* (3 vols., 1867, 1885, 1894), and *A Critique of Political Economy* (1859).

Mottershead
  British trade unionist.

Odger, George (1820–1877)
  English trade union leader. He set out as a cobbler. In 1862 he became secretary of the London Trades Council. In 1870 he served as general secretary of the I.W.A. A powerful speaker, he became the idol of metropolitan radicalism. He made five attempts to win a parliamentary seat, but was blocked each time by the Liberal party. His funeral became the occasion of a remarkable demonstration by London workingmen.

Pyat, Felix (1810–1889)
  French lawyer and politician. From 1849 to 1870 he lived as a refugee in London. Then he returned to France, became a member of the Paris Commune, was condemned to death in 1873, fled, and returned after the amnesty of 1880. In 1888 he was elected deputy. He published *Lettres d'un Proscrit.*

Ranvier, Gabriel (1828–1879)
  Blanquist delegate to the Hague Congress; refugee from the Paris Commune. He had served on the Central Committee of the National Guard. He was mayor of Belleville and the only mayor of a Paris *arrondissement* who came out for the Commune from the outset. He proclaimed its establishment and he posted its last proclamation. He directed the defense of Belleville to the very end, then fled to London.

Scheu, Heinrich
  One of the brothers of Andreas Scheu, eminent leader of Viennese Socialist labor. For a time he edited the Viennese *Volkswille*, a Socialist biweekly paper of the early 1870's.

Schuhmacher, Georg (b. 1844)
  Leatherworker in his native city of Cologne and later in London from 1860 to 1875. He became a Marxist socialist, joined the I.W.A., worked from 1876 until 1878 as a journalist for the Cologne *Freie Presse.* In 1879 he established himself as a leather dealer in Solingen,

where he became a leading figure in the labor movement. In 1884 he was elected to the Reichstag on the Social Democratic ticket.

Schwitzguebel, Adhémar (1844–1895)

Swiss anarchist watchmaker; follower of Guillaume and Bakunin. He was born in the Canton of Bern and lived in Sonvillier in the Jura mountains. He raised a large family and later withdrew from politics.

Sorge, Friedrich Adolf (1827–1906)

German-American socialist, Protestant pastor's son, who participated in the Badenia insurrection of 1849. He escaped a death verdict by fleeing to Switzerland and from there to Belgium. He immigrated to the United States in 1852 and made his living in New York as a music teacher. He was active in circles of German freethinkers and socialists and through study became a confirmed Marxist in the 1860's. He met Marx and Engels in London before the Hague Congress and sought in vain to build up a theoretically pure Marxist organization among New York workingmen. His energies were consumed in factional struggles. "He was not only the first authentic interpreter in the United States of Marxian socialism, but through Gompers and Adolf Strasser, who respected him, he exerted a profound influence upon the American labor movement."—Selig Perlman, *Encyclopedia of the Social Sciences*, Vol. VII, p. 264.

Swarm (pseudonym for Dentraggues)

Took up residence in Toulouse, France, in March, 1872. He became active for the International and managed to receive the mandate of four sections of Toulouse and environs. In 1873 he was arrested, and police found lists of Internationalists in his possession. Although he was probably not a direct agent of the police, he denounced others during his trial, allegedly for personal reasons. Engels informed Sorge in a letter of March 20, 1873, that "Dentraggues with the usual pedantry has kept a mass of useless lists [of names and addresses of members] which provided the police with all it takes. Now his trial is under way."—*Sorge Correspondence*, p. 98.

Tolain, Henri Louis (1828–1897)

French worker, engraver; follower of Proudhon. He attended the World Exposition in London in 1862 as a delegate of French workers. He was one of the leaders of the Mutual Credit Society of Paris Bronze Workers. As organizer and leader of the Paris group of Internationalists, he read the reply of the French workers to the appeal of the British workers at the inaugural meeting of the I.W.A. in St. Martin's Hall in September, 1864. He attended the Congresses of the I.W.A. in London (1865), Geneva (1866), Lausanne (1867), Brussels (1868), and Basel (1869). As deputy to the National Assembly at Versailles in 1871, he belonged to the camp of the anti-Communards. Hence in the eyes of the General Council he was a traitor to the cause and was expelled from the I.W.A.

Vaillant, Eduard (1840–1915)

French civil engineer and physicist who had studied in Heidelberg, Tübingen, and Vienna. He was a member of the Paris Commune and was put in charge of educational affairs. After the downfall of the Commune he escaped to Switzerland and subsequently went to London, where he joined the General Council of the I.W.A. He was a Blanquist. After the amnesty of 1880 he returned to France and became the leading Blanquist in the Chamber of Deputies.

Vesinier, M.

French writer, member of the I.W.A. from an early date, secretary of the French section of the I.W.A. in London.

Walter (pseudonym for van Heddeghem)

Bonapartist police spy who managed to infiltrate the Hague Congress. Ironically, he was chosen to serve on the Committee of Inquiry into the Alliance affair. He had managed to win the confidence of a Paris section, and with the support of Ranvier, member of the Commune and then of the General Council in London, he received a mandate for the Hague Congress. When in March, 1873, some twenty members of the I.W.A. were put on trial in France, the prosecutor named Heddeghem as the denouncer of the accused.

Weston, John

British Owenite worker. He invented the cylindrical sewing machine. At the inaugural meeting of the International in 1864 he was elected to the General Council of the I.W.A. He attended the London Congress of the International in 1865. He was treasurer of the Land and Labour League.

Wroblewski, Valery (1836–1908)

Polish general who served as military leader of the Paris Commune. After its downfall he escaped to London.

Abeele, van den, Henry, 11, 13, 51, 52, 54, 63, 70, 92, 104, 110, 113, 117, 119; 138, 148, 160, 165; 175, 177, 198, 199, 200, 205, 208, 219, 225, 228, 230, 233, 235; 246, 249, 253, 255; 260, 263, 269, 286, 287, 289, 291, 292, 293; 297

Abstention from political activity, 66, 88–89, 92–93; 206, 211, 217–18, 219, 220

Affair Outine, 81, 214

Alerini, Charles, 14, 15, 16, 24, 29, 30, 31, 34, 51, 52, 54, 61, 84, 101, 106, 108, 113, 118; 139, 141, 142, 163, 165; 177, 179, 184, 186, 187, 188, 189, 198, 199, 200, 204, 215, 224, 226, 227, 230, 231n, 233; 246, 247, 254, 255, 263, 287, 288, 289, 290, 291, 292, 293; 297

Algemeen Handelsblad, 236–37n

Alliance, xii; 25, 26, 27, 32, 33, 34, 35, 36, 37, 38, 42, 53, 61, 95, 105, 108, 109, 110; 125, 128, 141, 142; 184, 185, 188, 189, 190, 191, 194, 199, 204, 221, 225, 226, 227, 228; 242, 243, 247, 253–54; 262, 263, 284, 285, 290, 292

American Congress, 18, 19, 20, 21, 23; 181–82, 183; 263

American Federal Council, 14, 177

American Federation, 39, 40, 103; 192, 193, 224–25

Amsterdam, meeting at, 120, 167, 235–37, 255, 276, 284

Anarchists, xii, xiv

Apollo Hall affair, 39, 192

Arnaud, Antoine, xiv; 13, 51, 66, 78, 94, 118; 176, 198, 206, 212, 220, 234; 283, 286, 287, 288, 289, 293

Attack on International, discussed, 269–73

Autonomy of sections, 126, 242, 254

Bakunin, Michael, vi, xii–xiii, xiv–xv; 65, 93, 102, 105, 106, 108, 109, 110, 114, 116–18; 125, 127, 128, 131, 162, 163, 165; 185n, 206, 220, 224, 226–27, 228, 231, 232–34; 242, 243, 254, 255; 262, 275, 284, 285, 291; 297–98, 300, 301, 305

Bakuninists, 88, 217, 242, 243, 300

Barry, Maltman, vi, vii; 13, 15, 16, 28, 29, 41, 42, 51, 52, 94, 118, 119; 140, 141; 176, 179, 186, 194, 198, 199, 213n, 220, 231n, 234, 235; 246, 247; 261, 262–63, 268, 280, 286, 287, 289, 292, 293; 298

Bastelica, 31, 188